Introduction to
Computer and
Network Security
Navigating Shades of Gray

Richard R. Brooks

Clemson University
South Carolina, USA

CRC Press
Taylor & Francis Group
Boca Raton London New York

CRC Press is an imprint of the
Taylor & Francis Group, an **informa** business

A CHAPMAN & HALL BOOK

CRC Press
Taylor & Francis Group
6000 Broken Sound Parkway NW, Suite 300
Boca Raton, FL 33487-2742

© 2014 by Taylor & Francis Group, LLC
CRC Press is an imprint of Taylor & Francis Group, an Informa business

No claim to original U.S. Government works

Printed on acid-free paper
Version Date: 20130625

International Standard Book Number-13: 978-1-4398-6071-7 (Hardback)

Visit the Taylor & Francis Web site at
http://www.taylorandfrancis.com

and the CRC Press Web site at
http://www.crcpress.com

Dedication

It has been my good luck to have many helpful colleagues and talented students. I depend on my wife's extended tolerance. In addition, Penn State and Clemson are wonderful places to live, work, and study. This book is dedicated to these people, places, and institutions.

Contents

List of Figures

List of Tables

Foreword

This is a computer and network security textbook. I have studied, analyzed, and been mildly obsessed by this topic for over 25 years. Computer use and misuse has fascinated me since I first learned about Fred Cohen and computer viruses in 1984 copies of *Die Bayrische Hackerpost* [119].

This book is based on my experience teaching security to undergraduate and graduate students in computer science, computer engineering, industrial engineering, and electrical engineering. These courses were taught at both Clemson and Penn State Universities. While teaching *ECE449/649 Computer and Network Security* for the past nine years, I have progressively refined the course contents. The resulting course of study is intended to:

- Make students aware of current security exploits,

- Help them understand technical factors that enable attacks,

- Deepen their understanding of technology,

- Open their eyes to the economic and social factors determining the security of future systems,

- Foster creative thinking, and

- Make learning technical topics challenging and enjoyable.

This text should be appropriate for teaching both upper division undergraduate and graduate level courses. It is assumed that students master a higher level programming language. It would be advantageous if that language were a variant of C. Students should have a reasonable background in the design and implementation of computer systems.

Many topics, such as buffer overflows and viruses, depend on object code formats and the run-time behavior of executables. I will not assume that students have any fluency in assembly code programming. It will be unnecessary for students to write assembly code. This will be clear in the wording of course assignments. When the use of assembler is unavoidable, I will provide example code that make its use as simple as possible.

The mathematics in this book is straightforward and self-contained. The treatment of encryption is rather superficial. Students are expected to learn the basics of what encryption does and have a rough understanding of how it works. No effort is made to treat the mathematics of encryption in any depth. References are given for readers that have particular interest in that topic.

Although every effort has been taken to make this book accessible, it is a technical text intended for students of computer science and/or engineering. Technical details of attacks and security mechanisms are provided. This book is not intended as a superficial overview. It is intended as a university level technical textbook. This does not mean that the contents of this book are not valuable for working engineers, technologists, researchers, and other interested parties. The information given should be very useful for those readers willing to invest the necessary effort.

About the Author

Dr. Brooks' background includes managing computer networks that span continents, performing sponsored research, and teaching university classes. His research has been sponsored by both government and industry, including:

- The Office of Naval Research (ONR),

- The Air Force Office of Scientific Research (AFOSR),

- The National Institute of Standards and Technology (NIST),

- The National Science Foundation (NSF),

- The Army Research Office (ARO),

- The United States Department of State,

- The Defense Advanced Research Projects Agency (DARPA), and

- BMW Manufacturing Corporation.

He has a B.A. in Mathematical Sciences from The Johns Hopkins University Whiting School of Engineering, and a Ph.D. in Computer Science from The Louisiana State University.

He has worked in the United States, France, Germany, Africa, Eastern Europe, and the former Soviet Union. His consulting clients have included the World Bank and French stock exchange authority. Dr. Brooks was head of the Distributed Systems Department of The Pennsylvania State University Applied Research Laboratory (PSU/ARL) for seven years. He has been an Associate Professor with the Holcombe Department of Electrical and Computer Engineering of Clemson University since 2004.

Acknowledgments

This material is based upon work supported by, or in part by, the Air Force Office of Scientific Research contract/grant number FA9550-09-1-0173, NSF contract/grant numbers CNS-1049765 and NSF-OCI 1064230, U.S. Dept. of State award number S-LMAQM-12-GR-1033, and a gift from BMW Manufacturing Corporation.

The U.S. Government is authorized to reproduce and distribute reprints for Governmental purposes notwithstanding any copyright notation thereon. The author gratefully acknowledges this support and takes responsibility for the contents of this report.

The views and conclusions contained herein are those of the author and should not be interpreted as necessarily representing the official policies or endorsements, either expressed or implied, of the Air Force Research Laboratory, National Science Foundation, US Department of Defense, US Department of State, BMW Corporation, or the U.S. Government.

Preface

Computer and network security is a field in constant flux. There is an ongoing arms race. Attackers need new vulnerabilities to exploit. These exploits, in turn, provide business opportunities for companies to create security counter-measures. As long as the information processed by computers and networks has any value, this process will continue and evolve.

This constant flux presents dangers for anyone teaching or writing about security. Information quickly becomes outdated. Where the 1990s were domi-nated by a series of high profile network worms, these types of worms are no longer the threat they once were. Where botnets, phishing, advanced persis-tent threats, and cross-site request forgery are topics of current interest, it is likely that countermeasures will make them obsolete in the near future. There is a clear temptation to restrict discussions to the most recent topics in order to be relevant.

While this may provide instant gratification, it is unlikely to be useful in the long term. Serious analysis of security problems shows a disturbing ten-dency to see the same problems recur with minor variations.[1] For example, man in the middle and insertion attacks are well known problems. In spite of this, it seems these exploits come as a surprise to the designers of each new technology. There are underlying patterns that should be learned, recognized, and avoided in the future. This requires reasoning at a higher level of abstrac-tion and looking at recurring themes. The danger with teaching security at the higher level of abstraction is that subject matter becomes arcane, difficult to relate to current systems, and often boring (since it appears irrelevant).

This book tries to present a pragmatic middle ground. Basic principles and concepts are presented and current threats given as examples. By showing how basic principles can enable and/or neutralize relevant exploits, we show students the relevance of these concepts to present and future technologies.

This material is intended to be a "learn by doing" exercise. The course structure is built around a set of challenging core exercises. The exercises force students to work through a number of technical details so they can stage exploits, know which countermeasures effectively neutralize those attacks, and understand why. To be able to complete the exercises, students learn:

- how computer systems and networks operate,
- to reverse engineer processes, and

---

[1]In the words of Yogi Berra, "It's *deja vu* all over again."

- to use systems in ways that were never foreseen (or supported) by the original developers.

I have tested and refined these exercises over many years. These are not cookbook exercises that can be solved by rote following of instructions. Students are expected to think, experiment, and be creative. The results have been rewarding for most students.

The core of the course is the projects in Chapters 4, 6, 8, and 9. These chapters present tutorials and the background information necessary to complete the projects. Instructors are given example solutions and additional material in the Teacher's Guide. Many other chapters need not necessarily be covered in lectures, but provide important background information for students.

I also suggest having in-class discussions on at least two of the following topics: privacy, copyright, digital rights management, and/or economic factors. It is easy to find current events that show the relevance of these issues. They are also topics that many students are interested in. It is relatively straightforward to create controversial in-class discussions on these topics that get students actively involved in heated debates.

1

Brief History of Computers, Communications, and Security

CONTENTS

Humans have been in conflict since prehistoric times. The earliest known writings on warfare concentrate on the strategic importance of information and deceit, which illustrates the existential importance of information security [405].

This chapter provides a brief history of communications and information technology, concentrating on security issues. Since empirical observation shows technology advancing at an exponential rate [53], the amount we can present about information technology in ancient history is sparse. The slow rate of technical change in early days is more than made up for by the explosive rate of change experienced since the 1940s.

We explain how information technology and warfare have influenced each other over time. This has strongly influenced society over the ages. Our final sections discuss current trends. We will speculate some about future developments. In Section 1.7, we discuss *cyberwar* as an example of *asymmetric conflict*. Asymmetric conflicts occur when the two combatants are not evenly matched, in which case the weaker side usually needs to use stealth. It seems likely that information technology will be an important factor in future asymmetric conflicts. In future asymmetric conflicts we can expect it to be increasingly difficult to distinguish between warfare and criminal activity.

Technical information about security technologies will be provided in later chapters. This chapter provides perspective. It shows how computer security threats reflect broader trends in society.

1.1   Pre-Renaissance

The earliest known writings about war consider information and secrecy as primary sources of power. In *The Art of War*[1], Sun Tzu says "The entire art of war is based on deception" [405]. Early technologies for storing and transmitting information were very primitive. Paper was first introduced to Europe by Crusaders around 1200 A.D. Mass distribution of information was first enabled by Gutenberg's invention of movable type in 1454 [74]. Until then, information was stored using tokens, tablets, knotted strings, notched sticks or handwritten parchment. The conceptual basics of computing, binary (3000 B.C. in China), logic (300 B.C. by Aristotle), and algorithms (820 A.D. in Baghdad), were well known before the renaissance [74]. In spite of this, the only computation devices worth mentioning that were available in ancient times were the abacus (500 B.C. in the Middle East), the compass (Rome), and the quadrant (Greeks and Babylonians) [427].

Until the 1800s, technologies for long-range communication were severely limited. Most large empires had some type of relay system allowing mounted messengers, or sometimes voice communications, to travel up to 200 miles a day. There are records of fire or smoke signals being used to send information more quickly. Those signals were limited in the amount of information they could send and constrained to use mainly over fixed routes [409].

For warfare, these long distance communication technologies were of limited use. They were reliable only in well-defended regions and therefore irrelevant to offensive operations. Long distance messages were mainly used to warn of approaching troops and request reinforcements. They could only support minimal oversight of remote forces. Under these conditions, tactical command was only possible when the commander was present at the front with the troops. Up-to-date intelligence about the enemy was mainly gathered from travelers, local inhabitants, deserters, prisoners, and spies. The slow rate of information transmission meant that generals worked in isolation. They had very limited ability to coordinate their actions with allied forces [409].

Perhaps the best illustration of the importance of information security to ancient societies is the relatively advanced state of *cryptography* and *steganography*, technologies devoted to keeping information secret, when compared to the other technologies available for computing and communication. Cryptography is the science of writing in codes that are hard to decipher, and steganography is the art of hiding information to make it hard to detect.

Many ancient texts describe cryptographic applications. The bible lists three different systems for writing secret codes [360]. Indian texts, including the *Kama Sutra*, list many uses for cryptography [360]. In 405 B.C., the Spartan general Lysander used cryptography to hide information from the Persians. The Spartans had a mechanical cipher: the *scytale* was a pair of

---

[1]Written in the 6th century B.C., this book is one of the earliest treatises on strategy.

simple rods with the same diameter. A long strip of paper could be wrapped around one of the rods and written on. To be read, the paper had to be wrapped around a matching rod. If the rods do not match, the letters on the strip of paper will not match up properly [447]. In Rome, Julius Caesar used a simple substitution cipher to hide information from his enemies [313].

In spite of the general decline of scholarship in Europe during the middle ages, cryptography continued to prosper and advance in the region. Confidential communications were important enough for the Church that they employed a full-time expert in cryptography [338]. Cryptography advanced as well in the Middle East, which was the center of scholarship at that time. Instructions for administrators of the Abbasid caliphate, which started in 750 A.D., explained how to use substitution ciphers. At the same time, scholars in the caliphate discovered *cryptanalysis*, the art of breaking ciphers. Muslim texts of that era explain how frequency counting can easily break substitution ciphers [366]. Cryptographic methods in ancient times were usually primitive because they had to be executed manually.

Even more effort was devoted to finding tools for steganography. Recorded ancient approaches for information hiding include [130, 144]:

- Texts written on shaved skulls that were later covered by letting hair grow (Greece),
- Invisible inks (Rome),
- Pin pricks placed above letters in a text to indicate letters in a secret message (Greece),
- Messages hidden in images and hieroglyphics (Egypt), and
- Messages written on a thin sheet, rolled into a wax ball, and hidden or swallowed (China).

Ancient empires sometimes controlled large territories for long periods of time, in spite of their inability to effectively, promptly share information to coordinate actions. These empires were often successful due to the primitive state of their competition. Technology was far from irrelevant to the balance of power. Advances in weapons technology almost always provided their owners with a tremendous advantage, which usually led to a shift in power. Successful empires relied on advanced weaponry, intelligent generals, clever strategies, and reliable social control structures. For large empires, social control required allowing local officials adequate freedom of action; the delays incurred by centralized coordination were prohibitive. Successful military structures usually include trade-offs where top-down control allows for bottom-up reaction to changing situations [409].

1.2 Renaissance to World War I

The Renaissance[2] was a period of renewed intellectual activity in Europe starting in the 14th century. Among other things, the Renaissance was characterized by increased interest in science, mathematics, and engineering. This renewed vigor led to the industrial revolution. Technical innovations were accompanied by radical changes in the social and economic fabric of Europe. This increased Europe's technical superiority, which allowed the continent to colonize and dominate most of the Earth. This section describes the technical and social changes that are most relevant to computer and communications security.

During this period, a number of tools for computation were developed. In 1617, John Napier printed a tract explaining how a set of rods or sticks with multiplication tables written on them could simplify calculations. These sticks became known as *Napier's bones*, since the most elegant sets were made of ivory. These bones were used for multiplication, division, and finding square roots [427, 54]. In 1891, Henri Genaille improved upon Napier's bones to produce a set of rulers, simplifying the process even further.

Genaille's rulers resemble slide rules, which use logarithmic scales to make numeric calculation even more straightforward. Sophisticated slide rules can calculate multiplication, division, roots, powers, trigonometry, logarithms, and exponents. The first description of a slide rule, a simple mechanical analog computer, was published around 1620 [54, 427]. Slide rules were widely used until made obsolete by electronic calculators in the 1970s.

In the 1620s, a number of researchers developed the mechanical calculators that were early precursors of modern day computers. Around 1623 Wilhelm Schickhard, in collaboration with Kepler at the University of Tübingen, produced a mechanical device capable of calculating astronomical tables. The device used a set of gears to manipulate Napier's bones and logarithm tables. They automatically performed carry operations. The device even rang a bell to indicate when overflow errors occurred. Schickhard had a working copy. Unfortunately, the copy he was building for Kepler was destroyed in a fire [54, 427].

Independently of Schickhard, Blaise Pascal produced around 50 mechanical calculators starting in 1642. Designed to relieve the tedium of tax calculations, Pascal's machine had a more robust gear system than Schickhard's [427]. Schickhard's machine did addition; Pascal's machines did both addition and subtraction. In 1672 Leibniz extended Pascal's design to perform multiplication. These ideas were progressively refined and commercialized, eventually evolving into mechanical calculators [54].

In the 1700s mechanical technology advanced and textile production was automated. Jacquard used punch cards to program looms to reproduce so-

---

[2]Literally, French for rebirth.

phisticated patterns [74]. The use of punch cards expanded and in the late 1800s Herman Hollerith developed a punch card tabulation system for use in the U.S. census. The company he started for this purpose eventually became International Business Machine (IBM) Corporation [54]. Punch cards were a primary storage medium for programs and data well into the late 20th century.

Charles Babbage produced the first programmable machines, the difference and analytical engines, in the mid-1800s [54, 74, 427]. Like Pascal's and Leibniz's devices, Babbage's engines were mechanical: using arrays of gears. Unlike earlier devices, his had input, output, and control units. Punch cards were used for programming. Ada Lovelace's set of instructions for the analytical engine is widely credited as being the first computer program [74]. While the machines from Babbage, Pascal, and Leibniz were never widely used, they were important precursors of later computers.

Other analytical computational tools developed at this time became precursors of later tools. One impressive example was Lord Kelvin's tide analyzer. He constructed a mechanical device to iteratively solve differential equations [54]. This iterative approach is a direct precursor of current numerical methods for analyzing differential equations.

Communications technology also made progress during this period. Optical telegraphs were deployed across France starting in 1790. This technology quickly spread to other countries. After this success, the 1831 invention of the electric relay in the U.S. led to the electric telegraph. Morse and Baudot binary codes were quickly developed for transmitting messages [74].

These technical changes coincided with changes in economy, society, and warfare. Nation states emerged in Europe. After the French Revolution, Napoleon radically changed the nature of warfare. A major enabler of this change was Napoleon's ability to create, command, and control an army by an order of magnitude larger than previously possible. The new communications and transportation technologies also made it possible to coordinate the activities of different commanders. Napoleon used these technologies to decentralize tactical command of his forces, while centralizing strategic command [409].

The seminal work on military strategy, von Clausewitz's *vom Kriege*, was based on the Napoleonic wars [416]. This book introduced the concepts of *friction* (the inability to reliably control a conflict) and *fog* (the inability to know the exact state of a conflict). *Vom Kriege*'s description of society, conflict, and war has dominated Western society up to the present [410]. In this view, nation-states have a monopoly on power, war is executed by uniformed military representing nation-states, and war is an extension of politics into the realm of force [410].

As Europe approached World War I, national economies expanded as peasants moved to the city. At the same time, the size of the armies grew greatly. Military commanders used telegraphs to coordinate army movements and were for the first time placed far away from the troops under their command [409].

Napoleon's military dominance of Europe was followed by Prussian General Staff dominance of Europe. Prussian success was primarily due to command and control strategies that most fully exploited the use of telegraph and railroad technologies to coordinate timely troop movements [409].

During this time, cryptography and cryptanalysis remained the key juncture between technology and politics. In Europe during the middle ages, cryptography was mainly used to maintain secrets by the Church. By the start of the Renaissance, though, its use spread quickly. Scientists and alchemists used cryptography to safeguard discoveries [366]. Soon every court in Italy, France, and Spain used cryptography as a routine part of diplomacy [366, 338].

As is to be expected, cryptanalysis was rediscovered. One famous example of cryptanalysis in court intrigue was the sentencing of Mary, Queen of Scots. She was put to death when her secret messages encouraging the assassination of Queen Elizabeth were deciphered [366].

Cryptographic technology advanced greatly during this period. Monalphabetic substitution ciphers were replaced with more sophisticated schemes. In 1510, the first book on ciphers made publicly available was published. Trithemius' *Polygraphia* was a complicated scheme that provided twenty words or phrases that could be used to correspond to a given letter. The recipients could take the message they received and use their code-book to decipher it [366]. Other advances during this time include:

- Poly-alphabetic solution ciphers (we provide an example of this, the Vigenère cipher, in Section 3.3),
- Placing grids over texts with holes exposing letters in the true message, and
- Using rotating disks to aid in deciphering poly-alphabetic ciphers.

The use of rotating disks became increasingly important in the two world wars.

Blaise de Vigenère's *Traicté des Chiffres* written in 1586 is of particular importance. His cipher uses a table and a key phrase to encrypt messages. The table is a simple square of the alphabet, with each column starting with the alphabet starting at a new position. Details on Vigenère's cipher and how it can be cracked using cryptanalysis are in Chapter 3. We note, though, that the cryptanalysis used to decipher this approach is more sophisticated than previously necessary. No effective cryptanalysis approach for Vigenère's cipher was found for over 200 years [193]. Babbage found one method for breaking the cipher in the mid 1800s [366]. Vigenère's work inspired Count Gronsfeld whose variant of this approach was used by Frederick the Great of Prussia [193].

Another cryptographic algorithm that remained secure for over 200 years was the Great Cipher designed by father and son Rossignol. They worked for Cardinal Richelieu and King Louis IV in the 1600s and 1700s. They were hired as cryptanalysts by the French government to find new ways to secure official communications. Over time Rossignol's "Great Cipher" approach was forgotten, leaving a trove of encrypted historical documents that were unreadable. Two centuries later, a cryptanalyst deciphered their messages by discovering that their encoding substituted numbers for either single letters or entire syllables depending on the context. It is likely that solving the Great Cipher finally identified the name of the prisoner who was "the man in the iron mask" [193, 366].

The third president of the United States, Thomas Jefferson, invented an encryption approach that the United States Navy still used during World War II. Thirty-six wooden disks are divided into 26 sectors. The alphabet is written on each disk in a different random sequence. The disks are mounted on a common axle. To encrypt a message, the user rotates the disks to write the message in a row and then locks the disks in place. At which point, the sequence of letters spelled out by any other row on the device is the cipher-text. This cipher-text can be transmitted and easily decrypted by anyone with the same set of disks arranged in the same sequence. They need only rotate the disks to match the cipher-text, lock the axle, and then look for a row of letters that makes sense [236].

During the Napoleonic wars and the American Civil War cryptography and cryptanalysis were widely used. Unfortunately, cryptanalytic art had progressed to the point where the cryptography in use was rather weak. The leading generals were also more interested in the way new telegraph technologies allowed timely communications than in the risks posed by not securing those communications. This led to a number of errors in the Napoleonic campaigns that could have otherwise been avoided [193]. These failings were exacerbated by the fact that long telegraph lines were difficult to protect and eavesdropping on telegraph lines is relatively easy.

This era ended with the French discovery of the St. Cyr Cipher, named after their military academy, which both greatly advanced cryptography art and was easily executed in the field. This cipher used three alphabets written on a sliding device. A code letter was used to signal the correspondence between clear text and cipher-text alphabets. The code letter was changed daily. In contrast, British security during the same epoch was based on assuming that the enemy could not understand Latin [313].

1.3   World War I

Leading up to the start of World War I (WWI) in 1914, European society became increasingly urban and industrialized. Their economic expansion was accompanied by increasing militarization. Military command and control became centralized and methodical. The use of trains and telegraphs enabled clockwork coordination of troop and supply movements [411]. To administer these new armies almost all major powers, except Britain and the U.S. whose armies were smaller, created general staffs modeled on Prussia's military hierarchy. Military coordination was handled like an engineering problem [409].

World War I was a time of rapid technological evolution. Air warfare provided new techniques for surveillance and bombarding enemy positions. Air-to-air combat led to the development of other new technologies, such as synchronizing the forward firing of machine guns with propeller movements. Armored tanks were a new technology that caused defensive forces to panic. Both sides experimented with poisonous gas artillery payloads, with disastrous consequences [411]. Innovations were frequently made in response to enemy technical breakthroughs.

Given the large number of weapons innovations, it seems strange that there were so few advances in computing during World War I. The most notable computing and communications results were [74]:

- Establishment of the principles of automation in Europe,
- IBM's innovations in developing mechanical calculators, and
- The use of wireless communications.

This lack of advance in computing technology is even more striking when one notices the importance of cryptography and communications security for the war efforts. The period from 1900 to 1914 saw all the major powers struggle to create strong ciphers that could be used practically in the field. It also saw each side having great success in stealing information about each other's ciphers [338].

At the start of WWI, the German advance through the Marne was hindered by shortcomings in their cipher system, which was based on substitution-transposition. This approach works well for clearly written messages. When messages were sent over a teletype or using wireless, any error in a single character renders the whole message unintelligible. This meant that most German communications had to be retransmitted multiple times and frequently arrived too late.

On the other side, the Russians were aware that their cipher had been compromised, so they developed a new cipher. The new cipher was a highly guarded secret. Unfortunately, at the war's onset, some Russian troops only had the old cipher. Troops with the new cipher had destroyed the old cipher to avoid using a compromised cipher. In the ensuing confusion, which was monitored closely by German troops, the Russians eventually had to send all communications in clear text [338].

These early mishaps led to each side experimenting with two basic classes of approaches to compensating for the limitations of their technologies [409]:

- Undertake only operations that can be controlled using available tools, or
- Plan operations so that they do not require ongoing control.

English cryptanalysts quickly established their superiority, after the Russian Navy captured a complete set of German code-books. From then on, the British decoding department in *Room 40* were able to quickly decrypt all

German communications, in spite of German efforts to regularly change their cryptographic keys [338, 193, 313, 236].

However, by 1915 the Germans realized that their codes had been compromised and developed new ciphers. They also cracked the British and French codes. The Germans even sent fake coded messages to the Russian fleet in the Black Sea, instructing them to undertake operations far away from the sites German and Turkish naval forces were preparing to attack.

By 1917 both sides were changing keys and ciphers regularly every few days. In spite of this, German codes were sometimes compromised by operator error [338]. It was also easier to compromise the new ciphers, since they tended to be variations of 19th century codes that had already been broken. England convinced the U.S. to enter WWI in part by revealing the decrypted contents of a German telegraph to Mexico, the Zimmerman telegraph, that encouraged Mexico to attack the U.S. [366, 193, 313].

At the end of the war, the Germans were constructing automated encryption and decryption devices. Unfortunately, these devices were large, cumbersome, and sensitive to operator error. The U.S. tried to use Choctaw Indians speaking their native language to secure transmissions. Unfortunately, the Choctaw did not understand each other over primitive telephones and had trouble with many concepts, such as machine gun, which is not a normal part of their language [366].

By the end of WWI, all parties realized the importance of cryptography for securing military communications. They also realized the hazards involved. Codes have to be secret and executed with a precision most human operators are unable to attain. This set the stage for many of the advances in computation that would occur during World War II. The final lessons of WWI seemed to be [409]:

- Warfare was increasingly mechanized,
- Mechanization required greater coordination throughout the entire supply chain,
- Errors in the supply chain were less easily tolerated than before,
- Commanders needed to understand the limits of their technologies, and
- Forces at the lower layers of command needed to adapt to new realities.

1.4   World War II

There was a twenty-year period of peace between WWI and World War II (WWII) that was dominated first by repercussions from WWI and then by the tensions leading to WWII. Like WWI, WWII was a period of rapid technical innovation. Unlike WWI, WWII included major advancements in computing technology. As we will see, advances were directly tied to the war effort and communications technology. Many of these advances are due to the intellectual prowess of two very different men: John von Neumann and Alan Turing.

Combat during WWII was even more mechanized than WWI. There were numerous technical advances that were not directly related to computers and communications, which included [411]:

- Radar and sonar for remote detection and tracking of enemies,
- Improved navigation systems,
- Missiles,
- Jet aircraft, and
- Nuclear weapons.

This non-exhaustive list does not mention improvements in arms, like tanks, that came to dominate warfare in WWI. Increased mechanization tied the outcome of WWII more closely than ever to the industrial ability of participants to produce arms.

Most of the parties fighting in WWII wanted to avoid the horrors of WWI's war of attrition. During the period leading up to WWII, the best strategists realized the possibilities presented by new technologies. Where WWI era warfare was constrained by the use of rail and telegraph, the availability of internal combustion engines, aircraft, and radio communications allowed military operations to be much more agile. The German *blitzkrieg* at the start of WWII exemplified this approach. Forces could move quickly and surprise their opponents. The tactical and operational layers of command were much less constrained. Aircraft, submarines, and armored units dominated combat. In spite of this new agility at the low layers, the increased weight of the logistics necessary to support machinery meant that strategic planning still needed to be methodical and precise [411].

The early phases of the war saw major advances by axis forces. But in the end, the combined industrial powers of the allied forces, including nuclear weapons, prevailed. The final result of WWII was reduced power for existing colonial powers: Britain, France, Germany, Italy, Japan, etc. Their influence was replaced by the bi-polar world dominated by U.S. and U.S.S.R. spheres of influence that we will describe in Section 1.5.

Some computational advances during WWII were incremental. A variety of mechanical computation tools were developed for aiming artillery, targeting ground and ship targets, and aiming defensive weapons on bombers. These tools were extensions of Lord Kelvin's work, augmented by innovations from Vannovar Bush at MIT. Similar tools were in use at least until the 1990s [54].

A very important proto-computer was the Mark I designed by Howard Aiken at the Harvard Computation Laboratory. This device consisted of a sequence of punch card machines and calculators. The punch card machines were connected to each other by sets of cables. It was developed partly with corporate support from IBM. It included separate devices for multiplication/division, interpolation, logarithms, and trigonometry [54]. The Mark I had 72 mechanical registers that could store 23 decimal digits, including their sign. Sixty constant registers allowed numbers to be input using switches [427]. Programs were stored on paper tape. It was used mainly for performing classified calculations, including determining the blast effects of the atom bomb. The Mark I used only mechanical relays. Later machines in the series (Mark III) did use vacuum tubes, but Aiken was concerned about their possible unreliability [54].

Aiken had a very distinguished team supporting his work. Of particular importance was Lieutenant Grace M. Hopper. She left her faculty position in mathematics at Vassar to join the Navy during the war. She later advanced to the rank of admiral, developing the first compiler and being influential in the development of COBOL [54]. She is also known for coining the term *bug* to refer to errors in computer programs. In searching for the reason for an error in one of her programs, she found a cockroach stuck in one of the Mark I's mechanical relays [74].

During this era many separate research teams independently developed working electronic computers. Konrad Zuse in Germany developed a series of programmable computers, some of which were Turing complete [64]. The German government used his innovations in the guidance systems of glide bombs. In 1944 Konrad Zuse designed the *Plankalül*, which was an algorithmic programming language. It was intended to become a Ph.D. dissertation, containing many ideas that would later become functional and object-oriented programming. But since this design was not published until 1972, its impact was limited [64].

At roughly the same time, Atanasoff developed the Atanasoff-Berry Computer at the University of Iowa for solving sets of simultaneous linear equations. His computer was not fully programmable and was never reliable. Although Zuse continued developing and marketing computers in Germany well into the 1960s, his work was less influential than Turing and von Neumann.

We mention Atanasoff and Zuse mainly because they have legitimate claims to having produced the first electronic computers [74, 54, 427]. The issue of who invented the first computer is not entirely academic; a 1973 legal decision in a lawsuit[3] invalidated patents given to the ENIAC team (that we discuss shortly) due to Atanasoff's prior work [54]. This court decision is essentially an official decision that Atanasoff invented the first electronic computer.

In spite of this, the most influential breakthroughs in computing came from the mathematicians Turing and von Neumann. Turing graduated from Cambridge after having spent some time at the Princeton Institute for Advanced Studies. During the course of his studies, he was taught by the top mathematicians of his day: Church, Gödel, Wittgenstein, and von Neumann. He even received an assistantship offer from von Neumann that he turned down [56]. In his dissertation, which owes much to Gödel's results, Turing de-

---

[3]Honeywell vs. Sperry Rand.

veloped the general recursively enumerable model of computing. This model remains the basis of computational theory to this day.

During WWII, Turing worked with the British cryptanalysis group at Bletchley Park. German cryptographers secured their communications using the Enigma encryption device. This encryption device had a keyboard and a set of mechanical rotors that scrambled the message. This approach reduced the possibility of operator error. The original machine had three rotors, each of which had 26 possible settings. The rotors therefore had 17,576 possible settings. There were 6 possible orderings for the scramblers and a plug-board that allowed for over 100 billion combinations. Enigma's key-space therefore had on the order of 10^{16} possibilities. This setting was the encryption key for communications. The setting was changed daily. Each message had a new ordering. The ordering for each message was sent before the message using daily settings from a code-book. The Germans later added two more rotors increasing the key space to about $159 * 10^{18}$ possibilities [366].

British intelligence was able to receive a copy of Enigma before the war. The cryptanalysis group had to determine the new key settings each day. Turing was able to automate much of this process, which greatly increased the ability of the Bletchley Park team to decode secret German communications [366]. Turing also collaborated with U.S. engineers to create secure wireless voice transmission technologies. His team at Bletchley Park designed the *Colossus* machine, which was one of the first true electronic computers. Colossus was used to perform brute-force decryption of German ciphers [54]. Instead of performing arithmetic, Colossus's logic circuits were designed to perform sets of Boolean inferences. Colossus's precursors performed cryptanalysis by storing temporary data on paper tape. By storing intermediate data electronically, Colossus was able to perform the computations more quickly and reliably. At the end of WWII, ten Colossi were in use at Bletchley Park [54].

The Japanese had a cipher device that was their equivalent to Enigma. It was code-named Purple. U.S. cryptanalysts were able to reproduce the Purple device and decipher secret Japanese communications. Fewer details are known about the cyptanalysis of Purple [313]. The work of the Bletchley Park and U.S. cryptanalysts were a major factor in deciding the outcome of WWII. During much of WWII, the U.S. relied on using Navajo radio operators to secure their communications [366]. They learned from their mistake of using Choctaw in WWI, by having the Navajo come up with Navajo equivalents for concepts that did not exist in their native language. For example, mortars were called "guns that squat" [366]. It should be mentioned that cryptography alone was not enough to secure communications. Even if the contents of communications were secure, the transmission of information had risks. When submarines communicated with their headquarters, ships with directional antennas could locate their positions and attack them [411].

ENIAC, the *Electronic Numerical Integrator and Computer*, was developed by Eckert and Mauchly. Both worked at the University of Pennsylvania. ENIAC used vacuum tubes to store information. It required 550 tubes to store a single ten digit number. It had a total of 20 accumulators, a multiply-divide unit, a bank of 10 switches storing up to 100 numbers in temporary storage, as well as standard punch card readers and printers. It contained on the order of 18,000 tubes and consumed 15 kilowatts of power [54]. ENIAC could run up to 20 hours without a tube burning out. Because changes in temperature made the vacuum tubes more likely to fail, the ENIAC was almost never turned off [427]. This computer was developed at the U.S. Army's Ballistics Research Laboratory and was programmed by replugging cables. Its first application was a classified problem involving hydrogen bomb design. Afterward, it was used for applications ranging from number theory to meteorology [54]. ENIAC was over 100 times larger than any previous electronic device. Its primary task was calculating ballistics tables for the artillery [427].

John von Neumann was the most renowned mathematician of the twentieth century. He is credited with numerous discoveries. These include advances in measure theory, topology, Hilbert spaces, theory of lattices, quantum theory, nuclear energy, numerical methods, game theory, economics, dynamics, meteorology, computing, Monte Carlo method, automata theory, cellular automata, and probability. Von Neumann worked on the Manhattan Project with Oppenheimer to produce the first atom bomb and invented game theory with Oskar Morgenstern. He was the youngest professor ever appointed to the Princeton Institute of Advanced Study. He studied under Hilbert and Polya [406]. Where Turing's life ended in tragedy, von Neumann only grew in stature and influence throughout his life. Among his many contributions to computing, his publication *First Draft of a Report on the EDVAC* documenting the ENIAC computer and suggesting extensions for the next generation established the reference machine architecture. This *von Neumann architecture* has core memory and a central processing unit. Code and data are managed and processed in the same way [56]. Although the paper describing ENIAC documented the work of many participants, only von Neumann's name appeared on the paper. This led to acrimony among the team and was one of many reasons for Eckert and Mauchly leaving the University of Pennsylvania to start their own company [427].

Although important, the Colossus was less influential on future computers than were the Mark I and ENIAC. This is partly due to its being designed specifically for one particular application domain. It may also be due, in part, to the secrecy associated with cryptanalysis efforts. Very few people knew about its existence, because it was kept secret until the 1970s [352]. Later mainframe computers are direct descendants of the ENIAC design. This research is seen as the precursor of modern day computers. Open publication of von Neumann's paper could be a major factor as to why the ENIAC's design decisions had a larger impact on future generations.

Steganography advances during WWII did not require the use of computers. Codes were developed where the true message could be found by looking at every, for example, fifth letter in a decoy message. Also, microdots became available where large volumes of information could be stored in an object 0.05 inches in diameter [130].

1.5 Cold War

Cold War post WWII reality was militarily and politically dominated by the atomic bomb. Using the timetable in [411], the Cold War lasted from 1945 to 1991. World politics was dominated by Soviet and American spheres of influence. Asia, except for Japan, South Korea, and South Asia, was in the Soviet sphere of influence. The western hemisphere, except for Cuba, was dominated by the United States. Europe was split in half. Western Europe (including West Germany) was allied with the United States. Eastern Europe (including East Germany) was under Russian influence. In these regions there was no major warfare, mainly due to fear of nuclear confrontation [409, 411].

Computer technology made major advances during this period. The pioneers of the ENIAC project were very influential. After his report, von Neumann returned to the Princeton Institute for Advanced Studies. He worked increasingly in Washington, D.C. for the Federal Government. He was one of five Atomic Energy Commission commissioners and used this position to secure funding for a new generation of computers. These machines were built for many leading research institutes [55]. During the same time Eckert and Mauchly, in many respects bitter that their names were not on von Neumann's report, started a company to build computers for commercial applications. They produced the *UNIVAC* series of computers and eventually sold their corporation to Remington-Rand [427].

A concurrent MIT project produced the Whirlwind computer system for avionics applications. After the end of WWII, the Office of Naval Research modified the Whirlwind project to become the focal point of the U.S. Cold War air defense infrastructure [427, 345]. Whirlwind was a very successful project, influencing later IBM products.

During the 1950s Remington-Rand merged with Sperry, and remained a major computer manufacturer. It competed with National Cash Register (NCR), Burroughs, and IBM, who all had successful computer hardware businesses. In the 1960s IBM came to dominate the computer industry. Until the advent of the PC, the computer business primarily sold hardware products. In the 1970s the set of non-IBM mainframe vendors were Burroughs, UNIVAC, NCR, Control Data, and Honeywell, informally known as BUNCH [109].

As computer equipment became essential to national defense, a number of influential studies established core concepts for computer and network security. The Anderson Report outlined plans for developing systems that could process classified information securely [44]. The report includes a list of important security threats and available countermeasures. Many of the threats known in 1972 are yet to be adequately addressed. In 1976, while working for MITRE, Bell and La Padula wrote an access control framework for MULTICS that was designed to allow secure processing use of information with multiple levels of security classifications on computer systems [65]. Both the Anderson Report and Bell-La Padula Model built on the idea of a reference monitor verifying the validity of access requests. Bell-La Padula concentrated on avoiding information leakage that could cause classified data to be treated at any point as non-sensitive. The 1985 *Orange Book*, heavily influenced by Bell-La Padula, was even more influential. It prescribed specific classes of computer systems and the security requirements that each class of computers was expected to fulfill. Security policies were explicit and users were accountable for their actions [135].

The MULTICS project at MIT deserves special mention. MULTICS started operation in 1969. It was a joint project of MIT, Bell Labs, and General Electric (GE). It ran on GE hardware. The GE computer hardware division was eventually sold to Honeywell. MULTICS was the first operating system written in a higher level language (PL/1). It had no file system, *per se*; everything was stored in long-lived virtual memory. The operating system designers paid particular attention to system security. The system design included a set of eight concentric rings denoting security levels. Access to secure instructions required using well-defined application programming interface (API) calls. This is an early example of a *firewall* [279]. MULTICS security was formally evaluated by the U.S. Air Force. While some security problems were found (notably trap doors could be inserted), the general design principles were found to form a good basis for the development of a secure operating system [232]. One exploit discovered by the red team allowed them to install a system patch that bypassed all storage security mechanisms [412]. MULTICS was the first operating system given a B2 security level, using Orange Book criteria. No buffer overflow vulnerabilities were ever found in MULTICS, which may have been due to the use of PL/1 instead of C. Many feel that later systems are less secure [233].

In the late 1950s, a new generation of smaller *mini-computers* emerged. These machines were smaller, less powerful, and less expensive than mainframes. This allowed applications to be developed that would have otherwise been prohibitively expensive. Control Data Corporation (CDC) and Digital Equipment Corporation (DEC) became important minicomputer vendors. DEC's VAX computer series helped popularize the use of Unix [109]. The Unix operating system was developed at Bell Labs as a single user version of MULTICS. Although Unix is much more widely used, it does not have the reputation of security MULTICS earned. In particular, Unix is written in C, which is extremely vulnerable to buffer overflow exploits. Buffer overflows will be explored more fully in Chapter 8.

The advent of the transistor helped shrink the size of computers more quickly. Personal computers became available in the 1970s. As computers shrank, the software industry emerged on its own. Software was no longer sold mainly as optional additions by hardware vendors. Microsoft Corporation successfully marketed its DOS operating system, which evolved into Windows. Eventually Windows and variants of Unix became the dominant operating systems [109, 74].

As computers became ubiquitous, creating networks of computers connected via telecommunications lines was a natural extension. The U.S. Department of Defense started the ARPANET in 1969, which eventually evolved into the Internet. Commercial computer networks using the ITU X.25 standard became available in the 1970s. Computer manufacturers, like IBM (SNA) and DEC (DECnet), quickly developed networking software allowing clients to fully utilize these networks [74]. The ability to access computers remotely, naturally made them vulnerable to intrusion. The use of passwords emerged as the standard tool for preventing unwanted access [295].

The new availability of computers allowed the science of cryptography to make major advances. Considering the fact that Colossus was only declassified in the 1970s, it is clear that little can be said about advances in military cryptography during the Cold War era. In the United States, the National Security Agency (NSA) is in charge of cryptographic research for the United States government and has worked zealously to maintain its monopoly [366]. Cryptography also became available for civilian use. In the 1970s the U.S. National Bureau of Standards[4], with NSA approval, agreed to the release of the Data Encryption Standard (DES) with a 56-bit key-space. This cipher would have been impossible to execute without an electronic computer. It became available for use by commercial applications. It requires both parties to have the same key value, which required the development of secure techniques for key distribution [366, 236]. The development of public key cryptography is a major step towards solving the problem of key distribution. Public key algorithms allow each party to have two matched keys. When a message is encrypted with one key, it can only be decrypted with the other key. This allows each party to publish one key and keep the other key private. We discuss how this works in Chapter 3.

During the Cold War period there were a number of security and defense related security concerns. We can not discuss issues related to military cryptography and cryptanalysis, since they would be classified. There were, however, a number of issues that were public.

We first consider a side-channel attack. Technical issues related to side-channels are covered in Chapter 12. Cryptography algorithms secure data by transforming clear text information into corresponding cipher-text. Great care is taken to assure the difficulty of inferring the clear text message from its cipher-text. Side-channels circumvent this by collecting environmental information that leak information about processing internals. One important side-channel is provided by electromagnetic emissions from computer operations. This vulnerability was given the military codename *Tempest*. Collection

---

[4]Now the National Institute of Standards and Technology

of intelligence data from the electromagnetic spectrum is known as *signals intelligence* or *SIGINT*. In WWI, German, French, and British forces all used electromagnetic emissions from telephone lines to eavesdrop on opponents. All sides quickly developed precautions to avoid these problems. In 1960, British MI5 used the electromagnetic signals leaking from the French embassy to break the French ciphers used during negotiations about British entry into the European Economic Community. To negate this vulnerability, the NSA developed strict "tempest" standards for shielding machines performing sensitive computations. This includes *red-black separation*, where there are no direct connections between machines doing classified work and machines treating unclassified information. This problem was first mentioned in open literature in 1966, but the broader public first became aware of it in the mid-1980s [247].

Although the Soviet Union's access to computer technology was limited, the record shows that it was very active in attempting to exploit computer security weaknesses. Anecdotal evidence exists that during the 1980s many parts of Eastern Europe, especially Bulgaria, had very active computer virus development scenes [84]. While there is little evidence that this activity was coordinated by the government, it would have been unusual for this activity to have been unnoticed in these tightly controlled societies.

Also in the late 1980s, a systems administrator at the Lawrence Berkeley National Laboratory tracked systematic intrusions into his computer systems. Although the evidence of the intrusions was slight, he eventually uncovered a group of West German hackers who traded information to the Soviet KGB in exchange for drugs. Luckily, the laboratory they attacked had no sensitive information [381].

In spite of the tense peace in Europe and the Americas, conflicts did take place in Africa, Southeast Asia, Central Asia, and the Middle East. Traditional war between nation-states was limited mainly to the Middle East. Most of those conflicts involving Israel were decided in Israel's favor, in part due to their successful application of maneuver doctrine [409]. This approach inspired by insights from Korean War air combat emphasizes the *OODA Loop*[5]. When combatants follow this doctrine, they actively engage their opponent. They try to create opportunities that they can exploit. As long as they can react more quickly than their opponent, opportunities will arise eventually [266].

With the exception of conflicts, like Algeria, where the local populace opposed their former colonizers, most other conflicts were in essence proxy battles. One superpower battled with a local actor who was supported by the other superpower. These conflicts included Viet Nam, Afghanistan, and a number of skirmishes in Central America. Often these conflicts were asymmetric. The superpower's opponent acted as insurgents; hiding within the native population [401]. This neutralizes many of the superpower's advantages. It is difficult to respond to attacks without alienating the populace, since it is dif-

---

[5]The Observe, Orient, Decide, and Act (OODA) loop refers to the time it takes to react to events perceived during a conflict.

ficult to differentiate between insurgents and civilians. It took the U.S. a long time to find a successful counterinsurgency doctrine [169, 300]. The United States' problems in the Viet Nam conflict had many sources. These included relying on the veracity of official reports and attempting using computer systems to over-centralize control. This hindered the ability of troops to react quickly in the field [409].

The Cold War ended with the economic collapse of the Soviet Union. It is still unclear what the eventual international order will become. The past has shown, however, a clear connection between military needs and advances in computation [74]. We expect this trend to continue.

Dr. van Creveld's predictions in [410, 411] are well thought out and particularly relevant to this book. In his view, von Clausewitz's view of war is obsolete. Future conflicts are unlikely to be fought between nation-states by uniformed military. Modern weapon systems are too costly and nuclear weapons are also too deadly. Use of expensive weapons drains national resources and use of nuclear weapons invites deadly retaliation. This does not mean that there will be an end to violent conflict. Asymmetric wars are more attractive. With insurgencies, terror campaigns, and cyberwar it is difficult to attribute offensive acts to parties. In the future, it is likely that it will be increasingly difficult to distinguish between criminal activity and foreign aggression [410, 411].

1.6   Organized Crime and Botnets

Up to now, we have discussed the use and abuse of computers only by nation states. Criminal organizations depend, at least as much as nations, on keeping information secret. Which is why criminal organizations have used secret codes since at least the fifteenth century [313]. Needless to say, the ability of modern day computers to secure information has been exploited by criminal elements.

There is no clear record of the origins of computer criminality. As soon as computers started being used in commercial enterprises, it is likely that, in at least one corporation, a computer was immediately used to hide some type of malfeasance. It is unclear whether or not this type of delict is specifically "computer crime." One study shows that from 1958 to 1963, there were one or zero incidents each year. Between 1968 and 1972 the annual number of computer crimes increased to over 75 each year. The forms of computer crime listed in the study are: vandalism, information theft, financial fraud, and unauthorized use. Almost half the cases listed are financial fraud [448].

The first computer and network specific crimes were probably telephone service thefts by *phreaks*. Starting in the late 1950s, many individuals discovered how to make long distance telephone calls without paying [331]. One famous phreak, John Draper, used toy whistles found in Cap'n Crunch cereal boxes to make free phone calls. Eventually phreaks started to make and market electronic *blue box* devices that made the same tones as cereal box whistles. Steve Wozniak and Steve Jobs, who later founded Apple Computer, earned money while in college by selling blue boxes door-to-door in college dorms.

In the late 1960s professional research reports started being published on computer network security and data privacy. The early computer abuse cases were typically not driven by greed, rather introverted, intelligent individuals committed crimes while trying to solve intractable, personal problems [331]. By the early 1970s new forms of computer abuse emerged, as students at top universities started misusing university computer systems for amusement and entertainment. Finding novel uses of computer equipment was seen as an intellectual challenge [331]. These students became known as *hackers* or *crackers*.

By the mid-1980s, the ubiquity of computer systems let computer crime expand to include a much wider range of targets [430]:

- Four 13-year-old students altered cola shipping instructions to get 10 cases of free soft drink,
- Credit records of 1/3 of all working Americans were illegally accessed on a TRW computer system,
- The Mafia attempted to set up a shell software company to develop a funds transfer network for the Middle East that included a backdoor,
- The Chaos Computer Club in Hamburg illustrated a flaw in the German telephone company's video-text offering by reprogramming a bank computer to run up over $ 70,000.00 in charges, and
- British hackers tampered with the Royal Family's e-mail.

Although these incidents are only a brief sampling of the incidents on record, they are illustrative of hacker exploits in the 1980s.

Computers and networks allowed new types of malicious tools to be developed. First came programs that included hidden functionality. These became known as *Trojans*, due to their resemblance to the Trojan Horse in Homer's *Iliad*. The best example of a Trojan is Ken Thompson's 1984 Turing Award Lecture. He described how he wrote a version of the Unix login program that contained a backdoor exploit, which allowed him surreptitious access to any Unix system running the program. To make it more difficult to detect, he modified the C compiler so that the object code for any login program it compiled would include the backdoor. He further modified the compiler so that the object code for any C compiler it compiled would include the same malicious logic [395]. This shows that programs can include Trojans, even if their source code does not.

Viruses are programs that reproduce by inserting copies of themselves into other programs. Von Neumann documented models of machines that reproduce themselves. The design of a self-reproducing cellular automata can be found in this 1966 paper [417]. In 1972, a science fiction novel included the idea of a "virus" program [174]. There were also a few obscure exploits before the mid-1980s that resembled viruses, and in some respects even Thompson's exploit could be considered a virus. But the first real use of the term computer *virus* and the first working software implementation of a virus was in Fred Cohen's research for his Ph.D. dissertation [119]. By the end of 1985, viruses started appearing on personal computers. It is not clear who the early virus writers were, although many viruses came from Eastern Bloc virus factories [84]. Technical details concerning virus design are fully treated in Chapter 9.

Like viruses, computer *worms* first appeared in science fiction. John Brunner's *Shockwave Rider* describes a dystopian future where the protagonist releases networked computer program worms to help avoid detection [96]. The first worm implementation was a research prototype at Xerox PARC. It was a distributed system management tool that performed many useful tasks. The only problem Xerox had with the worm occurred when they tried to turn it off. To stop the Xerox PARC worm, they had to turn off all the computers on the network. The first worm attack was a proof of concept released by Robert Tappan Morris in 1988. At the time, he was a graduate student at Cornell. The Morris worm infected over 10 percent of the Internet within hours [397]. Over time worms became increasingly prevalent. The years 2001-2003 saw many major worm incidents, including Nimda, Slammer, Blaster, Code Red I, and Code Red II. While it is unclear exactly what damage can be attributed to these worms, possible collateral damage attributed to the worm attacks included Automated Teller Machines, airplane flight schedules, elections, and possibly a blackout in the Northeastern U.S. [322, 294, 66].

E-mail viruses were at one point widespread. They were emails with malicious attachments that spread by sending copies of themselves to other users. This approach blurs the distinction between worms and viruses [397]. This distinction has been academic ever since hybrid attacks like Nimda fit both categories [428].

Worms and viruses were often high profile events that caused disruptions and had news coverage. Trojans are by definition stealthy attacks that tried to remain unnoticed. The current generation of threats usually try to remain stealthy. Modern cybercrime has become a very lucrative business that includes an underground economy in goods and services. Current cybercrime technologies and techniques include [319]:

- botnets – networks of compromised machines,
- spam – unsolicited e-mail advertisements, usually fraudulent,
- phishing – attempts to fraudulently collect sensitive personal information,
- pharming – redirecting web traffic to a fraudulent site,
- identity theft and identity fraud – fraudulent use of personal information,
- cross site scripting – inserting script commands into another's website,
- cross site request forgery – tricking a user's browser to making requests on another party's website,
- underground forums, and

- money laundering.

Botnets have been estimated to include hundreds of thousands to millions of machines. Although the numbers are difficult to verify, the largest botnet in 2009 was estimated to have somewhere between 580,000 to 1,600,000 nodes [319]. Botnets consist of multiple compromised PCs working in harmony to steal private information, send spam, do phishing exploits, and launch denial of service attacks. The Torpig botnet in 2010 was reliably estimated as collecting between $8,300.00 and $830,000.00 per day [58]. Since botnets act as an ongoing source of illegal income, botnet *herders*[6] invest a lot of effort in avoiding detection. Hackers, viruses, and worms produced high profile exploits, gathered a lot of publicity, and were rarely more than a nuisance. The current generation of computer crime is less easily detected and has a significant economic impact.

1.7   Cyberwar

The term *cyberwar* is somewhat controversial. There are many valid interpretations of cyberwar. In many respects, as we have seen, communications infrastructure has been an important tool for defense and offense, since the times of Sun Tzu. In other respects, the damage done to a human being with a kinetic weapon can not be put in the same category as disabling a server.[7] The view we present here is that cyberwar is a natural evolution of the military role of communications and computation. It is not a radically new idea; it is a logical extension of the past.

The extended distributed denial of service (DDoS) launched on Estonia by Russians in April 2007 is generally considered the first true cyberwar [419, 18]. The Estonian government removed a statue honoring Soviet troops, which insulted many Russian nationals. Estonia was subjected to a (DDoS) [8]. Estonia was a particularly good target for this type of attack, since Estonia's government and economic sectors depend heavily on the Internet. It is suspected that the attacks originated in Russia, although there is no clear evidence of Russian government involvement [124].

Russian government involvement is, however, heavily suspected in the second true cyberwar incident. In August 2008 there was escalating tension between Russia and Georgia concerning the Georgian provinces of South Ossetia and Abkhazia. The population of both regions have large Russian ethnic populations, but are part of Georgia. Georgian government websites were attacked

---

[6]The administrator of a botnet is usually referred to as a botnet herder.

[7]In the future, it is likely that computer attacks could be deadly when computer controllers and computerized medical devices are compromised.

[8]DDoS attacks occur when a large number of computers coordinate their activities to overload the victim. Legitimate users no longer have access to the website.

shortly before the Russian military attacked Georgia [124]. This is the first time that there were coordinated cyber and physical attacks.

Cyberwar presents a number of practical and ethical questions. One question is whether or not the use of psychological warfare, disinformation, propaganda, and information operations should be considered cyberwar. Another important issue is the legal framework for cyberattacks. Under the Geneva convention, it is a war crime for the military to attack civilian targets. What are (or are not) civilian targets in cyberwar? Given that the U.S. relies more heavily on its computer infrastructure than likely opponents, is it wise for us to invest in offensive cyber-technologies? What sort of defenses are permissible in a cyber-war? In fact, what does defense mean in a cyber-conflict? There are no clear answers for these issues to date. Just as there is no clear definition for cyberwar.

We return to van Creveld's insights on the future of war [410, 411]. Modern war as defined by Clausewitz [416] has become overly expensive with each cruise missile costing over one million dollars. War between major nations is dangerous, since both states are likely to have weapons of mass destruction. This makes war between nation-states impractical. On the other hand asymmetric conflicts, also known as insurgencies, terrorism, and/or low-intensity conflicts, are cheap, easy to organize, and frequently effective against nation-states. Cyberattack is in many ways an ideal weapon in this type of conflict. One major reason for this is the difficulty of attributing a cyberattack to its source.

For these reasons we anticipate the number of security incidents to increase. It is also to be anticipated that the line between cyberwar and cybercriminality will become increasingly vague.

1.8 Problems

1. Outline the evolution of cryptology over time. Explain how this application has been a driving force in the creation of modern information technology.

2. Justify why or why not the computer and network attacks mentioned in this paper could not have been invented any earlier than they were.

3. List at least five issues related to cyberwar that are ethically ambiguous. Justify your selection.

4. This chapter tends to present the development of computers and communication technology as being fundamentally tied to the evolution of military technologies. Write a short essay explaining why, or why not, you find this position justified.

5. Are the development of computer and communications technologies primarily the result of advances in mathematics or advances in engineering? Justify your response.

6. Attempt to trace the evolution of computer crime over time. Extrapolate and predict the new exploits that are to be expected in the next 20 years.

1.9 Glossary

Atanasoff: Engineer who made one of the first computers.

Babbage: Completed plans for mechanical computer.

Bletchley Park: British cryptanalysis center during WWII.

Bush: Vannovar Bush was a prominent academic who envisaged ideas that resemble the World Wide Web.

bug: An error in a computer program.

Colossus: Groundbreaking computer used at Bletchley Park for cryptanalysis.

Cryptanalysis: Science of analyzing codes to decipher them.

Cryptology: Science of encoded writing. Includes cryptography and cryptanalysis.

Cryptography: Science of writing in codes.

ENIAC: Groundbreaking computer.

Hopper: Grace Hopper was an early programmer. Leading figure in COBOL definition.

Lovelace: Ada Lovelace, daughter of Lord Byron, is credited with being the first programmer.

Mark I: Groundbreaking computer.

Pascal: French mathematician who implemented an early mechanical computer.

steganography: Science of hiding information.

Turing: English mathematician and cryptanalyst. Invented theory of computation.

Vigenère: Famous French cryptographer.

von Neumann: Mathematician who wrote paper establishing the reference computer architecture.

Zuse: Engineer who constructed an early computer.

2

Security and Privacy Overview

CONTENTS

2.1 Introduction

This chapter provides a brief overview of security and privacy. Our goal is to define the terms we need later in the book and give a brief technical overview before discussing the technical details beginning in Chapter 3. At the end of this chapter, the reader should understand:

- What we mean by security,

- The different levels of security a system can have,
- Common vulnerabilities and exploits, and
- How attackers can combine vulnerabilities and exploit them to accomplish a larger goal.

These concepts are threads that run through the entire book. Each section in this chapter builds on its predecessors. Specific topics in this chapter are:

- *Section 2.2* – what is meant by security and the attributes of secure systems,
- *Section 2.3* – the role of *social engineering*; how human factors and deception help compromise systems,
- *Section 2.4* – how people and computers convince computers and networks of their identity,
- *Section 2.5* – system access controls that typically define what users can and can not do,
- *Section 2.6* – how log files track system events in order to maintain system security,
- *Section 2.7* – the importance of user interfaces for maintaining secure systems,
- *Section 2.8* – presents an essential, fundamental limitation to security implementation and verification,
- *Section 2.9* – presents a security taxonomy from the Carnegie Mellon Computer Emergency response Team (CERT) that provides a language for describing security incidents,
- In *Section 2.10* – the taxonomy from Section 2.9 is tailored to deal with mobile code security,
- In *Section 2.11* – the taxonomy from Section 2.9 is used to analyze automotive information technology security.

Sections 2.10 and 2.11 apply the same taxonomy to distributed and embedded systems. Since the desktop workstation market is saturated, these two domains will become increasingly important. Traditional security approaches are not particularly well-suited to these new systems. These sections provide readers with an understanding of new issues that will have to be dealt with.

The final section introduces on-line privacy issues. Unfortunately, the intuition most people use to preserve privacy in the physical world is not well-suited to on-line interactions. The topic of privacy will recur frequently in this book. The current state of affairs is not satisfying.

2.2   Security Attributes

Traditionally, security is viewed as maintaining the following attributes [375]:

- *Confidentiality* – Is keeping your data private and only accessible by authorized persons. (e.g., The fact that you purchased the book *I Can Has*

Cheezburger? A LOLcat Colleckshun from Amazon.com should only be available to you, Amazon.com, and your credit card company.)

- *Authentication* – The origin of information is correctly identified. (Ex. Amazon.com determines your identity before accepting your book order.)
- *Integrity* – Only authorized parties can change information. (Ex. Your roommates can not change the number of copies in your book order from 1 to 5.)
- *Non-repudiation* – Neither sender nor receiver can deny that they performed a transaction. (Ex. After your book is delivered, you can not deny having made the order.)
- *Access control* – Access to information is controlled and limited to authorized parties. (Ex. You can neither read nor modify the Amazon purchase histories of your roommates.)
- *Availability* – Users should have access to computer assets as needed. (Ex. You can check the progress of your book order when you want to.)

In this book, as in [90], we view these attributes as a proper subset of what it means to be secure. Some people use the mnemonic device *CIA* to refer to confidentiality, integrity, and availability [310]. This is more compact than the list above and less explicit.

Although *availability* is not, strictly speaking, a security issue, it is necessary. The other attributes all describe things that are not allowed to occur, which leads to security designs that are too restrictive. It is a common joke that the only secure system is one that is never used, but the reality is that security needs to be effective without obstructing the user's ability to work. If security hinders legitimate users from doing their tasks, users will find ways to circumvent security mechanisms.

A number of system availability properties are important to security, including:

- *Reliability* – defined by the expected time to system failure [93], also known as mean time to failure (MTTF) or mean time between failures (MTBF). If a network is operational only when all pairs of nodes can communicate, dependability decreases exponentially with the number of nodes. In the simplest case, with n components all of which have failure rate λ and expected time to failure[1] $\frac{1}{\lambda}$, and the system is down if any component is down, the dependability of the system will be λ^n.
- *Availability* – is the percent time that a system is operational. As with reliability, depending on what is meant by operational, this can decrease exponentially with system size. In general, if a system MTTF is $\frac{1}{\lambda}$ and mean time to repair (MTTR) is $\frac{1}{\mu}$, then system availability is $\frac{MTTF}{MTTF+MTTR}$, because MTTF is the amount of time the system works correctly until a failure occurs and the lifecycle of the system is MTTR + MTTF.

---

[1]This assumes that component lifetime follows an exponential probability distribution [93].

- *Safety* – is defined as a condition where a predefined set of error conditions never occurs. This is a concept from fault tolerance [168]. Note that safety and security are very different concepts.
- *Liveness* – is a condition where a system always eventually returns to a predefined set of desirable states; it has liveness [168]. Liveness is another aspect of fault-tolerance.
- *Self-Stabilization* – is when a system has the ability to recover from any possible fault condition [168, 357]. This is an extreme form of fault tolerance.

These properties can be verified using either statistical or static analysis. Depending on security issues and system design, some attributes may or may not be relevant. It is worth noting that the term *dependability* is used to refer to both reliability and/or availability.

Reliability and availability are continuous values. Markov analysis techniques are commonly used to derive these values [363, 342, 341]. These Markov chains may be derived from reliability graphs that decompose the system into combinations of serial and parallel components [363]. Alternatively, fault trees can be used to derive upper and lower bounds of system dependability. They have difficulty expressing subcomponents that are used by more than one subsystem, but their quantitative evaluation is more straightforward [264]. We discuss Markov process analysis for another application in more depth in Chapter 12.

Safety, liveness, and self-stabilizability are Boolean values. Model checking tools are commonly used to verify these attributes. These techniques are quite similar to the ones we use to verify security protocols in Chapter 4.

One important issue where security analysis goes beyond dependability is that dependability analysis primarily relies on statistical fault models, where security has to assume the presence of an intelligent, malicious adversary. Interestingly, there is a rich set of dependability literature which assumes that failures occur in the most unfavorable way possible and allows for intelligent collaboration among failing components. This is the *Byzantine Generals Problem* [252, 60, 92, 93], where participants try to create consensus among a distributed set of fault prone components. It is stated as a word problem where a set of generals, in an army renowned for its internal corruption, try to decide whether to attack a city or lay siege. Each of the n generals knows that some number t of their colleagues work for the enemy and are trying to cause confusion. The question is whether or not (and how) the loyal generals can reach agreement. In general, this is possible as long as $t < n/3$, subject to connectivity constraints [252]. Unfortunately, in security analysis, as with social interactions, the assumption that $2/3$ of your inputs are correct is rarely practical.

Another important security attribute is *attack surface* [211]. Since all software and hardware components are subject to failure and likely to contain errors, it is wise to minimize the number of components that an attacker can access. These components include [211]:

- Number of open sockets (network access points),
- Number of open pipes (inter-process communications entries),
- Number of open remote procedure call (RPC) endpoints,
- Number of services (Windows), daemons (UNIX/Linux), or equivalent processes; this includes services running by default,
- Number of services (Windows), daemons (UNIX/Linux), or equivalent running with elevated privileges,
- Number of web server scripts, filters, and applications,
- Number of accounts with elevated privilege, and
- Number of files, directories, etc. with weak access control.

Some of this is common sense. Attack surface minimization needs to be weighed against other good design practices. Simple programs are less likely to contain errors, so adding complexity to reduce the number of entities available to attack can be counterproductive.

Finally, systems should always follow the *principle of least privilege*. Each process and user should be given only the access rights necessary to perform its tasks. File access rights need to be restricted to only allow read, write, and execute access to the users/daemons/processes that should be accessing them. Network ports that are not needed should not be allowed to accept access requests. This list is not exhaustive, but the rule is pervasive.

2.3 Social Engineering

"It's human nature to trust your fellow man, especially when the request meets the test of being reasonable. Social engineers use this knowledge to exploit their victims and to achieve their goals." This quote comes from Kevin Mitnick's book *The Art of Deception* [290]. Mitnick is one of the best known hackers of the late 20th century. He was convicted for a number of exploits. He stole a Pacific Bell technical manual and a pre-release version of the Digital Electronics Corporation VMS operating system. He listened in on the voice mail of Pacific Bell security officials and broke into the computer of another security expert [213]. In his book, Mitnick attributes his success in infiltrating computers to the art of *social engineering*: the ability to deceive others and extract information. He considers social engineering to be a cyclical process with four phases[396]:

1. Research,
2. Developing rapport and trust,
3. Exploiting trust, and
4. Utilizing information.

Social engineers masquerade as repairmen, colleagues, clients, or even bosses. Role playing makes it easy to find useful information, including passwords and security mechanisms. To collect the information, attackers call on the phone; show up in person; send e-mails; loiter; shoulder surf; read passwords posted on sticky notes in the workplace; use forensic tools to analyze discarded computer equipment; or go dumpster diving. The attacker may use "reverse social engineering," creating a situation that allows them to "help" their victim. Once they "help" the victim by solving the "problem" that they created, the victim is grateful and willing to trust the attacker [142].

The human element is often the weakest link in a security system. Users need to understand security policies, why they exist, and how they work. Sadly, this is rarely the case and people are easily convinced by outsiders that there is a good reason to not follow the rules in a given instance. A statistical analysis of a cybercrime database found seven generic scam classes[374]:

1. *Low level trickery* – requires no planning or finesse. An example scam is an on-line merchant reimbursing a client for their purchase, which turns out to have been made with a bad check. Typically some amount of money is given to the victim.
2. *Story based application* – are more sophisticated scams that require planning and an elaborate background story. This class includes fake charities.
3. *Participation* – complex processes that enlist the victim as a participant. Frequently, this involves employing the victim for a period of time. The victim may be used as a mule for money laundering. Alternatively, by employing the victim the scammer receives their identity information, making the victim vulnerable to identity theft.
4. *Obligation* – requires victims to actively respond to the initial contact and receive unexpected charges. Example scams could involve the victim dialing a number starting with *72 (which activates call forwarding) or area code 809 (which is an area code with premium charges).
5. *Apparently authentic requests* – gather information about the user that can be misused. Examples of this class include spyware keyloggers and phishing.
6. *Merchant/customer exploitation* – abuse purchase interactions. This includes non-delivery of merchandise, shill bidding, non-payment, or bait and switch. These scams are planned and sophisticated.
7. *Marketing* – involve investment opportunities. This includes pyramid schemes, Ponzi scams, investment seminars, and get rich quick schemes. By advertising investment opportunities, the scammer tries to collect money and/or information.

These classes are differentiated mainly by four static factors [374]:

1. What the scam offers,
2. Role of the victim,
3. Scammer's goal, and

    4. Method of scam introduction.

These are the main factors used for planning by a social engineer. While the seven classes given in [374] relate mainly to theft, the same general approaches can be used to collect other types of information or circumvent system security mechanisms.

Technology sometimes makes it difficult to tell the difference between legitimate requests and fraudulent ones. Professor Ross Anderson at Cambridge recounts an incident where someone in his lab was investigating a suspected phishing[2] attack and contacted the bank concerned [46]. The bank verified that the email they were investigating was not an official communication. The bank was wrong: the e-mail was sent by another office. When banks can not differentiate between their own communications and fraudulent attacks, users can not be expected to be immune to social engineering.

Since these attacks are based on human nature, they are difficult to avoid. Awareness campaigns can help convince employees to be wary. Detailed security policies that address common social engineering problems can be useful. Policies need to be tested and enforced. Security audits that test users may be useful [227]. Many well known attacks are based on social engineering. We now discuss some of the most common social engineering based attacks.

2.3.1 Nigerian 419 scams

Nigerian 419 scams – are also known as advance fee fraud [319]. This fraud dates back to the sixteenth century, but the advent of email allowed it to spread worldwide [127]. The name 419 scam refers to article 419 of the Nigerian criminal code (financial fraud); fraud is the fifth largest industry in Nigeria. Typically, the victim receives an e-mail from someone claiming to require money or information to perform a financial transaction. They offer money to the victim for their help. Common 419 variants claim that the scammer received an inheritance; there is an investment opportunity; or the victim won a lottery [146]. It is difficult to estimate how widespread this scheme is; the crime is under-reported by victims that are ashamed [319]. A study from the Netherlands estimates global loss in 2009 from 419 scams to be \$9,387 million [214]. Although the practice started in Nigeria, it has spread globally. The top countries for generating 419 scams in 2009 were (in order) the United States, Ghana, The United Kingdom, China, and Spain [214]. For every 1000 emails sent by a scammer, about 10 people respond and about one person eventually sends money [146].

2.3.2 Spam

Spam– is unwanted e-mail advertising. In 2008, Symantec observed 349.6 billion spam messages on the Internet; they estimate that 90 percent of that

---

[2]We will define phishing later in this section.

spam was generated by botnets [319]. While not all unwanted email adver-tising is criminal, the majority of it is fraudulent, as illustrated by it being generated by botnets. The rush to eliminate spam has led to an industry that attempts to identify and eliminate spam automatically. Naturally, spam op-erators create programs that attempt to outwit spam filters [429] and there is reason to believe that statistical learning of spam profiles can never be secure [62]. Science fiction author Corey Doctorow has observed that legions of spam generation engines fighting legions of spam filters daily is the equivalent of programs evolving to pass the Turing test. He humorously hypothesizes that this industry is likely to beat artificial intelligence researchers in producing sentient machines [140].

As e-mail use is becoming less pervasive [402, 271], spam is naturally mov-ing to other technologies. Since social networks are replacing e-mail as a vehicle for on-line communications, they are increasingly attractive for distributing spam [199]. *Webspam* refers to spam content distribution via webpages. It is also used to mislead search engines into directing users to specific webpages, known as spamdexing [108], frequently by generating large numbers of web pages constructed solely to influence search engine rankings [158]. This in-cludes providing different web page content to search engine spider-bots than to normal users [114]. Not surprisingly, webspam targets searches which can be exploited for monetary gain [114]. Spamdexing can be used to support click-fraud when websites receive money for URL referrals [223].

Voice over Internet protocol (VOIP) is also being used to transmit un-wanted advertising, commonly known as spam over Internet telephony (SPIT). SPIT can be unwanted audio connections, instant messaging (spam over in-stant messaging SPIM), or presence spam sending unwanted messages through requests to join a "buddy" list [404]. Suggestions to date for stopping SPIT have been unsatisfying. Blacklists that block specific callers are easily circum-vented by generating a new identity. White lists that restrict calls to known identities are too restrictive [356].

2.3.3   Phishing

Phishing – is an on-line attempt to extract personal identity information from someone by masquerading as a legitimate organization [319]. Most commonly, an email is sent designed to mimic the style and logo of a well known orga-nization, such as a bank. The email contains an urgent request for the user to access a remote system and input personal information. For example, an alleged security breach at a bank requires the victim to log in, using a link en-closed in the email, to immediately change their password. The link connects the victim to a fraudulent machine, which collects personal information from bank clients. Often the link closely resembles a legitimate URL. For example, it can use a Unicode character that look like a normal Latin character, but with a different binary value. Visually, the real and fraudulent URLs will be identical. In the first half of 2009, an industry working group identified over

210,000 websites being used for phishing scams; in Australia alone there were over 30,400 victims of phishing scams in 2007 [319].

Tools exist that identify and flag phishing URLs, frequently relying on published black lists of known phishing sites. They are currently not very reliable. Ones that identify more than 50 percent of the blacklisted sites tend to have high false positive rates as well [443]. Most users will eventually learn to ignore these tools, when they realize that the information provided is unreliable. In spite of this, these tools could be effective at stopping users from giving information to phishers, if they could correctly identify phishing URLs [151].

On a positive note, economics-based analysis of phishing indicates that the more heavily phishers use this attack, the better known and less profitable it becomes. It appears that less than four people are victimized for every thousand contacted [196], which gives phishing a better hit rate than Nigerian 419 scam [146]. The analysts feel that phishing may result in attackers losing money, if you consider the possible revenues they could make by investing their time elsewhere [196].

2.3.4   Pharming

Pharming – resembles phishing, except it does not use a malformed URL to redirect web traffic. Traffic is redirected to a malicious copy of an authentic website. This can be done in many ways, including:

- Malware makes the local host redirect traffic to the wrong IP address [87];
- Host file entries hard-code erroneous symbolic name to IP address entries;
- Network settings point to a DNS server controlled by the pharmer;
- DHCP and WPAD parameters are corrupted, pointing to a rogue DNS server;
- DNS spoofing injects false redirection entries into legitimate DNS servers (cache poisoning);
- Pharmers legitimately purchase DNS entries when owners let them expire;
- Pharmers illegitimately hijack ownership of a DNS entry;
- DNS wild-cards redirect large ranges of entries to fraudulent domains;
- A number of other specific attacks on the DNS protocol make DNS cache poisoning and spoofing easier [320]; and
- Unprotected home wireless routers are attacked remotely to modify the DNS server or hard-code entries for specific sites [376].

We will discuss DNS attacks in detail in Chapter 4. That discussion belongs with our discussion of SSL/TLS, since X.509 certificates combined with SSL/TLS are the recommended solution for overcoming the lack of DNS authentication. This is the vulnerability exploited by most pharming attacks. Chapter 4 details common SSL/TLS weaknesses.

Like SPIT creating VOIP spam, voice pharming attackers hijack VOIP sessions. Unsuspecting users can be redirected to bogus voice mail systems, or simply have session initiation protocol (SIP) sessions redirected to another party. This can be a man-in-the-middle attack. Voice pharming mis-uses the trust we traditionally have in our telecommunications infrastructure; assuming the call we place goes to the telephone number we enter. With VOIP, this may no longer be true [420].

2.3.5 Spear-phishing

Spear-phishing – is a more sophistic form of phishing. Spear-phishing messages are crafted for specific targets [321]. The attacker has specific knowledge about the target and uses this to create messages that appear perfectly ordinary. The messages could be crafted to resemble common messages from human resources to employees. They may come to an employee spoofed to resemble a message from the boss. Alternatively, the attacker may prepare the attack by learning the victim's context [221, 222]. This may be as simple as googling social network information to find the person's likes and dislikes. It may involve sniffing network traffic to determine the names and network addresses of frequent contacts. Of particular interest would be communications partners that send MIME attachments. Adobe PDF, Microsoft Word DOC, and Microsoft PowerPoint PPT files can be constructed to trigger exploits, such as buffer overflows [37] (see Chapter 8).

Techniques for embedding malware in office documents can be found in [129]. Numerous vulnerabilities have been found in Adobe PDF format files resulting in numerous patches. Symantec wrote in 2011 that PDF files had become the attack vector of choice for targeted attacks [389]. This attack can be very effective and has been used to compromise the security of many security conscious organizations, including RSA security [85], and Oak Ridge National Laboratory [442].

2.3.6 Mules

The weak point of many current criminal activities is the difficulty of adequately laundering money. Because of this, criminals running botnets and identity theft schemes are in constant need of *mules* to accept payments and make money transfers that can not be traced. Work at home advertisements are placed that offer the victim a percent of the funds transferred. Unfortunately, the unwitting victim is frequently caught, prosecuted, and accountable for reimbursing the entire amount of the funds they received [392].

2.4 Authentication and Authorization

Authentication is performed when a computing session starts. In existing systems, a user is authenticated in one of three ways [448]:

1. *Knowledge* – something the user knows (ex. password),
2. *Possession* – something the user has (ex. smart card), or
3. *Identity* – biometrics (ex. fingerprint).

Each can be problematic. Passwords can be forgotten, sent over the network in clear-text, or revealed inadvertently. Simple passwords are easy to guess. Complex passwords are easily forgotten, or need to be written down. Smart cards, dongles, or other authentication tokens can be stolen. Voice-prints may have false negatives if the user has a cold. People are hesitant to use retina scans, since they seem invasive.

Biometrics can also be spoofed. For example, to protest Germany's use of biometric identification cards, the Chaos Computer Club posted the fingerprints of Wolfgang Schäuble, the German Minister of the Interior, on-line, making it possible for people to easily spoof his biometric identification [256]. The same group showed earlier how fingerprint-based payment systems can be fooled to purchase goods using another person's identity (for example Wolfgang Schäuble's) [51].

On a local machine, authentication is straightforward. If authentication uses knowledge, for example a password, the user is prompted directly for the information. If possession is used, the token (ex. smart card or dongle) can be interfaced directly to the computer. Some authentication systems give the user a device that displays a code value to enter into the system. For biometrics, a physical device has to interact with both the user and the computer system.

All these approaches assume the local system is trustworthy. If the local hardware or software is not trustworthy[3] this will compromise both knowledge and biometric authentication. *Two factor authentication* uses more than one authentication technique. Most frequently, the combination is knowledge and possession. This helps minimize the damage caused by key-loggers and related tools.

Authentication over networks is problematic. As shown in Chapter 6, data sent over the network in clear-text is easily read by third parties. Most secure remote systems rely on cryptography to encrypt a token or digital signature to identify the user [375]. Some of the most widely used tools for distributed system authentication are Kerberos and X.509, and the lightweight directory access protocol.

Kerberos is an authentication system where tickets control access control to data services. The system passes tickets between servers via the client that wants to be authenticated [306]. The simple Kerberos needs at least three different servers which can deal with tickets: authentication server (AS), ticket granting server (TGS), and service server (SS). Since Kerberos can be configured with multiple AS, TGS, or SS servers, the system can support multiple realm authentication. See Figure 2.1. Kerberos is based on the Needham-Schroeder key exchange protocol [301]; later versions of Kerberos can use public key encryption to generate session keys and tickets.

---

[3]For example, a key-logger has been installed to secretly record keystrokes

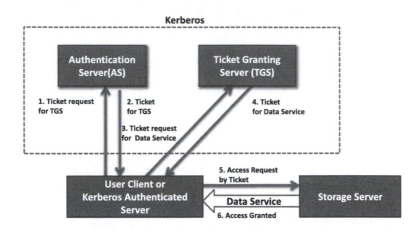

FIGURE 2.1
The Kerberos authentication process.

X.509 is the standard for public key infrastructure authorization and privilege management established by the international telecommunications union (ITU)[4] [408]. X.509 certificates are generated by a certificate authority (CA) who cryptographically signs a data structure containing the user's public key. The signature uses the CA's private key to attest to the validity of the certificate. The CA is responsible for verifying the identity of the party receiving the certificate. Distributed authentication can be supported through X.509 proxy certificates. Revocation lists need to be maintained on-line by the certificate authority to disqualify certificates that are known to be compromised [209].

Lightweight Directory Access Protocol (*LDAP*) is a descendant of the X.500 standards [440]. The International Telecommunications Union (ITU) developed the X.500 network directory standards uses the Open Systems Interconnection (OSI) network stack. The OSI stack model is not widely used, since the Internet Protocol (IP) stack has been widely adopted. This led to the implementation of the Lightweight Directory Access Protocol (LDAP), which adapts the X.500 Directory Access Protocol (DAP) to TCP/IP. LDAP provides a directory for finding user credentials. LDAP authentication can either be:

- Anonymous access – which requires no authentication and should only be used for non-sensitive information;

---

[4]Chapter 3 provides cryptography background for understanding this process. Chapter 4 describes common problems associated with X.509 certificate use. These are generally not due to cryptography or protocol errors. They are mainly due to X.509 relying on a number of unfounded assumptions

- Simple authentication – which requires a username and password sent in clear-text (see Chapter 6 for why this is not a good idea);
- Simple authentication with SSL/TLS – which requires a username and password sent through an encrypted channel (see Chapter 4 for potential problems with this approach);
- Simple Authentication and Security Layer (SASL) – which supports the four following security mechanisms for authentication: Kerberos, S/Key (uses a secure hash and is designed to not allow replay attacks), Generic Security Service Application Program Interface (GSSAPI) (provides the possibility of integrating other security mechanisms into LDAP), and External – which is a catch-all category for anything else.

LDAP vulnerabilities include the weakness of simple authentication sending clear-text username/passwords data over the network, inappropriate default configurations of some LDAP tools [440], and vulnerability to injection attacks [33].

Once the user has been authenticated, *authorization* determines the access level the user is allowed to the requested assets. Section 2.5 discusses the types of access typically allowed and how they are defined. For grids, clouds, and web services, distributed authorization infrastructure is required [225]. We will discuss two widely used distributed authorization frameworks: PERMIS and Shibboleth.

PrivilEge and Role Management Infrastructure Standard (PERMIS) is an authorization method that assigns roles and attributes to subjects and objects using policy enforcement points (PEP) and police decision points (PDP) [111]. To support distributed authorization, multiple PEPs and PDPs can be configured (see Figure 2.2). PERMIS provides cryptographically secured Privilege Management Infrastructure (PMI) using public key encryption technologies and X.509 certificates to maintain user attributes. PMI is like X.509 Public Key Infrastructure (PKI), except that it securely maintains mappings of identities to the user's privileges and access rights [225], in addition to identities.

Shibboleth is the Internet2 middle-ware solution for integrating authentication and authorization [13]. It uses the Security Assertion Markup Language (SAML) 2.0 standard. Federated identity management allows information about users in one security domain to be shared with other related organizations [153]. This supports cross-realm single sign-on. Content providers no longer need to maintain user names and passwords [302]. Shibboleth has two different server types, identity provider servers (IP) provide certificates for accessing restricted services, and service provider servers (SP) manage restricted services.

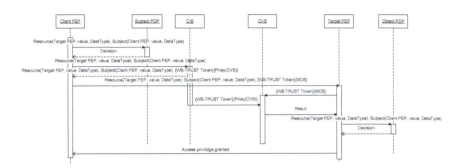

FIGURE 2.2
PERMIS security protocol sequence diagram.

2.5   Access Permissions

Authentication identifies the system user. Authorization provides the user with access rights to system resources. This section discusses access permissions. Permissions are typically associated with files, directories[5], or programs. We first discuss Unix file system access permissions and commands. Unix is widely used; most file system access modes are roughly equivalent. After discussing Unix permissions and access control lists (ACLs), we discuss contemporary access control standards defined by the Organization for the Advancement of Structured Information Standards (OASIS).

2.5.1   Unix file access permissions

Unix file systems typically allow three levels of file access: read (r), write (w), and execute (x). In general, the meaning of these access levels are obvious: files can be read, written, or executed[6], respectively.

    If the file is a directory, then:

- *Read* access allows listing files in the directory,
- *Write* access allows adding files to the directory, and
- *Execute* access allows opening files in the directory by name; this is also called search access.

To open a file on a Unix system, the user must have execute access to all directories in the file's path [379, 305].

---

[5]A directory is only a specific type of file
[6]Assuming that the corresponding file is a program or script

Nine bits are used for the file access permissions. The *umask* command defines default file access privileges for files created by a process. One bit for each access right for three different classes of users:

- *User* (file owner) is signified by octal values of 400 (read), 200 (write), and 100 (execute),
- *Group* is signified by octal values of 40 (read), 20 (write), and 10 (execute), and
- *World* (everyone else) is signified by octal values of 4 (read), 2 (write), and 1 (execute).

The superuser with effective user ID 0 has unrestricted access to all files. Access rights are verified in the order user, group, then finally world. Once the process is identified as a member of a class, it is given access rights for that class. The access rights for other classes are ignored. If the process's effective user ID makes it the file owner, access is defined by the user octal values; the group access rights are not even looked at. Each process can have multiple group ID's. For group access to be permitted, any of the process's group ID's must equal the file group ID [379].

For example, octal value 777 means all users have unrestricted access to the file. Octal value 420 means the file owner can only read the file, even though other members of the file group can write to the file. No other access is permitted [379].

When the set user ID (octal value 4000) and set group ID (octal value 2000) bits are set, executable files can run using the effective user or group IDs (respectively) of the file. This is typically used to temporarily elevate privileges for users [305]. This feature has been the source of numerous security incidents. The mount flag *nosuid* tells the system to ignore these bits for files on the volume being mounted [399].

The sticky bit (octal value 1000) originally was used to signify program files that would remain in memory once loaded. This use is obsolete on current machines, since they almost always have more memory and virtual storage. Its main use today is to modify the security properties of directories. If the sticky bit is set, most versions of Unix only allow the file owner to delete or rename the file, over-riding normal directory permissions. This allows users to share the tmp directory with more privacy than would otherwise be possible [305].

The use of common directories, like tmp, can be abused by malicious users. One attack is to create symbolic links to other files that have the names of files used by privileged users. Privileged users are thus tricked into modifying files they had no intention of changing [399].

Finally, each file has a four bit file-type identifier. The identifier is assigned to the file when it is created and cannot be modified after the fact. These identifiers signify files as being devices, pipes, normal files, etc. [379].

Access control lists, *ACLs*, exist in some file systems. They usually are an exhaustive list mapping user access rights to file system objects, or they can just list exceptions to the normal file system access permissions. ACLs exist in Windows NT and Unix variants [364, 170].

2.5.2 OASIS standards

The *Organization for the Advancement of Structured Information Standards* (OASIS) was originally a consortium of vendors of *Structured Generalized Markup Language* (SGML) created to encourage SGML use. The SGML markup language greatly influenced the development of HTML and XML. OASIS has become an influential standards organization that cooperates with the United Nations electronic business organizations. Some OASIS standards have been adapted by the International Standards Organization (ISO).

OASIS security standards are widely used by web services. Where Unix file system access controls define a security policy for a file system, OASIS standards provide a logical framework for expressing security policies. Among other policies, OASIS can define policies for multi-level security, role based access control, and hierarchical access control.

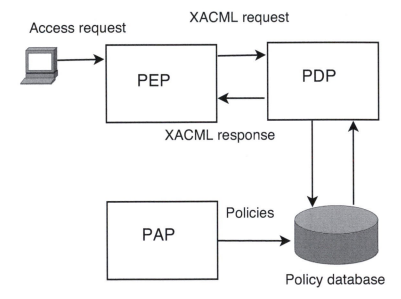

FIGURE 2.3
A user submits an access request to the Policy Enforcement Point (PEP). The PEP sends an XACML request to the Policy Decision Point (PDP). The PDP evaluates the request using a policy database maintained by the Policy Administration Point (PAP) to decide whether or not access should be allowed.

Important security standards frameworks related to the OASIS publications include:

- XML signatures *XML DSig* – is a standardized interface between XML documents and digital signatures [290]. In Chapter 3, we explain what digital signatures are and how they work.
- XML encryption *XML Enc* – is a standard describing how to encrypt XML documents. It is possible to encrypt either the whole document or only selected parts [299]. Refer to Chapter 3 for a fuller discussion of cryptology.
- XML Key Management Specification *XKMS* – is a set of simple object access protocol (SOAP) extensions that create a web services interface with public key infrastructure for use with XML Enc and XML DSig. It has sub-protocols for key registration/revocation and key discovery/retrieval [299]. XKMS will suffer from the same flaws as SSL/TLS, as discussed in Chapter 4.
- eXtensible Access Control Markup Language *XACML* – is an XML-based language for expressing access control policies. See Figure 2.3. The access control policy is a database of rules maintained by the Policy Administration Point (PAP). A Policy Decision Point (PDP) uses the database to make decisions as to whether or not access should be allowed. It is up to the Policy Enforcement Point (PEP) to make certain that these decisions are executed [134]. A policy is defined by a set of rules. Rules are evaluated based on the attributes of the subject requesting access, the resource requested, and the action desired [315] . Unfortunately, XACML rules and attributes can be arbitrarily defined, which makes automated evaluation challenging. Decidability issues can arise. This has led some researchers to suggest using subsets of logic that are decidable [242].
- XML Access Control Language *XACL* – The IBM Tokyo Research Lab developed a number of projects advancing web services and XML security. These were included in an XML security suite. Part of the suite was XACL, which was later incorporated into the OASIS XACML standard [191].
- Extensible Rights Markup Language *XRML* – is a language for digital rights management (DRM) [421]. In spite of its being focused on DRM, its technical details resemble XACML. XRML is part of the ISO MPEG-21 standard.
- Security Assertion Markup Language *SAML* – is an XML-based standard for exchanging authentication and authorization information between security domains. It is an attempt to create standards for an Internet-wide single sign on technology. Identity providers are supposed to use SAML to securely provide client identity information to service providers. SAML includes information exchange protocols and relies on XML-encryption standards to secure sensitive information [270]. The SAML design is compatible with web services technologies.
- Service Provisioning Markup Language *SPML* – The SPML OASIS standard is meant to support secure and quick deployment of interfaces for Web services and applications. SAML is used to exchange authorization information. SPML lets enterprise platforms such as Web portals, application

servers, and service centers generate provisioning requests within and across
organizations. This should automate user or system access and entitlement
rights to electronic services across organizations [316].

- Geospatial Access Control Markup Language *GeoXACML* – extends
  XACML to deal with dynamic geospatial data services. This includes sets of
  rules that express geometric services. Different regions have different access
  rules. Entities requesting access can also change roles dynamically [118, 197].

- Web Services Security *WSS* – are a set of simple object access protocol
  (SOAP) extensions that use XML enc and XML DSig to add authentication
  and end-to-end message integrity to web services [299]. WSS is independent
  of the use of HTTP-S (basically ssl/tls) for transport. WSS authentication
  may use Kerberos, X.509, SAML, or XrML.

2.6   Audit

Auditing business is common practice [90]. Independent experts verify finances
and business practices. Technical security audits, where independent experts
verify system security goals and implementation, should be part of this process. Audits evaluate the risks associated with a system and suggest measures
for minimizing these risks [397, 448]. A security audit may include penetration
testing where a team of experts, called a tiger or red team, tries to circumvent system security [33]. Penetration testing is common in the Department
of Defense [397]. The eligible receiver security audit found vulnerabilities in
the 911 emergency response systems in many cities [166].

   Computer systems and network appliances often maintain log files for discovering and diagnosing security breaches. Mainframes and minicomputers
commonly used to use teletypes as system consoles; security violations and the
use of privileged commands were printed on a paper audit trail. To change the
system log, an intruder needed physical access. Searching for security alarms
required manually leafing through reams of paper. Modern systems store log
messages in computer files, making detecting and isolating security alarms
easier. Unfortunately, intruders with access to privileged accounts can erase
or modify log files to hide intrusions. This can be counteracted by storing log
files on in-erasable media, like write once read many (WORM) tape, to make
a permanent audit log that can be used as evidence. Data forensics tools can
be used to identify modifications of log files and possibly recover the original
file [304].

   Audit logs may be maintained for multiple machines. Simple Network
Management Protocol (SNMP) allows events to be monitored throughout the
network. Management Information Base (MIB) messages, including security
alerts, are transmitted to a network management workstation [257]. MIB logs,
like other logs, can be subject to after the fact modification by intruders [340].

Unfortunately, the volume of information gathered can seriously impact network performance. In practice, these monitoring tools are frequently disabled. Network monitoring is a major part of any intrusion detection system (IDS). IDSs monitor network usage in order to infer system misuse. Although many commercial IDS packages exist, they are notoriously plagued by false positives. Not only are actual attacks buried in multiple events of no consequence, the volume of alarms can lead to systems crashing on their own [308]. Intrusion detection is an area of active research.

2.7 User Interface Issues

In addition to problems due to social engineering, there are many problems due to human computer interface issues. There are also many reasons why security interfaces are difficult to implement and use. Important issues include:

- Attackers intentionally attempt to trick users by mimicking interfaces,
- Many security issues are due to technical details that users can not be expected to be familiar with,
- It is difficult to describe cryptographic processes in layman's terms, and
- There is a natural tension between users (who are intent on getting tasks done with minimal work) and security personnel (who need to prohibit unsafe practices).

For a fuller discussion of security usability, please refer to the "Usability and Psychology" chapter in [49]. To give the reader a feeling for the issues involved, we discuss here some issues related to passwords and ssl-certificates.

One point where security theory frequently conflicts with usability is the use of passwords. The first academic paper on passwords, which appeared in 1979, stated that a simple dictionary attack found 81% of the user passwords [295]. Longer passwords are more difficult for attackers to guess with brute force attacks. Similarly, passwords with special symbols are more difficult to brute force. Passwords that are found in a normal dictionary are also subject to brute force attacks, which leads to policies requiring long passwords containing special characters.[7] Passwords should also be changed regularly [216].

Unfortunately, these measures make passwords difficult to use and remember. Users react by using a number of coping mechanisms. Passwords are reused on multiple machines. If frequent changes are required, users often add a number that they use as a counter. If these tools for remembering passwords are not sufficient, they write the passwords down. These coping techniques

---

[7]Advice is often given to substitute numbers that look like letters. This use of *leet* (1337) speak is not really effective. If anything, computer intruders are more adept at using 1337 than normal users.

make the system less secure. Security policies mandating frequent use of complex passwords and frequent changes encourage users to adopt these coping mechanisms, which then make systems less secure. A good case can be made for deploying single sign-on technologies that use one password for the entire network, reducing the cognitive load on the users [216].

Many web-sites use e-mail for password retrieval and/or reset. Since the DNS protocol is insecure, this is a major security flaw and easily exploited by intruders [230]. The intruder need only modify the DNS entry for the user's e-mail address and read emails sent to the IP address in the false DNS record. Since e-mail is almost always sent in clear-text, this is very easy.

Most web-browser security measures are based on transport layer security (TLS, which is the new name of the secure sockets layer SSL). We discuss SSL/TLS in depth in Chapter 4. These security measures suffer from a number of user interface problems. The following list from [91] is representative:

- Web browsers have put in place a number of visual clues to signal when a secure link is being used. Attackers can effectively mimic many of them.
- A valid SSL/TLS connection relies on a certificate that is cryptographically signed. The majority of valid certificates are signed by themselves. On the one hand, these certificates are valid and can be used to set up a secure connection. On the other hand these certificates do nothing to guarantee that the party being contacted is who they say they are, which can allow sessions to be hijacked. The browser user should be informed of this situation because of the potential risk; however, signaling an error for the majority of valid certificates teaches the user to ignore alarms. It is almost impossible to find the right way for the user interface to correctly inform non-experts about this situation.
- When certificates are not self-signed, they are part of a chain of trust. The certificate is either issued by a trusted authority or someone (recursively) given a certificate issued by a trusted authority. The root certificate authorities are given the responsibility of verifying the identity of people receiving certificates. There are problems with this: (i) many certificate authorities do not verify identities, (ii) there are hundreds of certificate authorities that browsers accept as valid roots of trust, (iii) many of these roots of trust belong to foreign institutions that many of us would not trust, and (iv) certificate authorities located in foreign countries[8] are subject to legal pressure. Browsers typically display neither the chain of trust nor the identity of the root of trust.
- When certificates are invalid, the browser needs to signal it. Early browsers gave a simple error message and offered to display the certificate. Since many fields of the certificate are the outputs of cryptographic hash functions, there is absolutely no possibility that a user can get any useful information from this display. The message to the user was that there was something complicated that the user could not understand, but which could be a problem.

---

[8]And the US

Users almost always ignored the error message. More recent browsers tend to display a sequence of error messages with alarmist warnings that tend to convince the user to give up and not use the web page. Since the error is often simply that the certificate has expired, this approach is often excessive.

These problems with passwords and certificates are illustrative of the issues faced when designing security user interfaces. Often security systems are designed with the desire of enforcing cryptographic protocols. When the interface restricts the user's ability to perform their tasks, users find ways of working around the security mechanisms. This can easily result in a less secure system.

2.8   On Trusting Trust

This section outlines an attack documented in Ken Thompson's Turing award lecture [395]. We present the attack as a simple thought experiment that illustrates basic limitations in the design and implementation of secure computer systems.

In the paper, Thompson starts by presenting a simple backdoor. The source code for the Unix login command can be modified so that a specific username/password will always be allowed to access the system. Normally, only username/password pairs that are registered in the password file will be allowed access. This backdoor could be detected by a simple code audit.

To avoid leaving traces of the back door, Thompson explains how the C compiler can be modified. The C compiler checks to see if it is compiling the login command. When it compiles the login file, the C compiler inserts object code that includes the backdoor. The backdoor can no longer be detected by inspecting the login source code. It can, however, be detected by auditing the C compiler code.

These traces can also be removed by making one additional change to the C compiler. The C compiler should also check to see whether or not it is compiling a C compiler. If it is compiling a compiler, the object code it produces should include the logic to produce login programs that contain the backdoor.

The result is a software development environment that produces insecure code and *there are no traces of the attack in the source code*. The final attack can only be detected by reverse engineering the executables, which is difficult. The lesson is that a trustworthy computer system can only be created when all the software and hardware layers are trustworthy.

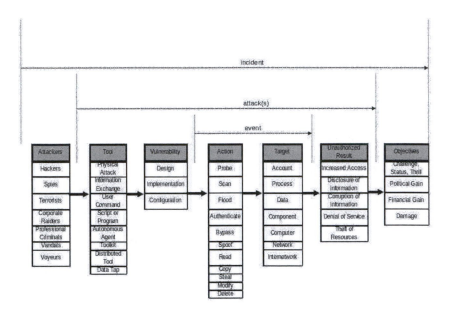

FIGURE 2.4
Taxonomy of security incidents used by the Carnegie Mellon Computer Emergency Response Team (CERT) [210].

2.9 Taxonomy of Attacks

To provide a structure for discussion of security issues, we adopt the taxonomy of security incidents shown in Figure 2.4 from [210]. It is a taxonomy and language for classifying security incidents. In each incident, an attacker abuses the system to achieve an objective. The incident is composed of one or more attacks. For each attack, the perpetrator uses one or more tools to exploit system vulnerabilities and create a result that helps achieve the attacker's objective. Single events represent ways of exploiting vulnerabilities. Each event consists of an aggressive action taken against a target.

2.9.1 Vulnerabilities

The set of attackers given in Figure 2.4 is inclusive and rather generic. Similarly, the tools listed are fairly complete. The list was developed in 1998 and changes could be made to better fit current threats. US Department of Defense (DoD) studies compiled the following list of 20 vulnerabilities in seven categories [45]:

Architecture/Design vulnerabilities are a direct consequence of the system structure. Correcting these vulnerabilities requires major modifications to the system.

- Components unique to this system may not have been thoroughly tested.
- Single points of failure can cause an entire system to fail and singular components that exist in one place can be exploitable.
- Centralization of system control on a single process.
- Network separability can allow components or processes to be isolated from the network and compromised using a divide and conquer strategy.
- If all component instances are homogeneous, the same attack can be repeated to disable all of them. They can be attacked one at a time.

Behavioral complexity vulnerabilities are characterized by how the system reacts to its environment.

- A system that is sensitive to variations in use may be vulnerable to attacks that pinpoint a specific aspect of its behavior.
- If a systems reaction is predictable, this can be used to construct attacks.

Adaptability and Manipulation in a system can lead to the system being used to aid an attack.

- It is hard to subvert a rigid system, but neither can the system adapt automatically to attacks.
- On the other hand, a malleable system can be easily modified and subverted.
- Gullible systems that do not verify inputs can easily be used to subvert other applications. The ability to spoof the Internet is an example.

Operation/Configuration changes allow systems to be used in attacks.

- Resource capacity limits can be used in attacks. Denial of Service (DoS) and buffer overflow attacks are examples.
- If a system takes an inordinate amount of effort to reconfigure or recover from failures this can be exploited.
- Systems that lack introspection are unable to detect attacks and correct the situation.
- Systems that are awkward and difficult to configure and administer can more easily be mis-configured.
- Complacency can result in there being a lack of effective administrative procedures.

Non-physical exposure refers to access to devices that does not involve physical contact.

- Remote system access is a stepping-stone to system misuse. Connecting a system to the Internet permits attacks, such as password guessing.
- The more open and transparent a system is, the easier it is to probe for vulnerabilities. Attackers have even subverted the network time protocol and postscript printers to access systems remotely.

Physical exposure refers to vulnerabilities requiring physical access to a device. These vulnerabilities are particularly important for embedded systems. The judicious use of tamper-proof hardware can mitigate some of these risks.

- Physical access to a system almost certainly guarantees the possibility of Denial of Service (DoS) through sabotage or destruction.
- Physical access also extends to attacks on power or communications lines.
- In many cases, the electromagnetic radiation emanating from computer equipment can be captured and used to compromise or steal information. Intrusion or equipment damage may also be possible using electromagnetic radiation. These attacks are often referred to by the code-name tempest.

Dependency on supporting infrastructure is an important vulnerability. Lack of electric power, air conditioning, network connections, etc. causes computer systems to fail.

Other studies of vulnerabilities have been made. The computer security incident taxonomy in [210] classifies vulnerabilities as being design, implementation, or configuration issues. Another taxonomy can be found in [253], where flaws are categorized using three different criteria:

1. *Genesis* – the flaws origin:

    •Intentional flaws are either malicious (Trojan horse, trapdoor, and logic bomb) or non-malicious (ex. covert channel).
    •Inadvertent flaws of several types exist, including the following errors: validation, domain, aliasing, inadequate authentication, and boundary condition violations.

2. *Time of introduction* – when the flaw was created:

    •During development errors can be made as part of the design, coding, or build processes.
    •Flaws can be introduced as part of maintenance.
    •Security flaws can also be created during system operation.

3. *Location* – components containing the flaw:

    •Software flaws can be in the operating system components, support environment, or application being used.
    •Hardware security can also be inadequate.

The list of vulnerabilities we provided from [45] is rather exhaustive but inconsistent. Systems should neither be rigid nor supple. Uniqueness and homogeneity can both be turned against the system. The taxonomy from [253] provides a similar lesson. Flaws can be introduced at any point in the systems life-cycle and they can be present in any component.

2.9.2   Attacks

Adopting the terminology from [210], see Figure 2.4, an attack exploits a system vulnerability to create an unauthorized result. For confidentiality, authentication, integrity, non-repudiation, access control, and availability, four general classes of attacks exist [375]:

- *Interruption*: Availability of an asset is disrupted.
- *Interception*: Unauthorized access to an asset.
- *Modification*: Unauthorized tampering with an asset.
- *Fabrication*: Creation of a fictitious asset.

Attacks can be passive or active. Passive attacks monitor systems. Active attacks change a system's state.

Information warfare threats have a larger scope than the traditional security issues [293]. DoD studies have found twenty-one information warfare threats in four categories [45]:

- *External passive attack* – wiretapping, emanations analysis (tempest), signals analysis, traffic analysis.
- *External active attack* – substitution or insertion, jamming, overload, spoof, malicious logic.
- *Attacks against a running system* – reverse engineering, cryptanalysis.
- *Internal attack* – scavenging, theft of service, theft of data. Attacks involving access to and modification of a system violation of permissions, deliberate disclosure, database query analysis, false denial of origin, false denial of receipt, logic-tapping, tampering.

These attacks describe the basic arsenal of cyber-warfare.

Known attacks on Internet Protocol based networks include:

- *Denial of service by flooding* – Multiple messages request packets for a particular address cause congestion and hinder delivery of correct packets. Smurfing is an example [45].
- *Denial of service by forging* – The network is sent incorrect routing update messages, intentionally inducing network congestion [45].
- *Packet sniffing* – Unencrypted traffic moving through the network can be intercepted [45].
- *Host intrusion* – Use of the network for unauthorized access to a network node [45].

- *Attacks on lower level protocols* – IP packets can be delivered using a number of physical and link layer protocols. Denial of service would be possible by attacking an ATM service [45].
- *Physical attacks* – Destruction of nodes or critical links [45].
- *Distributed Denial of Service (DDOS)* – Triggering a denial of service attack from multiple locations simultaneously is an order of magnitude more difficult to identify and correct than attacks from a single location [171]. For this reason we list DDOS separately.

Switched networks, like the voice telephone system, have known vulnerabilities similar to those of Internet Protocol networks [45]:

- *Sabotage* – Destruction of equipment, lines, or offices. These are physical attacks.
- *Line tapping* – The analog equivalent of packet sniffing.
- *Jamming transmissions* – This is indiscriminate tampering with wireless communications to provoke a denial of service attack.
- *Intrusion and tampering* – If unauthorized access is possible to a switch, the switch can be improperly reprogrammed. Eavesdropping and forging voicemails are also possible.

The attacks discussed so far are all fairly low-level attacks. There are also some slightly higher-level strategies that are widespread and deserve mention:[9]

- *Scavenging* – In many systems, freed or deleted storage space is simply de-allocated. No effort is made to actually erase the contents. It becomes possible to access confidential information by reading storage space that is allocated in memory and on disk.
- *Trojan horses* – Programs that do something different than what the user expects.
- *Virus* – Programs (typically malicious) that spread surreptitiously. Originally, viruses were considered programs that infect other programs. Later, the definition was changed to be malicious programs whose spreading required some user input. This change was caused by the advent of e-mail viruses, which did not conform to the original definition. Viruses are discussed in detail in Chapter 9
- *Worm* – Another class of surreptitiously reproducing (typically malicious) program. Originally, worms were considered programs that spread from machine to machine by reproducing themselves. They did not modify other programs. Later, the definition was modified to programs whose spreading did not require user input. Since the 1990's, many types of malicious code are hybrid attacks that can act as either a virus or a worm.
- *Covert channel* – An attack where communications occurs between two machines in violation of a security policy through use of a hidden communications mechanism. This can be done using some combination of steganography and side-channels.

---

[9]More details about all of these can be found in [90]

- *Side-channel* – A subtle attack where information is leaked from a computer due to the attacker measuring environmental consequences of program side effects. This is dealt with in detail in Chapter 12.
- *Man-in-the-middle* – In a data exchange between A and B, the attacker inserts themselves between the two parties by masquerading as the other end of the conversation. We discuss this in more detail in Chapter 4
- *Replay* – The attacker records network traffic, which is retransmitted at a later time.
- *Cryptanalysis and reverse engineering* – Analysis of data and or code to deduce information that the attacker was not meant to have. This is typically a very difficult and time consuming attack vector.

2.9.3   Advanced persistent threat

Advanced persistent threat *APT* refers to attacks that combine multiple attack vectors that allow the attacker to patiently search for vulnerabilities and tailor an attack to fit the victim's vulnerabilities. APT's are typically meant to be stealthy. Some of the more prominent APT attacks include:

- *Google China* – Attackers analyzed contacts in social networks and sent targeted attacks to friends of key Google employees. The key employees were then infected by messages from their friends. Google was one of 30 large companies infected. Information related to their authentication system was compromised [426].
- *Ghostnet* – Computers and networks used by Tibetan activists were infiltrated by variants of spear-phishing attacks. Malicious PDF and office documents were transmitted to activists in order to infect their computers. The system included a sophisticated command and control infrastructure. Infected systems included computers used by the UN and the Indian military [37].
- *Stuxnet* – Malware was crafted to spread over the network of an Iranian nuclear research facility and infect computers used for system control and data acquisition (SCADA). Some SCADA nodes were used to control centrifuges essential for the enrichment of radioactive material. It seems that the malware was introduced to the system via USB drives [97].
- *RSA Security* – A spear-phishing attack on RSA employees allowed some machines belonging to the security firm to be infected. The infection spread slowly through the network, eventually compromising machines including product source code and customer information [73].
- *Lockheed Martin* – Information gained by attackers from the RSA attack was used later, apparently in combination with spear-phishing, to attack defense contractor Lockheed Martin Corporation [110].

Other victims of similar attacks include Oak Ridge National Laboratory and the International Monetary Fund [349].

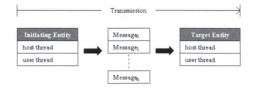

FIGURE 2.5
A transmission is a set of message exchanges.

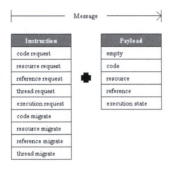

FIGURE 2.6
A message has an instruction and a payload.

FIGURE 2.7
An itinerary is a set of transmissions.

2.10   Case Study – Mobile Code

This section[10] adapts the taxonomy discussed in Section 2.9 and shown in Figure 2.4 to mobile code security issues [325, 89, 90]. This allows the correspondence between mobile code implementations and security issues to be naturally discussed.

---

[10]Parts of this section appeared previously in [325, 89]

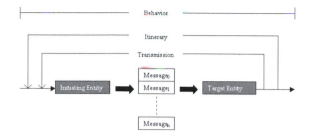

FIGURE 2.8

A behavior is a set of itineraries defining a complex network activity.

X: user thread at initiating client
Y: host thread at target server

(a)
[execution request, empty]
[resource request, empty]

X————————▶Y

(b)
[resource migrate, resource]

Y————————▶X

FIGURE 2.9

Remote evaluation transmits a program for remote execution.

As shown in Figure 2.5, in the mobile code taxonomy a transmission is a set of messages sent between two entities. An entity may be either a host thread bound to a specific machine or a user thread that may migrate from node to node.

A message (see Figure 2.6) is the basic unit of communication. It has an instruction and a payload. Many instructions request a service from the target and have an empty payload. In most cases, the target responds with a new message containing the appropriate instruction and payload. Payloads may contain a concatenation of many payload types. For example a thread migrate request for a mobile agent with strong mobility typically contains a payload containing code, data resources, and execution state.

An itinerary (see Figure 2.7) is a set of related transmissions, and a systems behavior (see Figure 2.8) is a set of related itineraries. Figure 2.8 thus presents the entire taxonomy showing the relationship between its parts.

We now discuss mobile code paradigms that are based on client-server concepts. In client-server, the first message has two requests: (access to node services, and execution of services). The second message returns the results of execution. In remote evaluation (Figure 2.9), the first message contains the program to be executed and the second message the results of execution. In the Java code-on-demand (Figure 2.10) approach, the first message requests the program and the second message contains the program.

Mobile agent systems are different. Figure 2.11 shows a multi-hop mobile agent with strong migration. Each agent hop consists of a single message transmission. The user thread migrates at its own volition from node to node.

FIGURE 2.10
Code on demand downloads a program for local execution.

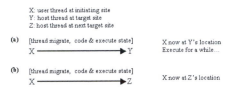

FIGURE 2.11
Agent migrates from node to node under its own volition.

Figure 2.12 describes the process migration approach, which is often used for load balancing. Migration decisions are made by the local operating system, which pushes processes to other nodes as needed. Finally, an active network approach has a mobile agent traversing the network, triggering software updates in its wake. The agent decides how code is executed on the infrastructure.

Let us map the security taxonomy in Figure 2.4 [210] to our mobile code taxonomy. Each security incident is a combination of one or more attacks, perpetrated by a group to fulfill its objectives. Attacks use tools to exploit system vulnerabilities and create an unauthorized result. Each unauthorized result is produced by an event. Events are the actions an attacker takes to exploit the vulnerabilities of specific targets.

The behavior of a malicious mobile code package results in a single security incident. The itinerary of the package behavior is a set of transmissions. Each transmission used by the malicious code is an attack, and every message is a security event. Each instruction is an action applied to a payload, which is a potential target. Unauthorized mobile code executions produce unauthorized results.

Where do mobile code security measures fit in? A sandbox contains code execution. It protects a target machine from unauthorized access. A firewall's goal is to protect a target sub-network from unauthorized access. Proof carrying code's goal is to allow target machines to reject offensive code before executing the code.

The security taxonomy shows that attackers use tools to exploit vulnerabilities. Actions are then taken against targets to produce unauthorized results fulfilling the attacker's objectives. Note how events in this taxonomy correspond to messages in the taxonomy illustrated in Figure 2.8.

Although a case could be made that these approaches remove vulnerabil-

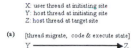

FIGURE 2.12

Process migration allows hosts to move programs to other nodes.

ities, in essence all these approaches protect target machines, or networks, from attacks.

Code signing works at a different level. By identifying the source of a program, code may be rejected as being unsafe. Alternatively if code is found to be malicious, the signature can be a forensics tool for proving culpability.

Some approaches for protecting code from hosts concentrate on fortifying components. Computing with encrypted functions and code obfuscation protect mobile code programs from being targets by making them difficult to decipher.

Tamper-proof hardware makes system corruption impossible, removing an entire class of vulnerabilities. This allows both host and code to trust the tamper-proof component. In the ideal case, this protects both from being targets of attack.

The use of itineraries, redundancy, and audit trails work at an entirely different level. Although each single event in a mobile code intrusion is of relatively minor importance, the consequences of the aggregate behavior can easily become catastrophic. These approaches look at aggregates of messages, and thus work closer to the incident or behavior levels of the taxonomies.

Most security measures fortify potential targets of attacks. While this is important and necessary, consider the larger picture. Many e-mail viruses do not perform actions that are forbidden by a sandbox. Worms primarily exploit software implementation errors. It is unlikely that software design will advance in the near future, if ever, to the point where we automatically foresee the abuses of software features or consistently produce bug-free systems.

Our network infrastructure enables distributed attacks. Increasingly fortifying individual machines on the network does not fortify the network. A metaphor can be made between worms / viruses and blitzkrieg. The advent of blitzkrieg made fortification of individual positions insufficient. In much the same way, fortifying individual processors is no longer sufficient. Distributed attacks have become widespread. Distributed countermeasures are needed to defend against them. Concentrating on fortifying individual processors is like building a stronger Maginot Line after WW II.

2.11   Case Study – Connected Vehicles

This section[11] presents another adaptation of the attack taxonomy. In this case, we adapt the taxonomy to automotive information technology [95]. Automobiles are now networks of embedded computers integrated into global information networks. Vehicles are often communication hubs with multiple wireless communications. Traditional automobile security tools (car alarms, key-less entry, power door locks, etc.) no longer adequately protect owners and their investments. The interests of many other stakeholders, such as automobile manufacturers, can also be compromised by attacks on automotive systems. We use the Computer Emergency Response Team (CERT) taxonomy [210] to systematically analyze the problem space.

Modern automobiles are networks of embedded computers, often with global connectivity. Communications can be either wired or wireless, either long-distance or short distance. This is the basis of many recent major innovative automobile applications. We roughly classify them into the following areas:

- Automobiles externally communicating with the environment or other automobiles for safe driving and other purposes.
- Automobiles connecting with manufacturer integrated business services.
- Electronic control unit (ECU) reprogramming for cost savings, easy maintenance, and/or better performance [258].
- The automobile's internal communications bus connecting embedded systems [258].

Each area brings new security concerns. Although most automotive security research concentrates on car theft, modern automotive systems are subject to a much wider range of potential abuses. We map automotive security research onto the CERT taxonomy to find which threats are not adequately addressed. In mapping, we tailor the taxonomy to our applications. This indicates gaps in the problem space, like inadequate protection of embedded software from invasive attacks [258]. It also finds common threads in the set of known vulnerabilities, like exploiting the use of inadequately long cryptographic keys [82, 42].

Individual consumers are not the only people concerned with the security of automotive systems. Automobile manufacturers and dealerships have large inventories of cars they need to protect. After-sale, unauthorized modifications to automotive software can have warranty and liability implications for manufacturers and suppliers. In addition, as automotive systems become increasingly dependent on embedded computers, manufacturers are forced to make large investments in software development. This intellectual property needs to be protected.

---

[11]Parts of this section appeared previously in [95]

Every automobile owner has common security needs: protecting their investment from theft, avoiding their systems being abused, and being certain their property is not used to launch attacks on others. However, fleet owners view automobiles as a commodity, and do not store sensitive personal or corporate information on vehicles. This contrasts with individual users who will store sensitive personal information (SIM card credentials, itineraries, calling and billing records) on their vehicle. These individuals should be concerned that personal information remains private.

On the other hand, service providers are concerned about vehicles as potential attack vectors. For example, the cloning of credentials, like the attack in [82], can be used to make fraudulent payments for gasoline, tolls, etc.

We can not assume the vehicle operator is not a potential attacker. Private owners typically have access to very few automobiles and lack incentive for executing most attacks. On the other hand, someone interested in attacking an automotive system could rent vehicles for short periods of time. They have less to lose should reverse engineering damage vehicle electronics and they would be able to collect a much larger set of data. Individuals working at automobile dealerships have access to an even larger set of automobile configurations; this can be useful for determining how to undermine network security measures. A vehicle in a repair shop is also exposed to invasive testing and modification using equipment that is typically not available to most attackers.

Automotive information systems can be accessed in many different ways. The most invasive interactions, such as removing or replacing vehicle components, require physical access. We place physical attacks in the category of wired access, since wires imply physical contact with the vehicle. Often physical contact with vehicles is unsupervised, for example in a repair or chop shop.

We divide wireless communications into low-power local communications and long distance connections. Multiple types of local communications are supported:

- It is increasingly popular to interface vehicle electronics with consumer electronics devices, including PDAs, MP3 players, and cell phones.
- Some manufacturers provide blue-tooth connections for easy interfacing with gadgets.
- RFID chips are used in engine immobilizers and other applications.
- Wireless key fob control of physical access to cars is commonplace.

Important security gaps have been found in these systems [82, 192, 42].

It is uncertain which technology will dominate automobile connections to wide area networks in the future. Current applications mainly use cell phone infrastructure. Widespread future acceptance of WiMAX is expected, due to its broad coverage area and capability to support network connection even when automobiles travel at speeds up to 70 mile per hour. IEEE standards exist for transferring sessions between Wi-Fi and WiMAX. Although some groups propose peer-to-peer VANet solutions [268], there are good security

Attackers	Objectives
Thieves	Steal cars and expensive components
Vandals	Enter vehicle to inflict damage
Hackers	Crack entry system for fun and challenge
Professional criminals	Carjack, chop shop, kidnap, theft, ...

TABLE 2.1
Attackers of auto entry systems and their objectives.

arguments for most applications to be between individual vehicles and a fixed infrastructure. Each technology has a different security profile.

2.11.1 Anti-theft systems

Common automobile anti-theft systems are key/keyless entry systems and engine immobilizers. Customers, fleet owners and leasing companies rely on these systems to protect their ownership. Manufactures rely on them to maintain their reputation and provide customer satisfaction. Usually, thieves use low-tech attacks to steal cars, such as breaking the window, jimmying the lock, cutting alarm wires, hot-wiring the ignition, or looking for keys left in automobiles by their careless owners, etc. However, vandals, hackers, or professional criminals are likely to adopt the high-tech attacks that are possible now as soon as it becomes cost-effective. There is some anecdotal evidence of high-tech car theft already being a reality. The attackers of automotive entry systems and their goals are summarized in Table 2.1.

Keyless entry is widely adopted to prevent unauthorized physical access to automobiles. Researchers have successfully cracked the Keeloq [80, 215] keyless entry used by many car manufacturers, such as Chrysler, Daewoo, Volvo, Toyota, etc. The key recovery attack in [80] exploits three Keeloq weaknesses: self-similar key schedule scheme, short block length, and existence of an efficient of linear approximation of the NLF Shift Register (NLFSR). The set of known Keeloq attacks are in Table 2.2.

The Digital Signature Transponder (DST) RFID device has been used by more than 150 million vehicle immobilizer keys, including 2005 model Fords and Exxon's SpeedPass gasoline payment. The DST uses Advanced Encryption Standard (AES) encryption and a 40-bit cryptographic key. DST interacts with a reader by emitting a factory-set 24-bit identifier, and authenticates itself by engaging a challenge-response protocol. The reader initiates the protocol by transmitting a 40-bit challenge. The DST encrypts this challenge under its key, truncates the resulting cipher text, and returns a 24-bit response.

Attack	Tool	Vulnerability	Action	Target	Unauth. Result
Slide attack step	Info. exchange	Design: similar key schedule and short 32-bit block	Read, authenticate	Key	Recover first 16 bits of 64-bit key
Correlation step	Info. exchange	Design: existence of a linear approximation of the NLFSR	Read, authenticate	Key	Recover bits 17-48 of 64-bit key
Linear step	Info. exchange	Design: existence of a linear approximation of the NLFSR	Read, authenticate	Key	Recover remaining 16 key bits

TABLE 2.2
Known Keeloq attacks.

Attack	Tool	Vulnerability	Action	Target	Unauth. Result
Reverse engineering	Info. exchange	Design: cipher structure and function design	Read, authenticate	Function detail of cipher	Recovering complete functions of the cipher
Key cracking	Info. exchange	Design: short 40-bit cryptographic key	Read, authenticate	Function detail of cipher	Recovering 40-bit cryptographic key

TABLE 2.3
Known DST attacks.

Researchers successfully cracked the ignition key of a Ford car which uses the DST [82]. Based on a rough schematic of the DST 40-bit cipher, they were able to clone a key and open the car with that fake key. They also compromised Exxon's SpeedPass gasoline payment that uses the DST. With their cloned card, they successfully purchased gasoline for free. The main vulnerability of DST was its short cryptographic key length. See Table 2.3.

Bypass kits can be an attack vector for anti-theft systems. Anti-theft systems are usually produced by an OEM and sold to manufacturers. Sometimes, manufacturers need an additional interface kit to allow an aftermarket (not installed at the factory) system to work properly. Bypass kits are interface kits used to momentarily bypass the anti-theft system to allow remote vehicle

Attackers	Objectives
Terrorists	Cause harm and hysteria
Drivers	Clear traffic paths
Hackers	Crack system for fun and challenge

TABLE 2.4
Attackers of VANets and their objectives.

starting. With the easy availability of by-pass kits and a growing market for stolen luxury cars, this mode of crime is expected to be cost effective in the near future.

2.11.2 Vehicular Ad Hoc Network (VANet)

Vehicular Ad Hoc Networks (VANets) are seen as a way to enhance safety (collision avoidance, traffic optimization, lane-changing assistance, etc.) and comfort (toll/parking payment, Internet Access, locating fuel stations, etc.) [344, 217]. VANets include vehicle-to-vehicle and vehicle-to-roadside communications [217]. The communications technologies (WiMAX, LTE, DSRC, GSM, ...) that will be used to create VANets is still uncertain. Likely attackers for VANets and their objectives are listed in Table 2.4. Terrorists could misuse VANet in the hope of creating traffic havoc. Greedy drivers that want to clear traffic along their path could fool other vehicles into choosing other paths [332].

VANets are prone to the attacks listed in Table 2.5. In a Sybil attack [434, 186], one vehicle may pretend to be hundreds of other vehicles to send bogus road congestion information, fooling nodes in the VANet. In denial of service (DOS) attacks a large number of spoofed packets absorb all network bandwidth making the system unavailable for legitimate users. DoS attacks can prevent vehicles from receiving urgent information, such as accident notification. Spoofed information can also be hazardous. An attack may fool one vehicle in front of a line to halt abruptly to create traffic accidents that may involve many vehicles rear-ending each other [332]. Currently, colluding vehicles do similar things in a common insurance scam. VANets could spread malicious code [434, 176, 303]. In [434], the author investigates parameters that govern how quickly active worms can spread.

Vehicle location information is also valuable. There are two types of attacks: location tracking [353] and location spoofing. In location tracking, an attack may use data mining technology to trace the location of a vehicle. There are cases that vehicles announce their coordinates, for example, geographical

Attack	Tool	Vulnerability	Action	Target	Unauth. Result
Sybil attack		Crypto or protocol	Spoof, authenticate	Identity	Multiple-identity forgery
Bogus information	Script or program	Crypto or protocol		Data	Data corruption
Denial of service	Distributed tools	Crypto or protocol	Flood	Resource	Theft of resources
Man-in-the middle		Crypto or protocol	Modify or eavesdrop	Data, identity	Data modification or eavesdropping
Location tracking	ID data mining	Crypto or protocol	Eavesdrop	Location information	Violation of privacy
Malicious code	Script or program				
Replay attack		Crypto or protocol	Bypass, spoof, authenticate	Identity	Identity theft, increased access, data corruption

TABLE 2.5
Anticipated VANet attacks.

routing, accident location, etc. Attackers may also send spoofed location information for their own benefit. In [435], on-board radar detects neighboring vehicles, to confirm advertised vehicle coordinates. It is worth noting that many automobile passengers carry mobile phones, which have similar issues with safeguarding location data.

One challenge for VANets is the trade-off between authentication and privacy [332]. To prevent Sybil or other ID spoofing attacks, it is advisable to bind each driver to a single identity. Such strong authentication also provides valuable forensic evidence and allows us to use external mechanisms, such as law enforcement to deter or prevent attacks on VANet [332]. However, drivers are likely to value privacy, so they may not adopt systems that require them to abandon their anonymity.

Another challenge for securing VANets is the fact that not all drivers are honest. There are incentives to lie about traffic or accident information. Researchers need to find ways of verifying the source of information they receive.

Current security research for VANets focuses on strong authentication, privacy, and encryption to secure data during transmission. The wireless media being used also needs to be considered, since different wireless communications media have different security designs. Securing data during broadcast constitutes only one part of an effective security system. The protection of the VANet automobile infrastructure from abuses is important as well. For road side units, physical protection from vandalism should be considered. Since people (friends, family members, etc.) other than the owner also operate the automobile, care needs to be taken to protect data stored on the vehicle. While it is desirable that these people can also use the communication system, for either safe driving or effective traffic, the system should be carefully designed so that they use the VANet only when operating legally. System misuse, such as tampering with data, should be forbidden or at least detected and not repudiated.

2.11.3   Electronic control units

Many vehicle functions, gear shift, servo steering, ignition system, electrical window lift, climate controls, etc. are controlled by electronic control units (ECUs). The number of these embedded processors varies from 40 in compact class automobiles, up to 90 in luxury class automobiles. A typical embedded system consists of a microprocessor with its programs stored in read-only memory (ROM). The ROM is often reprogrammable, to save cost. This allows bugs to be corrected, and new functionality to be introduced without replacing ECUs. This also reduces the number of hardware variants [258].

ECU software flashing comprises software development, software delivery, and software installation. Multiple parties with conflicting interests are involved in these processes, which makes flashing a challenge. ECU remote on-line flashing is being considered. Vehicles connected to the manufacturer back-end network could then have their ECUs flashed on-line. This makes secure flashing an even bigger challenge.

Confidentiality is important to software developers who want to protect their intellectual property. Confidentiality can be violated by both insiders and outsiders. The most highly motivated outsiders are corporate competitors. They covet proprietary information because they can benefit by applying it to their products or disclosing software bugs to besmirch their competition's reputation. Reverse engineering is one way to acquire the information. Insiders have easy access to data. Disgruntled employees may intentionally disclose information or employees may be tempted to sell information.

Authentication identifies the origin of software. Software from untrusted sources should not be used in critical embedded devices. They may degrade ECU performance. Automobile owners may sometimes use software of unknown provenance because of a lower price. To guarantee authentication, automobiles owners are notified of the hazards of using unauthorized software or ECUs can be designed so that only an authorized party can flash the processors.

Integrity prevents software modification by unauthorized parties. Automobile owners may intentionally have software modified to have more sportive shock absorber calibration, power enhancement, improved brake behavior, etc. [258]. Truck drivers in Europe may want to change data in the digital tachograph, which is used to record driving hours as required by law. Modifying software can also be lucrative. One typical example is changing the ECUs of vehicle immobilizers [258]. Non-repudiation keeps track of the software version, when it was installed and who installed it. This serves as a deterrent to unauthorized software flashing.

We summarize the attackers of ECU flashing and their objectives in Table 2.6. Possible attacks are listed in Table 2.7. Possible attacks on ECU flashing include more than reverse engineering and modifying code. Phlashing is a potential threat and with severe aftermath. Phlashing tricks a remote device into letting you flash its firmware so that the machine can never be rebooted, and must be pulled out and replaced [8]. It causes permanent damage. Phlashing may exploit unpatched vulnerabilities in embedded systems to gain access. Such access can be obtained by fuzzing. Fuzzing sends random packets to discover vulnerabilities in systems.

2.11.4 Integrated business services

In many vehicles, customers connect embedded systems in their automobile to the manufacturers back-end network to use the applications or services provided by manufacturers, such as remote tele-diagnostics, remote software

Attackers	Objectives
Customers	More sportive shock calibration, power enhancement, improved brake behavior, change digital tachograph readings, etc.
Corporate raiders	Steal code to obtain proprietary information.
Thieves	Disable vehicle immobilizers, entry systems, and other anti-theft protection.

TABLE 2.6
ECU flash attackers and their objectives.

Attack	Tool	Vulnerability	Action	Target	Unauth. Result
Modifying code	Script or program	Design, implementation	Modify	Data	Information corruption, performance degradation, destruction
Reverse engineering	Information exchange	Design, implementation	Probe, read	Data	Disclosure of information
Fuzzing attack	Script or program, information exchange	Design, implementation	Probe, modify	Computer	Information corruption, increased access
Phlashing attack	Information exchange	Design, implementation	Modify	Computer	Denial of service

TABLE 2.7
ECU flash attacks.

Attack	Tool	Vulnerability	Action	Target	Unauth. Result
Brute force	Info. exchange	Crypto or design	Authent.	Account, data	Increased access to data
Social attacks		People		Data, account	Increased access to data
Denial of service	Distributed tools, script or program, toolkit	Configuration, design	Flood	Resource	Resource consumption
Malicious code	Script or program, distributed tools	Configuration, design	Modify, delete	Process, data, component	Increased access, disclosure of information, data corruption
Reverse engineering	Information exchange	Design, implementation	Probe, read	Data	Disclosure of information

TABLE 2.8
Integrated business application client-side attacks.

update, entertainment, access to the third party applications (email, on-line banking, etc.).

Automobile manufacturers look at these innovations, not just to provide the most comfort to customers, but also to add revenue streams. GM is proud to present its subscriber-based OnStar services: vehicle diagnostic checks, OnStar Navigation, automatic notification of air bag deployment, hands-free calling, etc. OnStar uses mobile phone networks and GPS for communication. Similar services are offered by BMW, Mercedes-Benz, and LoJack.

Integration involves three entities, the client (vehicle) side, manufacturer's back-end network, and Internet Service Provider (ISP) in between. Sometimes, a third party (on-line banking, email, etc.) is also involved. The security of integrating business models entails securing all the entities involved. Attacks can be launched from both vehicle side (Table 2.8) and non-vehicle side (Table 2.9). Integration of business services into the automobile introduces the following risks:

1. Attacker gains access to the business platform in vehicle.

2. Attacker gains access to vehicle system.

3. Attacker gains access to user data.

Attack	Tool	Vulnerability	Action	Target	Unauth. Result
Phish and Pharm	Info. exchange	Configuration	Authent.	Account	Increased access to data, disclosure of information
Malicious code	Script or program	Configuration, design	Modify, delete	Process, data, component	Increased access to data, disclosure of information, data corruption
Wireless tapping, eavesdropping	Data tap	Design	Read	Data	Disclosure of information

TABLE 2.9
Integrated business application server-side attacks.

When an attacker accesses the business platform from the vehicle they get normal client-level access to the back-end. The attacker can use this as a stepping stone for other attacks on the server to increase their privilege level on the business system. The attacker can gain client-level through phishing and pharming attacks. They can also gain client-level access using malicious code. Once the attacker is able to run arbitrary software on the business platform in vehicle, then the attacker can take over embedded systems and gain access to other vehicle systems. Depending on how cryptographic checks are performed, the attacker may be able to send malicious code to other vehicle systems. The user may also have personal or corporate data at risk, which may be associated with the manufacturer or with third party applications such as on-line banking. Tools that an attacker could use include malicious code, social attacks, and wireless exploits.

Given the nature of the Internet, web access provides a path for malicious content to execute on the client and attack the vehicle (e.g., Trojan horse attack). Malicious content could originate from a man-in-the-middle attack or from the intended third-party server. Malicious code attacks will not be quite as likely if the vehicle platform is not based on the widely used Microsoft Windows or Linux operating systems.

Eavesdropping and tampering can leverage wireless network vulnerabilities to compromise the confidentiality and integrity of user messages. This is slightly less worrisome as long as the user understands the risks and necessary precautions to take when using wireless networks.

	Malicious code	Social engineering, phish, and pharm	Wireless tampering, eavesdropping
Client separation	X	X	-
Content filtering	X	X	-
VPN	-	-	X

TABLE 2.10
Security measures for different attacks.

Security mechanisms can reduce these risks. They include content filtering, client-side separation and trusted path, and network separation (VPN). A mapping of security mechanisms to attacks is given in Table 2.10.

When discussing security mechanisms, consider users connecting directly to third party applications through the ISP. This will require client-side security mechanisms, including content filtering and application separation. Client-side application separation includes data separation and the use of a trusted path. Trusted paths should be implemented in a manner outside of the application. Data separation provides a boundary between applications, so that malicious code is limited to execution within a single domain. Data separation involves either high assurance software development or machine virtualization. The quality of data separation determines the level of security, and secure separation is highly desirable. Software or hardware virtualization is a potential tool for maintaining safe separation. Since software analysis is more difficult than hardware analysis, the level of reliability in software separation is less than hardware separation. Also, software virtualization suffers from security risks and performance degradation due to monitoring and translation overhead. A benefit to software virtualization methods is that they do not require special hardware.

None of these options reliably remove vulnerabilities from third party websites. Session ID attacks, cross-site scripting attacks, social attacks, and other common attacks may be present in third party applications. This analysis is focused on protecting the system and preventing third party applications from being less secure than they would otherwise be over a wired network.

2.11.5 Connected vehicle summary

Security for connected vehicles differs from the traditional view of automobile security. We note that research to date has concentrated mainly on finding flaws in existing implementations. Little has been done to find ways to avoid creating flaws. Of the flaws found so far, many relate to either the use of

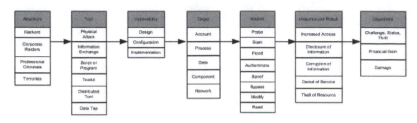

FIGURE 2.13
Modified attack taxonomy.

non-standard cryptographic protocols or the use of insufficiently long cryptographic keys. Current industry best practice is to rely on standardized cryptographic algorithms, as they are the most thoroughly reviewed. There is little excuse for using short cryptographic keys in the current environment.

We find that some columns in the taxonomy from [210] are not suited to the automotive security domain. A modified taxonomy is shown in Figure 2.13. Spies and voyeurs are not expected to attack automotive systems, nor is political gain a reasonable outcome from compromising the security of a single automobile. Most attacks are to be expected from professional thieves seeking financial gain.

The new computerized environment creates a natural tension between automobile enthusiasts and automobile manufacturers. Enthusiasts want to modify the manufacturer's proprietary systems. Attempts to secure these systems against modification provide incentives to hobbyists to break system security. A similar dynamic exists in the game console market. It is worth noting that the only console whose security has yet to be compromised is the console that provides a Linux interface supporting hobbyist modifications [32]. Perhaps automobile manufacturers should consider a similar strategy.

The sets of vulnerabilities and unauthorized results in Figure 2.13 vary little from those in the original taxonomy [210]. We expect them to remain unchanged for the long term.

On the other hand, we have not updated the sets of tools and actions in Figure 2.13 for the opposite reason. The new automotive security environment differs greatly from traditional systems. New attacks are to be expected, and it is probably premature to enumerate them. For example, fuzzing sends random packets at an embedded system hoping to find software flaws through trial and error, and phlashing is fuzzing with the goal of permanently breaking an embedded computer. These attacks did not exist when [210] was devised and we expect many new classes of attacks to emerge for attacking automotive and pervasive computing systems.

2.12   Summary

This chapter provides an initial introduction into computer and network security. There are a number of attributes that distinguish secure systems from insecure systems, notably: *confidentiality, authentication, integrity, non-repudiation, access control,* and *availability.* The definitions of many of these attributes overlap. Except for availability, there are no quantitative measures for these attributes. The following chapters deal with ways that we attempt to maintain these security attributes and why we often fail miserably.

A major issue in security is *social engineering.* Attackers deceive individuals and take advantage of them. We describe the more common social engineering attacks. In particular, *spear-phishing* is a powerful tool that is very difficult to stop.

We described a number of security tools, including file-system authentication and authorization and auditing.

There are limitations to the security we provide. User interfaces are too often ignored. It is difficult to translate mathematical and logical constructs into an intuitive representation for use by non-experts. This problem is made worse by the fundamental limitation pointed out by Thompson in [395]. Security decisions depend on information provided by software. If inputs are wrong, the wrong decision will be made. In practice, some layers of the system must be trusted. Security must always depend on a set of assumptions that may not be valid.

Section 2.9 provides a structured definition of computer and network security. We present an exhaustive discussion of vulnerabilities and attacks. The taxonomy we provide is a useful tool for describing the problem domain. We adapt this tool to mobile code and automotive systems. These classes of applications are increasingly important, since computer applications are moving from desktops to clouds and embedded devices.

2.13   Problems

1. A common way to install spyware on a computer is to advertise the malware as an anti-spyware tool. Which scam class does this belong to and what are the scam factors that define it?

2. Describe the approach you would take to avoid having users install spyware on their machine. How could you verify that your approach was effective?

3. Is pharming a social engineering attack? Support your answer by comparing it with phishing.

4. Two-factor authentication systems use two of the three (knowledge, possession, and identity) authentication factors to identify a user. Describe an attack that is able to foil two-factor authentication.

5. Would the use of tattoos or subcutaneous RFID chips as authentication factors make a system significantly more secure?

6. Create a directed graph of the OASIS standards showing which standards depend on other standards. Indicate where it is possible that two standards have overlapping responsibilities.

7. Explain what Unix file access values 777, 700, 241, and 017 mean.

8. Count the number of computer passwords that you have (include each webpage that requires you to have a registration password to access their service). Explain why or why not it is reasonable to assume that a person would be able to remember that number of random sequences of digits, letters, and random characters.

9. Explain how the problem described in the *On Trusting Trust* [395] could be removed from software development.

10. Pick eight information warfare threats and explain the vulnerability that they exploit.

11. Describe the advanced persistent threats from Section 2.9.3 using the taxonomy in Figure 2.4.

12. Describe at least one advanced persistent threat from Section 2.9.3 using the Case study in Section 2.10.

13. Rank the known attacks on automotive information technology systems by severity.

14. The smart grid concept uses computer technology to increase the efficiency of our electric power distribution network. Which of the attack taxonomies presented in this chapter is best suited to expressing threats to the power grid? Justify your answer.

15. Which would provide more anonymity: a system of 20 users all of which are equally likely to have generated a message, or a system of 1,000 users where the originator of the message is 10 times as likely to have generated the message?

16. There is debate as to whether or not anonymity should be permitted on the Internet. List ten reasons why anonymity should be allowed for information access. List ten reasons why anonymity should not be allowed.

17. Explain the relationship between *On Trusting Trust* and side-channel attacks.

2.14   Glossary

419 scam: A class of fraud that requests money from the victim as a down-payment on some future reward that never arrives.

Access control: Security attribute for limiting and controlling access to information.

ACL: Access control list.

Advanced persistent threat: Attack using multiple attack vectors over an extended period of time.

Attack surface: The set of components potentially accessible by an attacker.

Authentication: Security attribute for correctly identifying the origin of information, or the process of verifying user identity.

Authorization: Process of determining the access level a user should have to an information asset.

Availability: Security attribute denoting that the system needs to be usable. Availability also refers to the percent of time that a system can be used.

Byzantine generals problem: Refers to the ability to reach a correct decision even when a subset of the available information is intentionally deceptive.

CIA: Used to refer to the core security attributes: confidentiality, integrity, and availability.

Click-fraud: Fraudulent collection of URL referral fees through the creation of illegitimate web page accesses.

Cloning: Creating an exact copy of something. Frequently refers to credential duplication.

Confidentiality: Security attribute for restricting access to authorized persons.

Covert channel: Hidden communications between two machines in violation of a security policy.

Denial of service: An attack that makes system resources unavailable to legitimate users.

Distributed denial of service: A denial of service attack that is implemented using multiple attackers.

Engine immobilizer: Security device that electronically disables an automobile engine.

Fuzzing: Use of randomized data to discover system vulnerabilities.

Integrity: Security attribute for only allowing authorized people to change information.

Kerberos: A widely used authentication system.

Key-logger: Surreptitious software that records keyboard inputs.

LDAP: Distributed directory system based on ITU X.500 standards.

Leet: Use of numbers and other alternate characters to represent similar looking letters on-line.

Liveness: A system that is guaranteed to return to a known set of desirable states.

Man in the middle: An attack where an intruder inserts themselves between two parties and masquerades as the other end of the connection.

Mule: An individual used for money laundering of illegal funds.

Non-repudiation: Security attribute for not letting parties deny the existence of a transaction.

Orwell: George Orwell wrote *1984* and *Animal Farm*. The novel *1984* described a dystopia where individuals were constantly surveilled by a television camera and told they were being watched. Those people have more privacy than you.

PERMIS: An authorization system.

Pharming: Extracting personal information by using a malicious copy of a legitimate website, typically involving a malicious modification of the Internet addressing scheme.

Phishing: On-line attempt to extract personal identity information from someone by masquerading as a legitimate organization, typically using an email containing a malformed URL.

Phlashing: Attack where firmware is remotely rewritten in order to make it unusable.

Principle of least privilege: Each process and user should only have the access rights necessary for performing their role.

Reliability: The average time to a system failure. Related to availability.

Replay: An attack where the intruder records network traffic that is resent at a later time.

Safety: A system that does not allow a pre-defined set of errors to occur.

SAML: XML-based standard for exchanging authentication and authorization information between security domains.

Scavenging: Inspecting freed storage space for data that have not been erased.

Shibboleth: Middle-ware for authentication and authorization.

Side channel: Information leakage from a machine by environmental consequences of program execution.

Sniffing: Inspecting Internet packets traversing the network.

Social engineering: Deception in order to receive information or access.

Spam: Unwanted email advertising.

Spamdexing: Modifying search engine rankings to lead people to webspam.

Spear-phishing: A phishing attack crafted for a specific target.

SPIM: Spam over instant messaging.

SPIT: Spam over Internet telephony.

Spoofing: Using false data.

Sybil: An attack where one entity pretends to be multiple entities.

Taxonomy: A structured way of classifying a domain.

Traffic analysis: Study of network traffic flows to infer information about network usage.

Trojan: Programs designed to deceive the user by intentionally doing different actions than they are supposed to.

umask: Unix command for setting default file access settings.

Virus: Program that reproduces by inserting copies of itself into other programs.

Webspam: Spam distribution through webpages.

Worm: Network process that reproduces by creating new versions of itself on remote nodes.

XACML: XML-based language for expressing access control policies.

X.509: ITU standard for public key infrastructure authorization and privilege management.

XML Enc: Standard for encrypting XML documents.

3

Cryptography Primer

CONTENTS

3.1 Introduction

In Chapter 1 we discuss the history of cryptology, cryptography and cryptanalysis. *Cryptology* is the science of communicating using secret codes. It is subdivided into *cryptography*, writing in codes, and *cryptanalysis*, deciphering codes. As shown in Chapter 1, cryptography is of great historical, theoretical, and practical interest. It is an essential tool for developing secure systems.

This chapter provides a brief overview of cryptology. It does not deal with research issues in cryptology in any depth. It provides students with a basic understanding of what cryptology is, and is not. At the end, the student should have a practical understanding of how cryptography, and cryptanalysis work, and are used.

There is an apocryphal quote, which many attribute to Peter G. Neumann of SRI:[1] "If you think cryptography is the answer to your problems, then you don't understand cryptography and you don't understand your problems." In the realm of security, there is no magic bullet or "pixie dust" that solves all our problems. That said, cryptography is an important tool. You need to understand what it is and how it is used. Just as important, you need to know what it is not and what its limitations are.

Cryptography consists of *encryption* and *decryption*. *Clear-text* is the original version of the message, which is easily read. *Cipher-text* is an obscured version of the message, that unauthorized people should not be able to convert back into clear-text. Clear-text and cipher-text can be expressed in different domains. Encryption maps clear-text to cipher-text, while decryption maps cipher-text to clear-text. The range of possible values for clear-text (cipher-text) is the *message space* (*cipher-space*). These two ranges need not be the same.

As shown in Figure 3.1 [358], encryption and decryption mappings are found by executing algorithms that take as input both a text message (in clear-text or cipher-text) as well as a *cryptographic key*. The encryption and decryption algorithms may, or may not, be identical. Similarly, encryption and decryption may, or may not, use the same cryptographic key. When encryption and decryption use the same key, the cipher is called a *symmetric key* cryptosystem. When the two keys are different, the cipher is called an *asymmetric key* or *public key* cryptosystem [287]. The range of possible values for keys is the *key space*.

FIGURE 3.1
Illustration of encryption and decryption processes.

In general, cryptographic algorithms are not kept secret. It is felt that publishing cryptographic algorithms makes them more secure, since peer-review finds flaws in the algorithms. When flaws are known, they can be corrected. The use of secret algorithms is disparagingly called *security through obscurity*. Security through obscurity is found to produce less robust and secure systems. "Security should not depend on the secrecy of the design or the ignorance of the attacker" [439].

On the other hand, to keep the message secure some information must be hidden from potential attackers. The approach in Figure 3.1 shows the use of the cryptographic key, which is the one item that needs to be kept secret. Ideally, if the key is kept confidential, attackers can have free access to the

---

[1]I heard him attribute the quote to others with the caveat that they in turn attribute it to still other people. The quote is widely accepted, but of apparently unknown origin.

cipher-text and be able to determine neither the clear-text message nor the value of the key.

There are several classes of cryptanalysis attacks that are used to attack cryptographic systems [358]. This classification depends mainly on the information (in addition to the cryptography algorithm) available to the cryptanalyst. The four classical classes of cryptanalysis are:

1. In *cipher-text only attacks* the cryptanalyst only has cipher-text. The analyst tries to find as many message cipher-texts as possible. If the crytpanalyst can discover the cryptographic keys, then they can convert all past and future cipher-texts into clear-text.
2. *Known clear-text attacks* are easier, since the analyst has access to some clear-text messages. In these attacks, analysts are interested in using these example clear-text to cipher-text mappings to derive either the cryptographic key or an algorithm for inferring the cryptographic key.
3. In *chosen clear-text attacks*, the analysts not only know some clear-text inputs, they can choose the clear-text inputs that will be encrypted. For example, a secret document could be leaked in order to perform this attack. The analyst's goals are the same as with the known clear-text attack.
4. In *adaptive chosen clear-text attacks* analysts can also modify the choice of clear-text to be used based on results from analysis of previous chosen clear-text attacks.

We will not discuss in detail these less typical classes of cryptanalysis [358]:

1. In *chosen cipher-text attacks* the analyst can choose the cipher-text to be decrypted. This may be useful in black-box analysis of an encryption device.
2. A *chosen-key attack* does not mean that the analyst gets to choose keys, rather it occurs when the analyst gathers some knowledge about relationships between keys. For example, if an initialization vector is used as a seed for a pseudo-random number generator.
3. *Lead-pipe cryptanalysis*[2] [296, 390, 391] occurs when pressure is applied to humans to force them to reveal a cryptographic key. This may include force, bribery, social engineering, etc.

A survey of banking systems [47] shows that most civilian cryptosystems do not fail due to sophisticated cryptanalysis. Rather, they fail due to either implementation errors or management mistakes. In practical terms, the threat model commonly used for civilian cryptographic systems is not the most realistic one. Social engineering and lead-pipe cryptanalysis are more common attacks than sophisticated mathematical analysis. For military and diplomatic applications, the situation is likely to be different.

---

[2]This can also be called rubber hose cryptanalysis.

In the rest of this chapter[3], we first briefly discuss the main classes of cryptographic algorithms. We discuss each algorithm and mention known problems. We also discuss cryptanalysis of the substitution and Vigenère ciphers. This illustrates the general ideas behind cryptanalysis without being too onerous. Cryptanalysis of block ciphers and public key cryptography is outside the scope of this book. We then explain one-time pads; why they are secure; and why they are not very practical for most applications. This leads naturally into an introduction to key management. This is followed by a discussion of how to best verify the correctness of security algorithms. The chapter ends with discussions of steganography, obfuscation, and homomorphic encryption. Although steganography and obfuscation are not encryption, we will see that they have different assumptions, but are used for similar applications. Both steganography and obfuscation can be considered examples of security through obscurity. Homomorphic encryption and obfuscation are discussed together, in spite of the fact that one is encryption and the other is not, mainly because their application domains are very similar.

3.2   Substitution Ciphers and Frequency Analysis

The simplest cipher is a substitution cipher. This cipher replaces each letter of the alphabet with another letter. In the Caesar cipher, each letter is shifted three to the right. The letter "a" becomes "d," and "b" becomes "e." The end of the alphabet wraps around, with "x" mapping to "a'," "y" to "b," and "z" to "c" [358, 388]. If we number the letters from 1 to 26, this can be expressed mathematically as a mapping from the input character a_i to the cipher character a_c using modulo 26[4] addition:

$$a_c = a_i + 3 (mod 26) \tag{3.1}$$

If both characters are ASCII values, this can be written in the C programming language as:

```
char CaesarCipher(char input)
{
  char answer;
  if((input > 64) && (input < 91)){        /* Capital letters */
```

---

[3]We suggest that both instructor and students use cryptool software when studying this chapter [19]. Its visualizations of cryptography algorithms are useful in understanding the approaches. In addition, Cryptool's implementation of cryptography algorithms and cryptanalysis tools help teachers and students create experiments.

[4]Modulo arithmetic is simply normal arithmetic where there is a maximum number. For example, in arithmetic modulo n all multiples of n are set to zero and any numbers larger than n are set to their remainder when divided by n. For example, in modulo 8 arithmetic 10 is equal to 2, as is 18.

```
  answer = (((input - 64) + 3) % 26 ) + 64);
}else if((input > 96) && (input < 122)){ /* Lower case   */
  answer = (((input - 96) + 3) % 26 ) + 96);
}else answer = input;                       /* Non-alphabetic*/
return( input );
}
```

The ROT13 cipher is another cipher of this class, where each letter is shifted 13 positions:

$$a_c = a_i + 13 (mod 26) \qquad (3.2)$$

Verify that applying ROT13 a second time to a message gives you the original clear-text. A slight generalization of these two ciphers could use an arbitrary key k, with $k <= 26$. This would be a symmetric key encryption approach where encryption is:

$$a_c = a_i + k (mod 26) \qquad (3.3)$$

and decryption is:

$$a_i = a_c - k (mod 26) \qquad (3.4)$$

Cryptanalysis of this approach is easy. Since there are only 26 possible keys, it would be possible to write a program that uses all possible key values and compare the results with words in file /usr/share/dict/linux.words. If the input message is in English, the key could be found in seconds.

A more general encryption algorithm could use any one-to-one mapping from (to) a clear-text symbol to (from) a cipher-text symbol. For English, instead of there being 26 possible keys, there would be 26! (approximately $4 * 10^{26}$) possible keys [287]. An exhaustive search of this key space is more expensive. This kind of simple substitution cipher that uses a single alphabet when encrypting (decrypting) is called a *mono-alphabetic* cipher.

Mono-alphabetic ciphers are typically broken using frequency analysis [388]. We compute the frequency of each character in the cipher-text and compare them to the frequencies for a typical English text. In most cases, for reasonably long texts, this comparison is enough to provide us with the key with no further calculation[5]. This saves us from having to perform a brute force, exhaustive search of the $4 * 10^{26}$ alternatives in the key space.

This cipher was secure for Caesar not because of its complexity. It was secure in large part because many people were illiterate and unable to read clear-text.

---

[5]This could be problematic if the clear-text message was not representative of the language as a whole. For example, Georges Perec's 300-page French novel *La disparition* and Ernest Vincent Wright's English novel *Gadsby* were both written without a single use of the letter "e", the most common letter in both languages.

3.3   Vigenère Cipher and Cryptanalysis

We now describe Blaise de Vigenère's cipher from 1586 that we mention in Chapter 1. The Vigenère cipher is an example of a *poly-alphabetic* cipher where multiple alphabets are used.

To understand the cipher, consider Table 3.1 [388]. In Vigenère's approach, the key is a word or phrase. For a simple example, let's use the phrase *goldbug* as a key. We use this key to encrypt the message *EdgarAllenPoe*.

The message is encrypted letter by letter. We consider each character of the message and the key in turn. If the message is longer than the key, which is usually the case, we cycle through the key as many times as necessary.

Each letter in the message is replaced with the element in Table 3.1 corresponding to the column of the current key character and the row corresponding to the current message character. In our example, the first character of the encrypted message is *k* which is the character in column *g* and row *e*. The second character of the encrypted message is *r*, found at column *o* and row *d*. By repeating this simple process we encrypt the entire message, giving *Krrd-sUrrsySpy*. Decryption is performed by simply looking in the column specified by the key value at each step; finding the letter in the encrypted message; and replacing that letter with the letter corresponding to that row.

This can also be expressed mathematically [287]. For a message of length i, a key of length t, a clear-text sequence of characters $a_0, a_1, \ldots, a_{i-1}$, the encrypted text sequence of characters $c_0, c_1, \ldots, c_{i-1}$, and key sequence of characters $k_0, k_i, \ldots, k_t$, we have Equation 3.5.

$$c_i = a_i + k_{i mod t} (mod 26) \tag{3.5}$$

Cryptanalysis of poly-alphabetic ciphers is done by analyzing the cipher-text and finding ways to divide the problem into a set of mono-alphabetic ciphers.

To illustrate this, we downloaded a copy of Dostoevsky's *The Brothers Karamazov* from Gutenberg.org and encrypted it using the key *CRYPTO-NOMICON*. Figure 3.2 shows the auto-correlation of the resulting cipher-text[6]. We note the clear peaks at every 13 characters, which shows us that the key used in the Vigenère cipher is 13 characters long.

The symbol frequencies that were used to break the Caesar cipher cause these peaks to occur, since the same symbols occur more frequently when the key vlaues are the same. We can then separate the cipher-text into 13 unrelated Caesar ciphers. Solving them separately allows us to find the original key, which we use to find the clear-text message.

---

[6]This figure was produced using the cryptool software suite [19].

	a	b	c	d	e	f	g	h	i	j	k	l	m	n	o	p	q	r	s	t	u	v	w	x	y	z
a	a	b	c	d	e	f	g	h	i	j	k	l	m	n	o	p	q	r	s	t	u	v	w	x	y	z
b	b	c	d	e	f	g	h	i	j	k	l	m	n	o	p	q	r	s	t	u	v	w	x	y	z	a
c	c	d	e	f	g	h	i	j	k	l	m	n	o	p	q	r	s	t	u	v	w	x	y	z	a	b
d	d	e	f	g	h	i	j	k	l	m	n	o	p	q	r	s	t	u	v	w	x	y	z	a	b	c
e	e	f	g	h	i	j	k	l	m	n	o	p	q	r	s	t	u	v	w	x	y	z	a	b	c	d
f	f	g	h	i	j	k	l	m	n	o	p	q	r	s	t	u	v	w	x	y	z	a	b	c	d	e
g	g	h	i	j	k	l	m	n	o	p	q	r	s	t	u	v	w	x	y	z	a	b	c	d	e	f
h	h	i	j	k	l	m	n	o	p	q	r	s	t	u	v	w	x	y	z	a	b	c	d	e	f	g
i	i	j	k	l	m	n	o	p	q	r	s	t	u	v	w	x	y	z	a	b	c	d	e	f	g	h
j	j	k	l	m	n	o	p	q	r	s	t	u	v	w	x	y	z	a	b	c	d	e	f	g	h	i
k	k	l	m	n	o	p	q	r	s	t	u	v	w	x	y	z	a	b	c	d	e	f	g	h	i	j
l	l	m	n	o	p	q	r	s	t	u	v	w	x	y	z	a	b	c	d	e	f	g	h	i	j	k
m	m	n	o	p	q	r	s	t	u	v	w	x	y	z	a	b	c	d	e	f	g	h	i	j	k	l
n	n	o	p	q	r	s	t	u	v	w	x	y	z	a	b	c	d	e	f	g	h	i	j	k	l	m
o	o	p	q	r	s	t	u	v	w	x	y	z	a	b	c	d	e	f	g	h	i	j	k	l	m	n
p	p	q	r	s	t	u	v	w	x	y	z	a	b	c	d	e	f	g	h	i	j	k	l	m	n	o
q	q	r	s	t	u	v	w	x	y	z	a	b	c	d	e	f	g	h	i	j	k	l	m	n	o	p
r	r	s	t	u	v	w	x	y	z	a	b	c	d	e	f	g	h	i	j	k	l	m	n	o	p	q
s	s	t	u	v	w	x	y	z	a	b	c	d	e	f	g	h	i	j	k	l	m	n	o	p	q	r
t	t	u	v	w	x	y	z	a	b	c	d	e	f	g	h	i	j	k	l	m	n	o	p	q	r	s
u	u	v	w	x	y	z	a	b	c	d	e	f	g	h	i	j	k	l	m	n	o	p	q	r	s	t
v	v	w	x	y	z	a	b	c	d	e	f	g	h	i	j	k	l	m	n	o	p	q	r	s	t	u
w	w	x	y	z	a	b	c	d	e	f	g	h	i	j	k	l	m	n	o	p	q	r	s	t	u	u
x	x	y	z	a	b	c	d	e	f	g	h	i	j	k	l	m	n	o	p	q	r	s	t	u	u	w
y	y	z	a	b	c	d	e	f	g	h	i	j	k	l	m	n	o	p	q	r	s	t	u	u	w	x
z	z	a	b	c	d	e	f	g	h	i	j	k	l	m	n	o	p	q	r	s	t	u	u	w	x	y

TABLE 3.1

Vigenère table.

Number of characters that agree

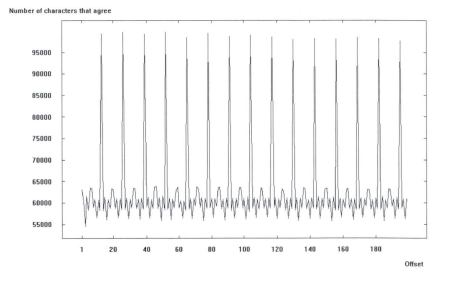

FIGURE 3.2
Example auto-correlation of Vigenère encrypted message.

3.4   Block Ciphers

The main weakness of both mono-alphabetic and poly-alphabetic ciphers is the one-to-one correspondence of clear-text characters to cipher-text characters. This gives cryptanalysts information to exploit. To overcome this, block ciphers encrypt and decrypt blocks of n bits at a time.

Most currently used symmetric key cryptography algorithms are block ciphers. The advent of the Data Encryption Standard (DES) block cipher is widely viewed as the birth of modern day cryptography. Today, as we will discuss, DES is no longer considered adequately strong. It has been replaced with another block cipher, the Advanced Encryption Standard (AES).

This section provides background information followed by summary descriptions of DES and AES. It ends with a brief discussion of cryptanalysis for block ciphers. Our goal is to provide a brief introduction to these tools, so the reader can have a general understanding of how they work. People interested in implementing, improving, or attacking block ciphers need a more in-depth understanding and should refer to our references.

3.4.1   Operations

Block ciphers encrypt clear-text messages by processing them in sequential chunks of n bits. Typically, n is a power of 2. DES uses a block size of 64 bits. AES uses 128-bit blocks [388]. Block sizes smaller than 64 bits would rarely be used, since the cipher would not be significantly different than a cipher processing one character at a time.

Symmetric key ciphers are typically built by combining the following atomic operations [287, 358, 388]:

- Boolean logic – The following operations will be used on bits, bytes, or words: AND, OR, XOR, NOT, NAND, and NOR.[7]
- Substitution[8] – Replacement of one value by another value. This may be specified as a vector. For example, if 0 is to be replaced by 2, 1 replaced by 0, and 2 replaced by 1, the vector would be [2, 0, 1]. We note that DES uses least significant bit order in this operation [388].
- Permutation[9] – Changing the bit order of the data. This may also be specified as a vector. For example, if bit 0 is to be put in bit 2, bit 1 placed in bit 0, and bit 2 moved to bit 1, the vector would be [2, 0, 1].
- Shift registers – A set of n registers collected to a common clock controlling the movement of data between, into, and out of the registers [194]. The path of movement between the registers is fixed. New data values of registers may include functions of the contents of other registers. *Linear feedback shift registers* are a common way of producing sequences of pseudo-random numbers.

Symmetric ciphers tend to be a networked combination of these operations. The symmetric key is used to parametrize these operations for transforming clear-text into cipher-text. It is essential that there is an efficient way of computing the inverse of the resulting encryption algorithm.

Feistel structures are a common way of networking these atomic operations [194, 287, 358, 388]. The clear-test input is divided into a sequence of blocks. If the blocks are not full, the last block will be padded. Each input block is divided into a left half L_0 and right half R_0. The Feistel network defines a number of computation rounds. Each round i has the same structure and an associated key K_i. Equation 3.6 gives the computation at each round, where $\oplus$ is the XOR function and $f()$ is a known function repeated at each round.

$$(L_{i-1}, R_{i-1}) \Rightarrow (R_{i-1}, L_{i-1} \oplus f(k_i, R_{i-1})) \tag{3.6}$$

Figure 3.3 is a flowchart for Equation 3.6.

---

[7]We assume the reader understands these operations, if not refer to [388]

[8]The component that performs a substitution operation is referred to as an *S-box* [358, 388]

[9]The component that performs a permutation operation is referred to as a *P-box* [358, 388]

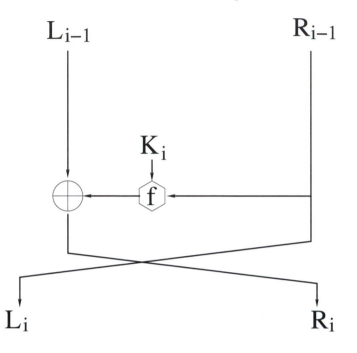

FIGURE 3.3
Diagram illustrating one round of a Feistel structure.

Round	1	2	3	4	5	6	7	8	9	10	11	12	13	14	15	16
Bits	1	1	2	2	2	2	2	2	1	2	2	2	2	2	2	1

TABLE 3.2
Number of key bits shifted at each round of DES.

3.4.2 Data Encryption Standard

The Data Encryption Standard (DES) is a block cipher that uses a 56-bit key K [358]. Any 56-bit number can be a key. There are a small number of known bad keys that must not be used. The key is usually expressed in 64 bits, but every eighth bit is a parity check and ignored by the computations.

The first step in the DES algorithm is a data permutation. The last step is the inverse of this permutation. Since this step has no effect on the security of the algorithm and is frequently skipped by software implementations [358], we ignore it here. Interested parties can refer to [358].

DES has 16 rounds. Each round i uses a different 48-bit sub-key k_i where $1 \leq i \leq 16$. To calculate k_i, k_{i-1} is divided into two 28-bit halves and each half is circularly shifted by 1 or 2 bits each round, following Table 3.2.

After the shift operation, a permutation operation (called the *compression permutation*) is performed using 48 bits from the shifted key. Because of the rotation operation, a different subset of the bits is used at each round [358, 287]. Another permutation operation (called the *expansion permutation*) takes 32 bits from the right half of the data and writes a 48-bit output.[10] The compressed key is XOR-ed with the output of the expansion permutation. These processes create a different key for each round and ensure that the dependency of output bits on input bits spread quickly.

The 48 bits resulting from the XOR of the outputs from the compression and expansion permutations are divided into eight sets of six bits. These six bits are input to eight separate *S-Box* circuits. Each S-Box inputs 6-bits and outputs 4-bits. They can be implemented as table look-ups. DES has eight unique S-Box circuits. The S-Box outputs are concatenated into a single 32-bit block. The S-Box step is non-linear, difficult to analyze, and largely responsible for DES's security.

The 32-bit block output from the S-Boxes is subjected to a simple permutation operation using a *P-Box* circuit. The results are then XOR-ed with the left half (32 bits) of the data for this round. This result becomes the right half for the next round. The unmodified right half of the data for this round becomes the left half of the data for the next round. Note that this is a Feistel structure as shown in Figure 3.3.

DES decryption is done using exactly the same algorithm as encryption. The only change is that the round keys are used in reverse order.

3.4.3 Advanced Encryption Standard

The Advanced Encryption Standard (AES) was chosen by NIST to be the successor to DES in 2001 [318]. Some of the reasons for this update will be discussed in Section 3.4.5. The original name for AES was Rijndael, which comes from the names of the two inventors. AES uses 128 bit blocks and supports key sizes of 128, 192, and 256 [388]. For brevity in this book, we only discuss 128 bit key AES[11].

AES starts processing each 128-bit byte by creating a *state* matrix, as shown in Figure 3.4. Each element $S(i, j)$ in the state matrix is an 8-bit byte. Each row of the matrix is a 32-bit word [318, 388].

AES has four basic operations [318, 388]:

1. *SubBytes* – Each element of the state is run through an 8-bit S-Box, which is usually implemented as a look-up table. This means each

---

[10]Tables of the bit positions used in these permutations will not be provided, because this level of detail is not relevant for our discussion. They are easily accessed, either from references [358, 287] or on-line at http://www.itl.nist.gov/fipspubs/fip46-2.htm. A sample implementation of DES can be found at http://www.cryptool.org. The visualization provided by the cryptool package is useful for understanding DES.

[11]We note that cryptool [19] has an AES implementation for reference and test. It, unfortunately, does not have a visualization

S(0,0)	S(0,1)	S(0,2)	S(0,3)
S(1,0)	S(1,1)	S(1,2)	S(1,3)
S(2,0)	S(2,1)	S(2,2)	S(2,3)
S(3,0)	S(3,1)	S(3,2)	S(3,3)

FIGURE 3.4
Row and column byte ordering for the AES state.

byte in the state is replaced with another byte value. See [318] for a table giving the replacement values in hexadecimal.

2. *ShiftRows* – The bytes in the last three rows are rotated to the left. The first row is not changed. The second row is rotated one byte to the left; the third row is rotated two bytes; and the fourth row is rotated three bytes.

3. *MixColumns* – Operates on the state column by column. In essence, the matrix multiplication in Figure 3.5 is performed where the operation $\otimes$ is *binary XOR long division modulo 128*. Refer to [318] for details on implementing binary XOR long division modulo 128.

4. *AddRoundKey* – XOR the state with the round key.

$$
\begin{bmatrix} S(0,i) \\ S(1,i) \\ S(2,i) \\ S(3,i) \end{bmatrix} = \begin{bmatrix} 2 & 3 & 1 & 1 \\ 1 & 2 & 3 & 1 \\ 1 & 1 & 2 & 3 \\ 3 & 1 & 1 & 2 \end{bmatrix} \otimes \begin{bmatrix} S(0,i) \\ S(1,i) \\ S(2,i) \\ S(3,i) \end{bmatrix}
$$

FIGURE 3.5
Matrix algebra representation of the AES MixColumns operation.

When using a 128-bit key, AES has 10 rounds. The AES algorithm is [318]:

1. Do AddRoundKey
2. For each round, except the last:
   - Do SubBytes
   - Do ShiftRows
   - Do MixColumns
   - Do AddRoundKey
3. Do SubBytes
4. Do ShiftRows
5. Do AddRoundKey

Each round uses a different key. When AES uses a 128-bit key, it has 10

Round	1	2	3	4	5	6	7	8	9	10
Bits	1	2	4	8	16	32	64	128	27	54

TABLE 3.3
Value of first byte of round constant for AES key schedule.

rounds. The 128-bit key is four 32-bit words long. The key scheduler has to generate 47 words to satisfy the algorithm. The first four words generated by the AES key scheduling algorithm are simply the original key. At which point, the following algorithm is performed [318]:

1. Write the last word output by the key scheduler into a temporary variable t.
2. Rotate the bytes of t one byte to the left and overwrite t.
3. Send each byte of t through an S-Box and store in t.
4. XOR the temp variable with a four-byte round constant whose last 3 bytes are zero. The first byte is 2^i modulo(283); these values are listed in Table 3.3.
5. XOR this temp variable with the first word in the last iteration of this algorithm and write this as one of the words to use as a round key.
6. For each of the three other words output in the last iteration of the algorithm, XOR them with the word just output as a round key and output them as the next word to use as a round key.
7. Go back to step 1 until 47 round key words have been output.

AES decryption is similar to DES encryption. The operations are done in reverse order, with a reverse key schedule, and inverse operations for SubBytes, MixColumns, and ShiftRows [388].

3.4.4 ECB and CBC modes

In practice, block ciphers are implemented using one of two modes:

- Electronic code book *ECB* – In ECB mode, each block's cipher-text is calculated by applying the encryption algorithm directly to the clear-text using the cryptographic key. Similarly, the clear-text is recovered from the cipher-text by executing the decryption algorithm with the cryptographic key on the cipher-text one block at a time.
- Cipher block chaining *CBC* - To use CBC mode, both sides need to start with a common *initialization vector* (IV) [12]. The IV is a random bit string as

---
[12]The IV is sometimes referred to as *salt*.

long as a single block. The first block is XOR-ed with the IV before encrypting. Each subsequent block is XOR-ed with the cipher-text of the previous block before encrypting. To decrypt the stream of blocks, the first block of cipher-text is decrypted and then XOR-ed with the IV. Each subsequent block is decrypted and then XOR-ed with the cipher-text of the previous block.

ECB mode is susceptible to replay attacks, where the attacker records cipher-text for use at a later time. For some applications replay attacks are possible, because the application will see that the cipher-text was encrypted with the proper key. Note that the attacker does not need to perform any cryptanalysis for this to work. The use of the IV (salt) makes replay attacks infeasible, as long as both sides use different IV values each time.

3.4.5   Cryptanalysis

In Section 3.1, we list the classes of cryptanalysis. Cipher-text-only attacks are the most damaging attacks to cryptographic protocols.

The simplest attack, conceptually, is a brute force attack, where the attacker tries different possible key combinations until they find one that correctly decrypts the cipher-text. For a key of n-bits, there will be 2^n possible keys. If all keys are equally likely, then there is a 50 percent chance that a brute-force attack will discover the key within 2^{n-1} guesses. Note that each bit added to the key doubles the number of possible keys and doubles the time needed to guess the solution.

It was vulnerability to brute-force search that forced NIST to replace DES with AES. DES was designed with a 56-bit key-length. A custom hardware design was published in 1993 which could find a DES key from known cipher-text and clear-text in 3.5 hours on the average (7 hours worst case) at a cost of around one million dollars. In 1998, the Electronic Frontier Foundation (EFF) published a book detailing a custom hardware and software design that would be able to find the DES key using 8-byte clear-text and cipher-text samples within one week at a cost of around \$ 200,000 [163]. The book detailed how to build low-cost devices tailored to quickly performing DES operations so that they could be used in parallel to find the DES key used to encrypt the data. After publication of this document, NIST opened competition to find another cryptography standard. This approach assumed a small amount of known clear-text but if the attacker has some knowledge of the format of the clear-text this approach would still be feasible. It would, however, require more cipher-text samples.

Another feasible attack on DES is *differential cryptanalysis* [388, 71]. The concept behind differential cryptanalysis is that differences in clear-text inputs will cause differences in cipher-text outputs. This is a chosen clear-text attack. Picking inputs correctly allows the attacker to target paths through specific S-boxes. Running a large number of samples through the encryption algorithm allows the attacker to derive a probability distribution relating input differences to output differences. See [388] for a fuller treatment of how differential cryptanalysis works and [71] for application of differential cryptanalysis to DES. They analyze 2^{36} cypher-texts in 2^{37} time.

Linear cryptanalysis has also been successfully used against DES. It is similar conceptually to differential cryptanalysis [388, 284]. Linear cryptanalysis assumes a linear expression can describe a relationship mapping bits of clear-text and cipher-text data to individual key-bits. Large sets of clear-text are input to the algorithm with different keys and the resulting cipher-text collected. Clear-text and cipher-text combinations are mapped to individual key-bits. Probability density functions are calculated. If the probability differs from 0.5 then the data provides information about the key. In the attack, cipher and clear-text pairs are input to the probability density functions to calculate the probability of different bit combinations for the key. The most likely key is chosen. The work in [284] shows DES can be broken using 2^{45} random plain-text inputs.

It is also possible to combine linear and differential cryptanalysis to aid in inferring keys. One can also do "higher-order" differential cryptanalysis by looking at the differences between differences in cipher-text. All of these approaches can be useful in cryptanalysis of block-ciphers [388].

In addition, all cryptographic approaches are vulnerable to *side-channel attacks*. A side-channel attack takes advantage of the fact that algorithms are implemented on physical machines. Machine instructions will not have identical time, power, space, etc. needs. Measuring these environmental interactions provides the attacker with enough information to break the basic assumptions behind the cryptographic protocols. We discuss side-channels in depth in Chapter 12.

The design of AES took advantage of lessons learned when analyzing DES. AES is very resistant to linear and differential attacks [139]. In spite of this, some possible vulnerabilities may exist in AES. Structural attacks can leverage the flow of information specified by the cipher. For AES, there is structural information that is predictable every three rounds. Algebraic attacks are also possible in theory that create sets of quadratic equations over the Galois field 2^8, which could be solved to infer some key bits using chosen text attacks [139].

AES has been shown to be vulnerable to the injection of physical faults. Power spikes, errors in clock timing, and electromagnetic radiation can all either modify the contents of memory or code execution causing the AES computations to be incorrect. For example if the attacker can set key bit i to zero (one) and observe that the other side accepts (rejects) the resulting cipher-text, then the attacker knows that the correct value of key bit i is zero. These ideas are used in [78, 175] to extract 128-bit AES keys. These attacks are typically countered by physically hardening cryptographic devices. A related concept is the idea of *related key attacks*, where the attackers can inject perturbations on the key and see how that changes the cipher-text. Some researchers have found related key vulnerabilities in AES [75].

3.5   RSA Public Key Cryptography

In public key cryptography the key used to encrypt data is different from the one used to decrypt the cipher-text. This asymmetry makes it easier to maintain system security, since users need only maintain the secrecy of their *private key* and can freely distribute the *public key* without fear of compromising system security. Since public key approaches are typically more expensive computationally than symmetric key cryptography, it is common to use the public key approach to securely exchange a random, temporary, session key that is used by a symmetric key algorithm, like AES, to encrypt/decrypt the data exchange [358].

This section will not provide mathematical details. We provide only brief, higher-level descriptions of the important public key encryption algorithm RSA. Elliptic curve cryptography is also important, but will not be presented, since it would require more mathematical detail than appropriate for this book.

The RSA algorithm's name comes from its inventors: Rivest, Shamir and Adleman. It is based on the difficulty of factoring large numbers [358, 287]. First find two large prime numbers p and q of equal length. Find the product n:

$$n = pq \tag{3.7}$$

Find a number e that is relatively prime to $(p-1)(q-1)$ and $1 < e < (p-1)(q-1)$. The encryption key is e. The decryption key is a number d where:

$$ed = 1 mod(p-1)(q-1) \tag{3.8}$$

which means that

$$d = e^{-1} mod(p-1)(q-1) \tag{3.9}$$

The public key is n and e. The private key is d.

To encrypt a message m:

1. Divide m into j blocks m_j of size 2^i where i is an integer and $2^i < n$.
2. The cipher-text block c_j is set to $c_j = m_j^e mod n$.

Decryption is simply:

$$m_j = c_j^d mod n \tag{3.10}$$

One way to break RSA would be to factor n directly [358, 287], but as long as n is large there are no efficient factoring algorithms. Current suggestions are to use keys of at least 1024 bits [249].

There are some known weaknesses in RSA:

- If similar messages may be sent over time, then it is inadvisable to use a small value for e [287],
- Choose d to be approximately the same size as n [287],

- For small messages, pad the message with random bits [287],
- It is possible for a message to have the same clear-text and cipher-text values. This should be avoided [287],
- Chosen cipher-text attacks can be used to trick users into mistakenly decoding messages [358],
- Re-use of the value n makes it easier to infer d [201],
- RSA is sensitive to related plain-text attacks [201], and
- Like symmetric key algorithms, public key encryption is subject to side-channel attacks [238]; see Chapter 12.

A thorough discussion of RSA weaknesses can be found in [201]. Issues related to hardware implementations of public key systems can be found in [63].

It is worth noting that for a public key approach like RSA to provide the same security as a symmetric key approach like AES, the public key approach typically requires a significantly larger key [358]. This is because constraints on the possible public key values reduce the size of the key space for a given key length.

3.6 Hash Functions

A hash function $h = H(M)$ is a mapping of a binary value M to a binary value h, where h has fixed length m. Common examples of hash functions are parity bits and cyclical redundancy checks. The use of hash functions in cryptography is similar to their use for error detection and correction [194]. Cryptographic hash functions are commonly referred to as *one-way hash functions*. A one-way hash function should have the following attributes [358]:

1. Easy to compute (find h given M),
2. Hard to invert (find M given h), and
3. Difficult to create collisions (find M' given M where $H(M') = H(M)$).

It is worth noting that both parity bits and cyclic redundancy checks are not hard to invert. They are, therefore, also prone to collisions.

One important issue in designing a hash function is finding the right value for m. The third property implies m should be large enough that different values of M are unlikely to have the same value. Recall the birthday paradox [424]. The probability that another person has the same birthday as you is $1/365$. The probability that they have a different birthday is $(365 - 1)/365$. Let's replace 365 with variable d. This lets us express the probability Q_1 that n people all have different birthdays as:

$$Q_1(n, d) = \frac{d!}{(d-n)!d^n} \tag{3.11}$$

So the probability $P_2(n, m)$ that there will be at least one collision among n messages M mapped to a hash function of size m is:

$$P_2(n, m) = 1 - Q_1(n, m) = 1 - \frac{m!}{(m-n)!m^n} \qquad (3.12)$$

This can be generalized as the *birthday attack*, which states that the expected number of random trials needed to construct a collision to a hash function of range m is:

$$1.2\sqrt{m} \qquad (3.13)$$

The two main classes of cryptographic hash functions are [287]:

- *Modification detection codes* (MDCs) – are un-keyed hash functions that are used as *fingerprints* to detect tampering. These are often constructed from block ciphers. NIST is currently evaluating proposals for a new family of cryptographic hash functions, since weaknesses have been found in SHA-1. Current advice is to use SHA-256 or SHA-512.
- *Message authentication codes* (MACs) – are keyed hash functions. They are used both to verify that the data has not been tampered with and the data source. MACs are often constructed from MDCs. MACs use a shared key for authorization, so they are not suitable for non-repudiation.

We will not discuss implementation details, since implementations of standard cryptographic hash functions can be found in Cryptool [19] and OpenSSL [22].

If non-repudiation is needed, then it is possible to use public key cryptography to encrypt a MDC value with the secret key.

3.7 One-time Pads

There is one theoretically secure, and totally impractical, cryptography algorithm. A one-time pad encrypts a message M of length m by XORing it with its key K. The key K is a random bit-string of length m with each bit set to 1 with probability $1/2$. K is used only once [194]. This approach goes back to Shannon and is perfectly secure against cipher-text only attacks, since all keys (and therefore cipher-texts) are equally likely. The cipher-text gives no information about the clear-text message, unless the attacker knows K.

This system loses its security, should K be re-used. The main drawback is the need to distribute the keys. You would need a secure, secret channel for distributing information with sufficient bandwidth to handle messages of size m. If you were to have that channel, it would be wise to transmit M directly.

3.8 Key Management

The issue with one-time pads is the difficulty of securely distributing key values. This is a general problem, which is quite different for symmetric and asymmetric key cryptography. We look at each in turn. The primary issue is how to transmit keys between hosts using untrusted channels, without compromising them.

3.8.1 Notation and Communicating Sequential Processes (CSP)

To describe protocols, we use notation from Ryan and Schneider [351]. The notation is based on Hoare's Communicating Sequential Processes (CSP) [203] as modified to create Abadi's [35] *spi calculus* that represents cryptographic protocols. This is a straightforward way of logically representing logic, message passing, cryptographic operations, and parallel operations.

For example, a sending b a message that contains a data element with session key k_{ab} concatenated with a's address, where the data element has been encrypted with key k_b, is represented by:

$$a \rightarrow b : \{k_{ab} \bullet a\}_{k_b} \tag{3.14}$$

CSP can be used to automatically check these protocols for deadlock and similar errors [203]. Theorem proving tools can be used to verify the soundness of protocols against a large number of attack scenarios [35, 351].

3.8.2 Symmetric key distribution

It is possible for two hosts (a, b) to securely establish a key over an open channel [287]. *Shamir's no-key protocol* starts with a and b publishing a prime number p. Node a and b choose random numbers r_a and r_b, respectively. Node a initiates the following protocol to send session key K to b:

- $a \rightarrow b : K^{r_a} mod p$
- $b \rightarrow a : (K^{r_a})^{r_b} mod p$
- $a \rightarrow b : (K^{r_a r_b})^{r_a^{-1}} mod p$

At which point, b exponentiates the last message by r_b^{-1} and retrieves K. Note that the protocol we present does not authenticate the hosts involved and only protects against passive eavesdropping. It is vulnerable to man-in-the-middle attacks.

A major problem with this approach is the lack of authentication. If the two nodes a and b do not already share a key, it is difficult for them to authenticate each other directly. If they both share keys with a trusted key server s, then they can use the Yahalom protocol [351]. In this protocol, n_a

and n_b are random values chosen by a and b, respectively. In the future, we will call random values like these *nonces*. The protocol uses the following keys:

- k_{as} – session key shared by a and s,
- k_{bs} – session key shared by b and s, and
- k_{ab} – session key to be used by a and b, chosen by s.

The following messages are exchanged:

- $a \rightarrow b : a \bullet n_a$
- $b \rightarrow s : b \bullet \{a \bullet n_a \bullet n_b\}_{k_{bs}}$
- $s \rightarrow a : \{b \bullet k_{ab} \bullet n_a \bullet n_b\}_{k_{as}} \bullet \{a \bullet k_{ab}\}_{k_{bs}}$
- $a \rightarrow b : \{a \bullet k_{ab}\}_{k_{bs}} \bullet \{n_b\}_{k_{ab}}$

This allows both parties to know the session key for direct communications. All messages are authenticated and no information is exposed in clear-text. The use of nonces guards against replay attacks.

The main issue with establishing a common key, using symmetric key algorithms, is that both parties need to have a common key-server that verifies their identities.

3.8.3 Asymmetric key distribution and public key infrastructure (PKI)

In many ways, key distribution is much easier when using public key cryptography. The public key can be sent in clear-text without compromising security. A major problem remains, how to authenticate that the party delivering the public key is the node we wish to communicate with.

Standards exist for public key authentication. The International Telecommunications Union[13] developed a number of computer networking standards. These included the X.500 directory services standards designed to support the X.400 electronic mail exchange standards. X.400 has been largely dominated by Internet SMTP technologies. The part of the X.500 standard that is most widely used is the X.509 standard, which defines *public key infrastructure* (PKI) approaches used for distributed authentication.

X.509 defines a format for *public key certificates*. A public key certificate is a data structure with two parts: data and signature [287]. The data part includes at a minimum a public key and string identification for the entity being authenticated. It may also contain, among other items:

- A termination date for certificate validity,
- Additional key information (algorithm and use), and
- Additional information about the entity being authenticated.

---

[13]The ITU is a special agency of the United Nations, which is responsible for making communications standards.

The signature is made by using the private key of a trusted party (called the *certificate authority* (CA)) to encrypt a cryptographic hash of the data part.

The X.509 key exchange protocol for nodes a and b to authenticate each other is [287]:

- $a \to b : cert_a \bullet t_a \bullet r_a \bullet b \bullet data_1^* \bullet \{k_1^*\}_{pb} \bullet \{t_a \bullet r_a \bullet b \bullet data_1^* \bullet \{k_1^*\}_{pb}\}_{sa}$
- $b \to a : cert_b \bullet t_b \bullet r_b \bullet a \bullet r_a \bullet data_2^* \bullet \{k_2^*\}_{pa} \bullet \{t_b \bullet r_b \bullet a \bullet r_a \bullet data_2^* \bullet \{k_2^*\}_{pa}\}_{sb}$

where $cert_x$ is a certificate from an accepted certificate authority binding x to its public key, px is x's public key, t_x is an expiration time-stamp generated by x, r_x is a nonce generated by x and sx is x's secret key. Both a and b verify each other's certificates and encrypted data items. This provides strong two-way authentication.

We will revisit PKI security and the use of certificates in Chapter 4. That discussion will illustrate how security flaws remain even when strong cryptography is used.

3.9 Message Confidentiality

The assumptions behind cryptography are:

- Keys, with the exception of asymmetric encryption public keys, are kept private,
- The encryption algorithms execute quickly when the key and data are known,
- Encryption algorithms are difficult to invert,
- Cipher-text provides little information about keys and clear-text, and
- Key size is large enough that a brute-force search of the key space will take long enough that the clear-text is not worth the effort.

We presented examples of how these properties can be justified. It was also shown that these assumptions are not always valid. Cryptanalysis is able to extract information from cipher-text and invert the Caesar and Vigenère ciphers (see Sections 3.2 and 3.3). The EFF (see Section 3.4.5) was able to design machines that allowed for a fast brute-force scan of the DES key-space. Moore's law that computation and storage capacity will double every two years presents a danger to designers of cryptographic systems. It is not enough to show that systems can not be broken with current CPUs, since more powerful computers will be available in the near future.

In addition, cryptography depends on sound protocols. In Section 3.8.1, we refer to a notation for expressing cryptographic protocols that is derived from existing protocol analysis techniques. This approach has been used to produce tools for automatic protocol verification [351] that use mathematical expressions of common attacks [35]. Protocol and attack descriptions can then

be input to theorem provers, which either show that the protocols are sound
or they find counterexamples. The counterexamples are traces of legitimate
protocol interactions that are vulnerable to attack.

Cryptography is a very important tool, but we need to be clear about
the guarantees that it does, and does not, provide. In Chapter 4, we will discuss in depth a number of vulnerabilities that have been found in the Secure
Sockets Layer / Transport Layer Security (SSL/TLS) system. In Chapter 12,
we will discuss the use of side-channel attacks to break the security guarantees provided by cryptography by attacking these systems at another level of
abstraction.

3.10   Steganography

Steganography is a security through obscurity concept. It is the science of
hiding information. One piece of data is hidden within another. For example,
changing the lower order bits of an image or music file is unlikely to noticeably
change the original item. White-space characters in documents or computer
source code can also contain hidden information. Comparing the original and
modified data items allows the hidden data to be retrieved easily.

Herodotus documented the use of steganography for covert communications. Recent concerns about the use of Steganography for secret communications by terrorist organizations is most likely overstated [4, 16]. In addition
to being used for covert communications, steganography is applied to digital
watermarking. Information hidden in images, sound, or other data can be used
to verify the origin of the data. This is used to protect intellectual property
rights.

Note that steganographic information is secure because others are unaware
of its presence. Once a hiding place is detected, recovery of the information is
usually fairly straightforward. Steganalysis refers to discovering and recovering
hidden information. Removal of hidden information is often straightforward,
once it has been detected. Typically, the attacker finds features that can be
embedded with minimal disruption of its host. Researchers are looking at ways
of detecting these disturbances, which limits the volume of information that
can be hidden without detection [333].

3.11   Obfuscation and Homomorphic Encryption

To obfuscate is to make a concept so confused and opaque that it is difficult
to understand [29]. Obfuscation in software design is not always intentional.

Examples showing effective obfuscation of computer code can be found in the results of the annual obfuscated C code-writing contest [17]. We will revisit obfuscation and computing with encrypted functions in the polymorphic virus project (see Chapter 9).

With obfuscation, object or source code is deliberately scrambled in a manner that keeps it functional but hard to reverse engineer. Sometimes obfuscation is derided as being an inferior form of encryption. Obfuscation tries to hide information without providing the formal complexity guarantees of modern encryption techniques. Many types of obfuscation exist. The obfuscation taxonomy in [120] can be summarized as:

- Layout obfuscation - these are simple, straightforward, irreversible, and fairly ineffective,
  - Replace identifier names in source or intermediate code with arbitrary values,
  - Remove formatting information in source or intermediate files,
  - Remove comments explaining code.

- Data obfuscation - makes data structures less obvious,
  - Store and encode data in unusual forms,
    * Create a transformation that maps a variable into a domain requiring multiple inputs,
    * Promote scalar values to objects or insert into a larger data structure,
    * Convert static data into a procedure that outputs the constant values desired,
    * Change variable encodings into an equivalent domain,
    * Change variable lifetime and scope.
  - Change the grouping of data structures,
    * If the range of two variables is restricted they can be joined into one variable with a larger range,
    * Modify inheritance relations between objects, including inserting useless classes in the class structure,
    * Change the dimensionality of arrays.
  - Reorder program instructions and data structures in a random manner,
    * Data declarations can be randomized,
    * The order of instructions can be randomized, so long as this does not change program meaning,
    * Positions of data in arrays can be randomized.

- Control obfuscation- changes program flow adding execution overhead,
  - Aggregation - combine unrelated computations into one module or separate related computations into multiple modules,
    * Replace a procedure call with an in-line copy of the procedure,

  * Take two separate code components and insert them into a common procedure,
  * Take two separate code components and interleave their statements in a common procedure,
  * Make multiple copies of a single subroutine to make calling patterns less obvious,
  * Modify loop structures by combining, splitting, or unrolling the loop.
  − Ordering - randomize the order computations are performed,
    * Reorder statements,
    * Reorder loops,
    * Reorder expressions.
  − Computations - modify algorithms,
    * Insert dead code that is irrelevant into a program,
    * Use native or virtual machine commands that can not be expressed in the higher-level languages,
    * Make loop exit conditions needlessly complex without affecting the number of times a loop is executed,
    * Parallelize the program,
    * Include an interpreter in the program that executes code native to that non-standard interpreter,

• Preventive transformations,

  − Targeted - explore weaknesses in current decompilers,
  − Inherent - Explore problems with known de-obfuscation techniques.

Obfuscation has been suggested as a method of protecting mobile code from attacks by malicious hosts. If code (data) is modified to remain valid only for a short period of time, the time needed for reverse engineering may be longer than the period of time the code (data) is valid. Unfortunately, it is difficult to quantify the time needed to reverse engineer obfuscated code and robustly establish the code validity time periods [224].

Homomorphic encryption resembles obfuscation in many ways. Code and data are executed on remote nodes. Details of the execution process and results are hidden from the user. An early example of homomorphic encryption was found in RSA [287]. The encryption of the product of two numbers is the same as the product of two numbers encrypted with the same key. Following this, Yao looked for ways of modifying Boolean circuits so that they could be executed without revealing the underlying function [437]. Another approach uses coding theory to express numbers in a format that is secured in a way that could be considered cryptography [273].

Finally, Gentry's Ph.D. dissertation at Stanford produced a fully homomorphic encryption scheme [173]. This scheme makes it possible for a machine to compute arbitrary functions of data using an encoding of the function that accepts encrypted inputs, produces encrypted outputs, and is opaque to the machine executing the function. Like the approach in [273], Gentry's approach introduces a limited amount of noise into each computation. At each step, though, the system can decipher the actual value by re-encrypting the result. This is done by performing more than one layer of encryption on the data. The approach in [173] is still computationally intensive, but holds great promise.

3.12 Problems

1. The instructor will provide you with a text encrypted using the Caesar cipher. Use Cryptool [19] cryptanalysis tools to decipher the text. What is the smallest amount of cipher-text you need to decipher the text? Why?

2. The instructor will provide you with a text encrypted using the Vigenère cipher. Use Cryptool [19] cryptanalysis tools to decipher the text. What is the smallest amount of cipher-text you need to decipher the text? Why?

3. Is there a one-time pad that performs a specific Vigenère cipher for a given text? If so, provide an example. If not, explain why not.

4. Use Cryptool [19] to encrypt two documents where the first 3 kilobytes are identical using DES in ECB mode with the same key. Examine the resulting cipher-texts. Is there any information that could be utilized in a cryptanalysis?

5. Under what conditions could a replay attack be performed on an AES encrypted data stream?

6. Use RSA to design a replacement protocol for Shamir's no-key protocol. Justify the security of your approach by showing that it is at least as secure as Shamir's approach.

7. Do RSA encryption manually for a very small message and with a very small value of p.

8. How many operations will it take to break the encryption in the previous problem? Justify your answer.

9. Is obfuscation necessarily less secure than encryption? Justify your answer.

3.13 Glossary

Asymmetric key: An encryption algorithm where encryption and decryption keys differ. In this approach, one of the keys (public key) can be widely distributed while the other key (secret key) must be kept secret. These are also called public key cryptography. RSA is a public key approach.

Block cipher: Encryption algorithm that creates mappings between large sections of clear-text and cipher-text. These are typically symmetric key approaches.

Cipher-text: Data in encrypted form.

Clear-text: Data in a usable format.

Decryption: Translation from cipher-text to clear-text.

Encryption: Translation from clear-text to cipher-text.

Hash function: A mapping of binary strings of arbitrary length to binary-strings of a fixed length.

Homomorphic encryption: A system that allows computation directly on encrypted data without decrypting it first.

Key: The value that uniquely defines the cryptographic mapping between clear-text and cipher-text.

Message authentication code (MAC): Hash function used to verify data source and lack of tampering. MACs are keyed hash functions.

Modification detection code (MDC): Hash function used to detect tampering. MDCs are un-keyed hash functions.

Obfuscation: Technologies to obscure the purpose and functionality of software.

One-time pad: A random bit-string of the same length as the message to be encrypted. When used as a key for one time only, provides perfect encryption when XORed with the message.

Poly-alphabetic cipher: Cipher that does character by character translations; however, multiple mappings are used in the same cipher. One example is the Vigenère cipher.

Public key infrastructure (PKI): Technology for distributing public keys and authenticating users. X.509 is the ITU PKI standard.

Substitution cipher: An encryption algorithm with a one-to-one mapping between characters in clear-text and cipher-text. One example is the Caesar cipher.

Symmetric key: An encryption algorithm where the encryption and decryption keys are the same. Security in this approach depends on the key being secret and shared only with the communicating parties. DES and AES are symmetric key cryptography algorithms.

4

SSL/TLS – Case Study Project

CONTENTS

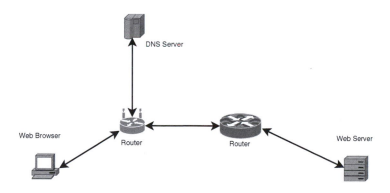

FIGURE 4.1

Typically, SSL/TLS is used when a web browser accesses a page containing sensitive information. The browser uses the Internet Domain Name Service (DNS) to find the webserver's Internet Protocol (IP) address. It then communicates directly with the webserver, tunneling HTTP through SSL/TLS through TCP through the underlying IP protocol.

4.1　Introduction

This chapter considers the technology that is the basis of most e-commerce[1]. The Secure Socket Layer (SSL) was created by Netscape Communications to provide web browsers with methods for secure communications. The first public SSL release was version 2.0, which in 1994 was bundled into the Netscape Navigator browser. SSL version 3 was the basis of the Transport Layer Security (TLS) protocol defined in RFC-2246. While TLS is not strictly compatible with SSL, it is as similar with SSL version 3 as SSL version 3 is with earlier versions of SSL [394] and may reasonably be considered as a new SSL version. In any case, TLS falls back to SSL when the other side does not support TLS [241].

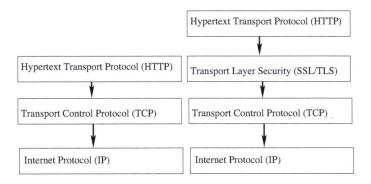

FIGURE 4.2
Normal web traffic (left) consists of HTTP packets being inserted into a TCP session, which provides reliable transport over the unreliable IP layer. SSL/TLS secured traffic (right) inserts an extra protocol layer to authenticate participants, encrypt, and decrypt traffic.

In this chapter, we consider SSL/TLS use within a web browser (see Figure 4.1). We will not consider security issues on the client machine, such as man-in-the-browser, cross site scripting (XSS), and cross site request forgery (XSRF) vulnerabilities. Neither will we discuss security issues due to possible corruption of the web server. We assume both of these machines work correctly, and will therefore discuss solely how SSL/TLS secures network communications. We will concentrate on the numerous security issues that remain unresolved.

SSL/TLS is bundled into web browsers to secure their communications with web servers. SSL/TLS is not solely used for web browser Hypertext

---

[1]Much of the information presented in this chapter is based on a paper published at the 6th annual CSIIR Workshop held at Oak Ridge National Laboratory in April 2010 [91].

Transfer Protocol (HTTP) traffic. For example, SSL/TLS can also be used to create Virtual Private Networks (VPNs) [241], as we will discuss in more detail in Chapter 6. SSL/TLS creates a protocol layer beneath HTTP, or other network applications, by tunneling connections through lower layer protocols, as shown in Figure 4.2.

Ignoring session initialization issues, a higher level protocol is usually tunneled beneath a lower level protocol by inserting the higher level packet inside the lower level packet's payload field [380]. With SSL/TLS, the tunneled protocol (in this case HTTP) is hashed for authentication and encrypted [394]. When block ciphers are used, the message may also insert padding to fill empty blocks.

In Sections 4.2, we describe the SSL/TLS protocol, which is followed by Section 4.3 showing how to verify SSL/TLS (and by extension other protocol) security properties. Sections 4.4 through 4.7 discuss unresolved security issues related to SSL/TLS. As we will see in Section 4.8, these issues tend not to be tied to the security of the underlying protocol. Almost all of these issues are due to unjustified assumptions made in the protocol design. We finish with Sections 4.9 and 4.10 giving student laboratory assignments and problem sets.

4.2 Cryptographic Protocol

SSL/TLS has four sub-protocols:

- *Handshake protocol* – Does authentication, exchanges encryption information, and initializes the session.
- *Record protocol* – Does fragmentation, compression, encryption, decryption, hashing, etc. between the application and TCP/IP layers.
- *Change cipher spec protocol* – Runs on the record protocol to tell the remote host to change security settings.
- *Alert protocol* – Runs on the record protocol and alerts the remote partner.

Figure 4.3 is a UML sequence diagram showing the TCP and SSL/TLS messages exchanged when initializing the secure connection. When consecutive messages have the same source and destination, they are typically bundled into one TCP segment. Due to possible fragmentation, it is impossible to know how many packets this will become. Each SSL message contains length information, which allows the protocol to correctly reconstruct the original messages [394]. Handshake protocol messages include:

- ClientHello – Highest SSL/TLS version supported by client, ciphers supported in order of preference, data compression methods supported, random data, and session ID (0 for a new session).
- ServerHello – Security services that will be used for session.

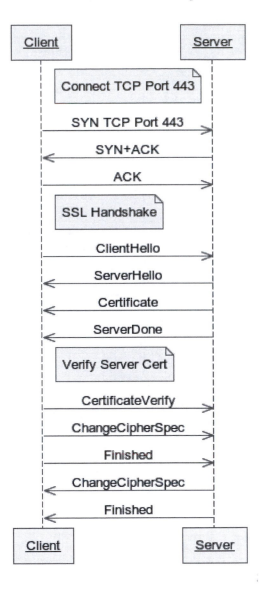

FIGURE 4.3
The client and server exchange these messages to set up an SSL/TLS tunnel

- Certificate – Includes sender's X.509 certificate.
- ServerDone – Server signals that it has completed all client requests for establishing session.

- CertificateVerify – Client verification that it knows private key associated with public key in certificate.
- ChangeCipherSpec – Indication to start using agreed-upon security services.
- Finished – Indication that negotiation is complete and secure communications started.

The record protocol takes each HTTP message, encrypts it, packages it to fit properly within the TCP segments, and deciphers it on the other end. It works on each application layer message in turn. The change cipher and alert protocols amount to the insertion of single out of band messages within the record protocol [394]. Due to the simplicity of these three protocols, no sequence diagram is given.

4.3 Verification

Using automated logic tools, we can check whether or not a security protocol provides its promised security properties. Should it fail to enforce a security property, a counter-example will typically be generated. We analyze security protocols by using Communicating Sequential Processes (CSP) and Failure Divergence Refinement (FDR). CSP, proposed by C. A. R. Hoare in 1985 [203], is a mathematical framework for description and analysis of systems interacting through message passing.

Security protocols are message flows within a network. CSP can explicitly model an intruder's abilities. To analyzing a specific security property of a security protocol, a CSP model of the security protocol is created, which include the protocol's message flows, the security property, and the explicit capacities of attackers, such as message dropping, message modification, etc. The CSP model is fed into FDR, which is an automated model checker [20]. FDR determines whether or not a security property is enforced. If the property is not assured, FDR returns a counter example.

"The construction of FDR code for a security protocol requires specialist skill" [351]. A compiler called Casper is used; with Casper, only a high level description information of the security protocol is needed [274]. Casper automatically constructs FDR code. FDR automatically verifies the security properties of the protocol using both CSP and logic. FDR uses CSP to generate all possible sequences of messages, and uses logic to verify that the desired properties are true at all times.

We now analyze Transport Layer Security (TLS) using Casper and FDR. We first extract the relevant portions of the SSL/TLS protocol suite from Figure 4.3. The items we retain are:

1. Client initiates a TLS session by sending random number nc.
2. Server responds with random number ns and its X.509 certificate.

3. Client responds with its X.509 certificate, *pms* (Pre-Master Secret key) encrypted using the server's public key, CertificateVerify, and Finished messages. The master key is derived from *pms*, *nc* and *ns* by both client and server. The client knows the public key of the server from the Certificate. The CertificateVerify message includes a digest of the previous messages signed using the client's private key. After receiving this message, the server uses the public key of the client to prove that the client has the private key corresponding to the certificate. The Finished message contains a hash and MAC over previous messages. It is encrypted using the master key. The server will attempt to decrypt the client's Finished message, verify the hash and MAC. If decryption and verification fail, the session failed and the connection will be terminated.

4. Server sends Finished message encrypted with the master key. The Finished message contains a hash and MAC over previous messages. The client performs the same decryption and verification as the server in the previous step.

A Casper script for modeling TLS follows (for Casper Syntax see [5, 274])[2]:

```
#Protocol description
0.    -> C: S, {C, PK(C)}{SK(CA)} % certc
1. C -> S: nc
2.    -> S: {S, PK(S)}{SK(CA)} % certs
3. S -> C: ns
4. S -> C: certs % {S, PK(S) % pks }{SK(CA)}
5. C -> S: certc % {C, PK(C) % pkc }{SK(CA)}
6. C -> S: {pms}{pks % PK(S)}
7. C -> S: {f(nc,ns,pms)}{SK(C)} % vrfy
[decryptable(vrfy,pkc)]
8. S -> C: {MK(nc,ns,pms) % mk }{pkc % PK(C)}
9. C -> S: {f(nc,ns,pms)}{mk % MK(nc,ns,pms)}
10. S -> C: {f(pms,nc,ns)}{MK(nc,ns,pms)} % finished
[decryptable(finished,mk)]
#Free variables
C, S, CA: Agent
nc,ns: Nonce
pks,pkc : PublicKey
pms: PreMasterSecret
PK: Agent -> PublicKey
SK: Agent -> SecretKey
MK: Nonce x Nonce x PreMasterSecret -> MasterSecret
mk: MasterSecret
```

---

[2]In the script C stands for client, S for server and CA for Certificate Authority. − > shows message flow direction

```
f: HashFunction
InverseKeys = (PK, SK),(MK,MK)


#Processes
INITIATOR(C,CA,nc,pms) knows PK(C), SK(C), PK(CA)
RESPONDER(S,CA,ns) knows PK(S), SK(S), PK(CA),MK


#Specification
Secret(C,pms,[S])
Agreement(C,S,[])
Agreement(S,C,[])


#Actual variables
Client, Server, CertAuth, M: Agent
Nc, Ns,Nm: Nonce
Pms,Pmsm: PreMasterSecret


#Functions
symbolic PK, SK, MK


#System
INITIATOR(Client,CertAuth,Nc, Pms)
RESPONDER(Server,CertAuth,Ns)


#Intruder Information Intruder=M IntruderKnowledge={Client,Server,
   CertAuth, M, PK(M),SK(M), PK(CertAuth),Nm,Pmsm}
```

We now explain the Casper script:

- In Flow 0 (2) the client (server) obtains its certificate from the environment. A certificate is modeled as a signed *id* and public key belonging to the *id*, signed using the CA private key. The client's X.509 certificate is $\{C, PK(C)\}\{SK(CA)\}$. Casper uses notation $\{A\}\{B\}$ to denote that A is encrypted using B. PK(C) is public key of C and SK(CA) is the private key of CA. Since certificates are obtained outside TLS, it is appropriate to model them as environmental variables. After receiving a certificate, both client and server decrypt it and obtain each other's public key. (Client and server knowledge about CA is given in #Processes.)

- In Flow 7, the client sends a CertificateVerify message. We express CertificateVerify in Casper as f(nc,ns,pms)SK(C). The client secret $SK(C)$ key is used to sign a hash f of *nc*, *ns*, and *pms*. The line after Flow 7 states that after receiving the CertificateVerify message, the server decrypts it with the client's public key. If the decryption is successful, then continue; otherwise terminate the protocol.

- In Flow 8, $MK(nc, ns, pms)$ is the master key and MK is the function to derive the master key. The server sends the master key encrypted using the client public key $PK(C)$. TLS specifies that both client and server know how to derive the master key from nc, ns, and pms. The derivation is performed independently by both client and server. Even though attackers know the algorithm, they cannot compute the master key because they do not know pms.

- In Flow 9, the client sends the server the Finished message. In Casper we express this as $\{f(nc, ns, pms)\}\{mk\%MK(nc, ns, pms)\}$, the hash of nc, ns, and pms encrypted using master key $MK(nc, ns, pms)$.
- In Flow 10, the server sends the client the Finished message as in Flow 9. We use different hashes in Flows 9 and 10 to prevent replay attacks.

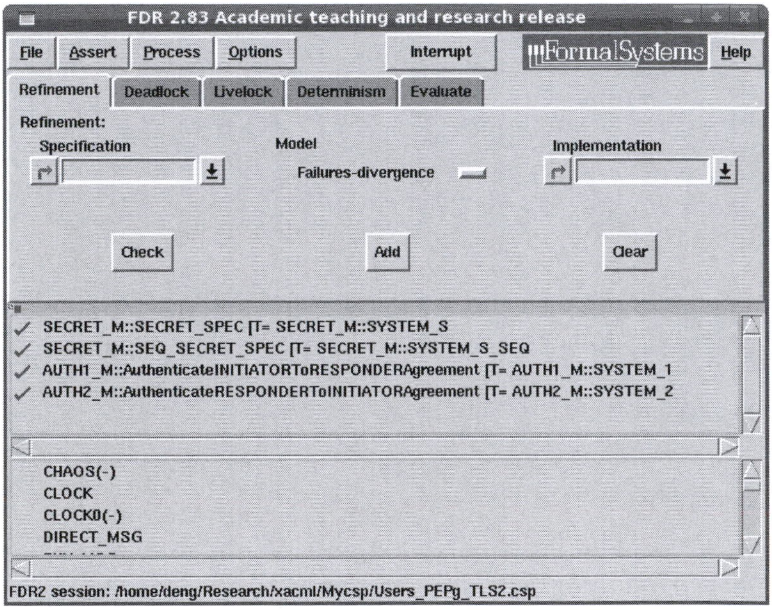

FIGURE 4.4
When we use FDR to verify the protocol, no errors are found.

The security properties to be verified are in "#Specification". We check that pms is only shared between client, and server. We verify that server and client are mutually authenticated. "#Intruder Information" models the attacker capacity. It suggests that the attacker is a legitimate user trying to obtain user credentials, including the secret key. When we give the Casper script to the FDR model checker, the results in Figure 4.4 show that the protocol is found to be sound.

We have described SSL/TLS, its goals, and its internals in some detail. Since SSL/TLS can support a number of standard cryptographic tools, we will assume (for the most part) that they are sound. We used tools to automatically analyze the protocol and verify that the data being sent between nodes remains secure. We will now discuss security issues that keep SSL/TLS from fulfilling its mission.

4.4   DNS and Routing

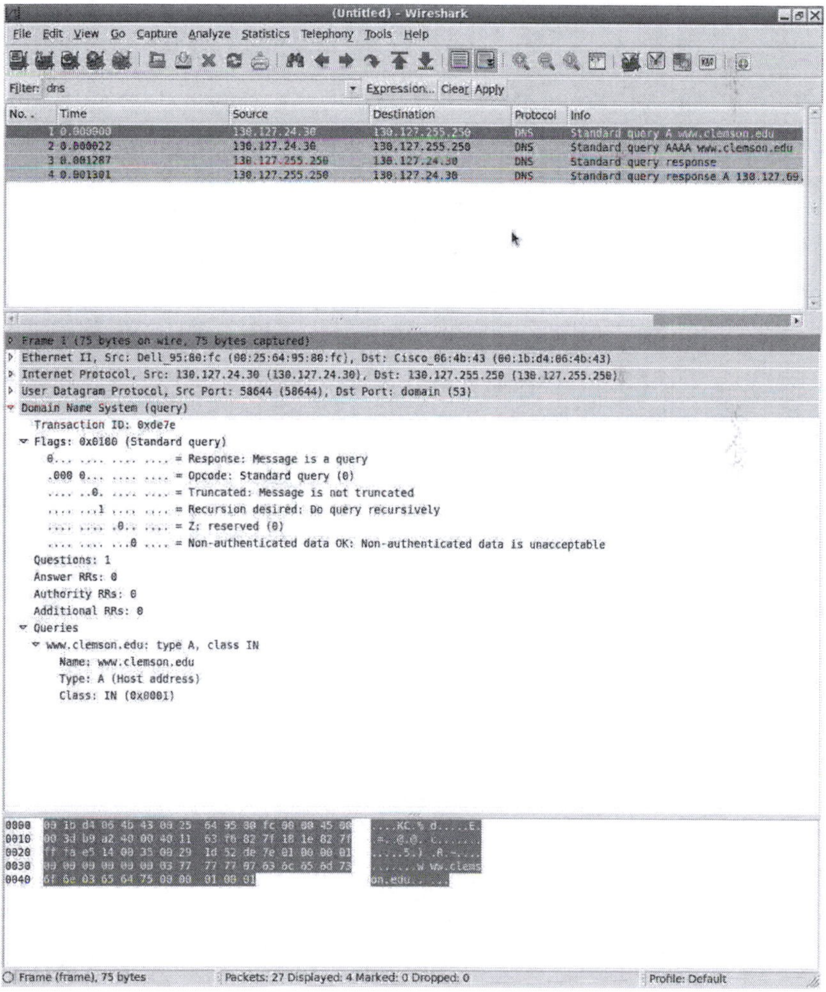

FIGURE 4.5
Wireshark capture of a DNS query packet.

```
#include <stdio.h>
#include <stdlib.h>
#include <netdb.h>
#include <sys/socket.h>
#include <netinet/in.h>
#include <arpa/inet.h>
int main(int argc, char *argv[])
{
  struct addrinfo *result, *cur_addrinfo;
  int error;
  char addr_str[INET6_ADDRSTRLEN];// IPV6 addresses
  char host_name[1025];
  if (argc != 2){
    printf("Wrong number of arguments. Usage: DnsExample <node-name>\n");
    return(EXIT_FAILURE);
  }
  error = getaddrinfo(argv[1],NULL,NULL,&result);
  if(error !=0){
    fprintf(stderr,"getaddrinfo error: %s\n",gai_strerror(error));
    return(EXIT_FAILURE);
  }
  printf("Address(es) are :\n");
  cur_addrinfo=result;
  while(cur_addrinfo!=NULL){
    inet_ntop(result->ai_family,
      &((struct sockaddr_in *)result->ai_addr)->sin_addr,
      addr_str,INET6_ADDRSTRLEN);
    printf("\t%s\n",addr_str);
    if(cur_addrinfo->ai_next !=NULL)
      cur_addrinfo = cur_addrinfo->ai_next;
    else cur_addrinfo = NULL;
  }
  printf("Node name(s) are :\n");
  cur_addrinfo=result;
  while(cur_addrinfo!=NULL){
    error =getnameinfo(result->ai_addr,result->ai_addrlen,host_name,
        1025, NULL, 0, 0);
    if(error !=0){
      fprintf(stderr,"getnameinfo error: %s\n",gai_strerror(error));
      return(EXIT_FAILURE);
    }
    if(*host_name != '\0')
      printf("hostname: %s\n",host_name);
    if(cur_addrinfo->ai_next !=NULL)
      cur_addrinfo = cur_addrinfo->ai_next;
    else cur_addrinfo = NULL;
   }
  freeaddrinfo(result);
  return(EXIT_SUCCESS);
}
```

Algorithm Description 4.4.1: – Use of addrinfo

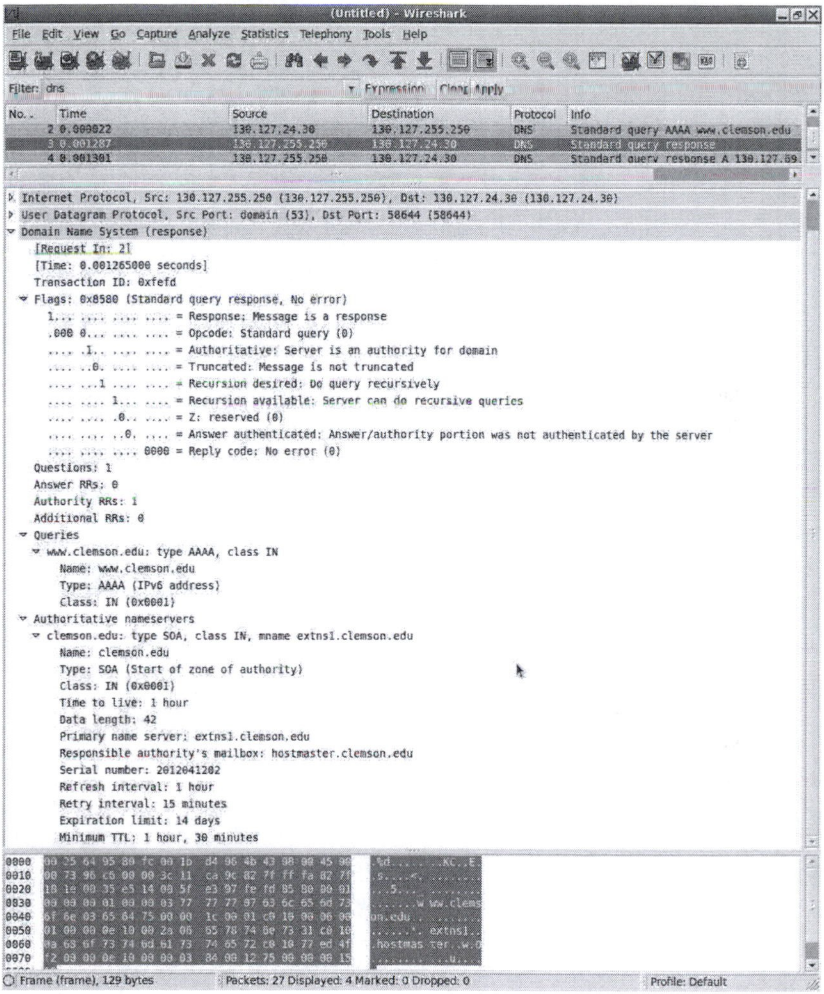

FIGURE 4.6
Wireshark capture of a DNS response packet.

.

This section considers the route taken by packets between the user's machine and the machine the user wants to access. This relies on two processes. The first process is using the domain name system to find the computer's IP address. The second process is finding the route between the two machines. We discuss in turn how each process works and unresolved security issues.

The first step in connecting to a remote host is determining the network address of the host. Typically, a host is known by a symbolic name, such as www.clemson.edu. However, network traffic is sent to nodes using numeric addresses, such as 130.127.69.75[3]. The *Domain Name System* (DNS) is a distributed database that maps symbolic names to numeric IP addresses.

The C function *gethostbyname* for requesting the IP address of the host from DNS [378] has been deprecated. It has been replaced with *getaddrinfo* [3]. Program 4.4.1 shows how addrinfo is used to retrieve the IP address of a computer from DNS by sending its symbolic name, and vice versa. The *getaddrinfo* command sends a command line input to DNS. The address of a data structure containing the node's IP addresses is written into the *result* pointer. Similarly, *getnameinfo* finds the symbolic name(s) associated with a given IP address.

Figures 4.5and 4.6 illustrate what happens when Program 4.4.1 is run with command line:

```
$ DnsExample www.clemson.edu
```

In Figure 4.5 and 4.6, Wireshark has been set to only show DNS packets. Two query packets are sent from 130.127.24.30:

- *Standard query A* requests the IPv4 address, and
- *Standard query AAAA* requests the IPv6 address.

Similarly, two response packets (the first for IPv4, the second for IPv6) are given by DNS server (130.127.255.250). In Figure 4.5 we see fields and values for the IPv4 query in the main window. The lower window contains the hex values. Figure 4.6 shows response values. Multiple IP addresses are usually returned. Typically, entries will be given for TCP (protocol 6), UDP (protocol 17), and IP (protocol 0). If IPv4 and IPv6 protocol stacks are both active, then addresses will be provided for both IPv4 and IPv6.

The first security issue is that packets sent to and received from the DNS server are in clear text. In addition to allowing unauthorized persons being able to monitor the computers being visited, it is easy for intermediates to create spoofed DNS responses. This requires constant monitoring of the victim's network traffic and fast response. If the DNS server is subjected to a denial-of-service attack [440] at the same time, to slow down its response time, this exploit becomes easier.

A more common exploit is DNS cache poisoning [440] . When an address is requested from a server, the server first checks in its local cache to see if it has a copy of the desired record. If the response is present, it simply forwards the address in its cache. If the address is not present, the DNS server queries another DNS server closer to the top level domain (TLD) server. This means that if the attacker sends spoofed responses to the DNS server, instead of the user, the DNS server retains the faulty information and returns the wrong IP address to queries. This also means that when the IP address for host *example.com* is spoofed at a DNS server higher up in the DNS hierarchy,

---

[3]This address is in the IPv4 format. IPv6 has a larger address space and a different address format. We use IPv4 in our examples, since IPv4 is prevalent. Most issues we discuss here will not be affected by migration to IPv6. The programs given work for both IPv4 and IPv6.

then all servers depending on the spoofed server get the wrong address for *example.com*.

In 2008 Dan Kaminsky identified a major flaw in the current DNS implementation. Outstanding transactions were given a transaction of a randomly chosen 16-bit number. This value was small enough that attackers could perform brute force attacks on the number and successfully perform a cache poisoning attack [?, 230]. During the Summer of 2008, the DNS system was rewritten to fix this problem. The patch has been widely deployed.

Another popular attack is DNS hijacking, where the attacker modifies the address of the DNS server for the network to point at a counterfeit DNS server. This can be done, for example, if a wireless router is not properly configured. The DNSChanger (or Zlob) malware performed this type of attack [244, 347]. Other more rare DNS exploits include [440]:

- Abuse of client-side dynamic DNS update mechanisms that allow modification of DNS records by normal Internet hosts,
- Exploitation of buffer overflow vulnerabilities in server software, and
- Use of spoofed messages to modify DNS registration records.

There are two basic flaws that make DNS vulnerable:

1. Traffic to and from DNS servers is typically in clear-text (proxy connections can be used to avoid this), and
2. DNS information is typically not authenticated.

DNS Security Extensions (DNSSEC) have been developed [10, 11, 12], but are not widely deployed. This is partly due to inertia and partly due to the difficulty of configuring the new system. There is also concern that the distributed use of cryptography in DNSSEC could be leveraged to enable large-scale DDoS attacks [136]. At this point, DNS is largely insecure. There is no guarantee that the address returned is correct.

The fact that DNS can not be relied on is compounded by the fact that IP routing can also be spoofed. On local networks, IP addresses are associated with MAC addresses using the address resolution protocol (ARP). When a machine boots, it broadcasts an ARP packet containing its IP and MAC addresses. Machines on the local network segment cache this information. In the future, messages destined for a local IP address will be sent directly to its associated MAC address. Since this protocol is not authenticated, it is possible to sniff ARP packets. Once an ARP packet is received, an attacker can send an ARP packet associating the victim's IP address with the attacker's MAC address. This poisons the local ARP cache, allowing the attacker to stage a simple man-in-the-middle (MITM) exploit [440]. Instructions for performing an ARP cache poisoning attack with the Metasploit penetration testing tool can be found in [128].

On the larger network, similar attacks can be staged to hijack TCP sessions and create MITM exploits. These typically require *sniffing* traffic to read a sequence of legitimate packets and *spoofing* packets to insert incorrect information into the data stream [440]. Route table poisoning is possible using roughly the same techniques as DNS cache poisoning [440]. Packet sources and destinations can be creatively modified to enable MITM.

4.5 X.509 and SSL Certificates

SSL/TLS is designed to create secure connections between two nodes on the Internet. In Section 4.4, we explained why we can not be certain that the IP address returned by DNS is correct; nor can we be certain that a packet sent to a given IP address is sent to the node that legitimately should have that address.

Since DNS directory and IP routing systems are insecure and can not be trusted, additional techniques are needed for authenticating and securing the network communications. X.509 certificates are used to authenticate the remote host. The certificate contains the following fields in this order [394]:

1. *Version* – The version of the ITU X.509 standard that the certificate conforms to. Since numbering of this field started with zero, version three of the standard would be signified by a two in this field.
2. *Serial Number* – A unique value assigned to the certificate by the certificate authority (CA) that issued the certificate.
3. *Signature* – Field identifying the algorithm used to sign the certificate in the *encrypted* field. This information is repeated in that field, leading most implementations to ignore this field.
4. *Issuer* –The CA that issued the certificate.
5. *Period of validity* – The start and stop dates for certificate validity.
6. *Subject* – The entity receiving the certificate from the CA. This typically includes the node's symbolic name.
7. *Subject's Public Key* – The public key and cryptography algorithm to use when communicating with the subject.
8. *Issuer Unique Identifier* – This field can distinguish between two issuers with the exact same name. This field is rarely used.
9. *Subject Unique Identifier* – This field can distinguish between two subjects with the same subject field. This field is rarely used.
10. *Extensions* – Allows issuers to add extra private information.
11. *Encrypted* – This field includes an algorithm identifier, a secure hash of the other fields, and a digital signature of the hash. A signature is obtained by using the private key of a public key cryptography algorithm to encrypt the hash value. Anyone with the public key should be able to verify both that the secure hash value to certify

that the certificate was created by someone knowing the private key and that the certificate has not been modified.

The certificate is designed to guarantee that the party you are communicating with, the *subject*, is the party you think you are communicating with. The certificate also provides a public key, *subject's public key*, for communicating securely with the *subject*. The identity of the *subject* is guaranteed by a certificate authority, the *issuer*, whose job is to verify the identity of the *subject*. The *subject* and/or *subject unique identifier* fields may or may not contain a uniform resource locator (URL) for a network entity. If it contains the URL, the CA says that by verifying the certificate the client may safely trust the server that the server providing the certificate owns the URL. The certificate authority uses its private key to sign the certificate, in the *encrypted* field. If you have the certificate authority's public key, you can use the proper public key cryptography algorithm to verify that the certificate has not been tampered with.

In some cases, it is useful for a *subject* to certify other users. For example, a university may need to issue certificates for machines within its domain. In this case, a *certificate chain* or *certificate path* is created [287]. Starting with the certificate of the *subject*, the certificates of certificate's *issuer*s are retrieved recursively until a certificate authority is found that is trusted. This certificate authority is typically a trusted *root certificate* [164]. Trust for a set of root certificates is usually embedded in a web browser.

Certificates can become compromised or issued in error. For example, in 2001 Verisign was tricked into issuing two certificates for Microsoft to an impostor [259]. When a certificate that is correctly signed is found to be erroneous, the issuer needs to prevent the erroneous certificate from being used in the future. Certificate revocation lists (CRLs) are designed to serve this purpose [164]. The issuer can provide an on-line list of certificates that are no longer valid. Revocation uses the On-line Certificate Status Protocol (OCSP) [312].

Revocation lists are problematic. Successful use of CRLs assumes:

- The person verifying user identity has a network connection,
- The server hosting the revocation list is on-line, and
- The person verifying user identity bothers to check the revocation list.

Each assumption is dubious. In particular, assumptions about network connectivity can easily be foiled by denial of service attacks. In practice, revocation lists may have issues with performance, timeliness, and scalability [343, 312, 245]. RFID applications can not assume network connectivity [312], and Certificate Authorities may be concerned about liability when taking responsibility for identifying compromised certificates.

Another problem with OCSP is3's. On the other hand, the attack used real world data; it was performed within a few days; and the forged certificate was accepted by all major web browsers [155]. MD5 is weak and should no longer be used. Unfortunately, it is still used by many CAs and supported for backwards compatibility. A 2010 survey finds that the relatively weak MD5 and SHA-1 hashes are the most widely supported by servers (over 95 percent each). The cryptographically stronger hashes are supported by a minimal number of nodes [250]. Backwards compatibility serves as an effective attack vector.

Other cryptographic attacks are known that may be more difficult to exploit in practice [61, 413, 104]. But, as we know, cryptography is typically the strong point of the system. Most systems fail due to either human or implementation errors [47].

Some issues are due to implementation problems. A recent study of SSL/TLS certificates used in practice found that a relatively small percent (about 0.38) of the key pairs in SSL/TLS certificates share a common factor and therefore provide no security [52]. This is probably due to using faulty random number generators.

One interesting problem was discovered by two different researchers in 2009. It was possible to get certificates where the subject field contained a NULL character. Consider someone who controls domain malicious.by that wants to masquerade as cia.gov. Alternatively, bot.net may want to masquerade as ebay.com. They could purchase or generate certificates for (respectively):

```
cia.gov\0.malicious.by
ebay.com\0.bot.net
```

When the cryptographic verification is performed, the entire subject field is used in the computation. Unfortunately when the browser compared the machine name with the subject field, C library strcmp() calls were used. These calls use the NULL character to denote the end of the string. This means that the malicious.by and bot.net certificates would be accepted as being valid for cia.gov and ebay.com, respectively [229, 282]. Although this vulnerability was fixed in all major browsers in 2009 before public disclosure, it has been rumored to reappear as a common implementation mistake [147].

Implementation problems can also be due to the complexity of the certificate data structure. For example, the extensions field can be problematic. It contains multiple attributes, which may be ignored or improperly parsed. The extensions field is defined in RFC3280 [6]. *BasicConstraints* is a critical attribute that defines whether or not the owner of the certificate can act as a CA. In a number of SSL implementations this field has either been ignored or used incorrectly even by major browsers [281, 147]. When not properly parsed, the SSL/TLS implementation will accept as valid any certificate for any network location generated by anyone with a valid leaf certificate. This error is somewhat forgivable, since much of the SSL/TLS documentation either ignores *BasicConstraints* entirely [394] or describes it in a form that is not easily understood [323, 81][4]. These errors, when they do exist, negate all SSL/TLS security and trust guarantees.

In a preview of Chapter 8, SSL implementation errors can create buffer overflow vulnerabilities. In 2002, a buffer overflow vulnerability in Open SSL was exploited by the Slapper worm [346]. Here we note that SSL/TLS certificates may be made more prone to buffer overflows by their use of Abstract Syntax Notation ASN.1. In ASN.1, many data fields are preceded by an integer stating the length of the field. Lazy programmers would use this number to allocate storage for the contents of the data field. This can be exploited by an attacker stating an incorrect value for the data field length. In Chapter 8, we discuss buffer overflows in some depth so that students can understand how easy this mistake is to exploit in practice.

The main vulnerability of SSL/TLS certificates, though, is due to the CAs that generate the certificates. A recent survey found that over 651 different organizations were authorized to generate certificates that would be trusted by Internet Explorer and Firefox [149, 148]. Trusted CA's are located in about 52 different countries, including China, Russia, Arab Emirates, Singapore, India, United States, and Tunisia. Branches of the Chinese, US, and Arab Emirates governments are able to generate certificates, although it should also be noted that any sovereign country with a trusted certification authority located within its borders has the legal means, under certain conditions, to force that certification authority to generate certificates that will be trusted by a browser [370], not that it should be surprising that nation states can circumvent these security measures.

More surprising is how unreliable the CA's are. In [149, 148] they found over 6,000 different certificates for *localhost*. These certificates were generated, in part, by many of the largest CA's. No individual or corporation should have a legitimate claim to the name *localhost*. It is also worth performing a quick experiment by using a search engine to look for "cheap SSL certificate." The author did so in May 2012 and found a number of offerings. Some were for free. A large number of CA's only required an email address and phone number as proof of identity. It is worth noting that many services offer email addresses with absolutely no background search. It is possible to purchase a pre-paid SIM card with cash that gives you a telephone number with perfect anonymity. It is, therefore, fairly easy for legitimate SSL certificates to be purchased for most *subject* fields for at most ten dollars. This fact has been noted elsewhere [155].

The fact that bogus SSL certificates can be purchased so cheaply has not stopped intruders from invading legitimate certificate authorities to generate bogus certificates. In 2011, the certificate authorities DigiNotar and Comodo

---

[4]Some documentation says that it must be set to True for CA's and otherwise may be set to False or left out, although some software may not work if it is left out. Other documentation says, "If the extension is present and has the value TRUE, then this cert is taken to be a CA cert. Otherwise it is not (except that trust flags may override this...)" [323, 81]. Neither description is particularly lucid.

(among others) were compromised by someone that was believed to be tied to the Iranian government [86]. The most amazing part of this exploit is that the attacker was willing to invest a lot of work to avoid paying a minimal amount of money to buy bogus certificates.

To summarize this section, SSL certificates are designed to certify the identity of the remote host. This certification is not very reliable for many reasons, some of the most egregious are:

- Many certificates are self-signed, providing no certification,
- Some of the hash functions accepted in the signature process can be compromised given a reasonable (if fairly large) amount of computation,
- Some certificates generated with bad random number generation provide no cryptographic security,
- Some SSL implementations do not verify the extensions field properly and accept forged certificates,
- Thousands of certificate authorities are trusted and a breach in the security of any certificate authority compromises the entire infrastructure, and
- Many certificate authorities do little to verify that the person purchasing a certificate has any right to the identity.

4.6   Man-in-the-Middle Attacks

In addition to the basic flaws in SSL shown in Section 4.6, there are a number of simple ways to create man-in-the-middle attacks (see Chapter 2).

Perhaps the simplest way to perform an SSL man-in-the-middle exploit is to purchase a network appliance that does the exploit for you [370]. Companies have been found that advertise network devices for intercepting and deciphering SSL/TLS traffic. These automated tools are advertised as inexpensive enough to be "disposable."

A more complicated attack could use the tools sslsniff and sslstrip [283]. This requires downloading and installing software. sslsniff is used in conjunction with an ARP spoofing attack (see Section 4.4). The software is installed; the ARP address redefined; and the null prefix attack (among others) used to intercept and read SSL traffic.

sslstrip [283] is simpler and more ingenious in some ways. It also requires ARP spoofing. When a request is sent for a web page, sslstrip retrieves the remote web page. It replaces https links with http links and forwards the new web page to the user. User inputs to the web page are sent in clear text to the attacker, who then uses SSL to communicate with the web server. The server sees a normal https session. The user sees a normal http session. All security is removed from the session with no perceptible changes.

Other possible man-in-the-middle exploits have been found. The ones presented here illustrate how inexpensive and simple it is to foil the SSL/TLS security guarantees.

4.7 Usability

Another problem with SSL/TLS is its complexity. The application of cryptography to web security creates a human factors problem. When security policies are violated and issues arise, most users are ill-prepared for understanding these problems.

In early browsers, problems with certificates were signaled by a field stating that there was an error. The error was explained in terms that were indecipherable to a layman. The user was then presented with an error message that amounted to "would you like to use the web page anyway?" Since the user was trying to access the webpage, and the error is indecipherable jargon, the user response was almost always "yes" [188]. The user was also given the option of viewing the certificate but, since few users can detect errors in cryptographic signatures by calculating in their head, it is unclear what the user was supposed to infer by looking at the certificate.

Modern browsers have changed the error dialogs. Now to actually access the web page, the user is forced to navigate a large number of screens. These screens force the user to state that they understand the potential threats and similar questions. It seems that the goal is to force the naive user to give up in frustration before accessing the page. While this may be better than the previous approach, users still are poorly informed as to why and how problems have occurred.

A number of visual cues, padlocks, green bars and the like are used to signal the use of SSL to secure traffic. sslstrip [283] shows how easily these cues can be presented by an attacker.

Vendors have developed a set of certificates that can be displayed by web sites to show users that they are trustworthy. Unfortunately, a survey has found that sites displaying certification that they are secure are more likely to be malicious [150]. This is likely to be due to the fact that malicious sites have much to gain by users feeling secure. They are therefore more likely to pay for certification. Also, this is due to the fact that the certifying agencies do not actually verify that the site is secure.

4.8   Summary

This chapter has done a case study of SSL/TLS certificates. We outlined the cryptographic protocol for certificate transfer, which is sound. We showed how to logically verify the security of protocols of this type, at which point we explained how the IP routing and DNS addressing infrastructure is insecure. There is no guarantee from DNS or IP routing that messages go to the intended party. X.509 certificates were developed to certify the identity of the party being contacted. The X.509 data structures were given and explained. With a few minor exceptions, the cryptographic tools are valid and appropriate for this application.

We then explained how implementation and design errors have made this approach largely ineffective. Probably the largest flaw is the set of 6,000 certification authorities that are trusted. Some authorities have been compromised. Some authorities appear to do little to seriously verify the identity of their clients. In addition, we explained a number of man-in-the-middle exploits that violate the security model.

In addition, the system was not designed with the users in mind. Error messages are confusing and frustrating. It is unlikely that normal users could understand the cryptography errors that would be caused by attackers.

4.9   Assignment

For this assignment, students should have access to a network segment with an "air gap." The instructor (or students) should set up a DNS server on this isolated segment. For packet capture and inspection, either Wireshark [28] or tcpdump [24] should be installed on the workstations. The sslstrip and ARP poisoning software described on the sslstrip webpage [283] is needed. One server should have a web server with a simple web page. The web page should have a certificate. I suggest getting one of the free certificates from an on-line service.

At the instructor's discretion, this assignment could follow the assignment in Chapter 6. That assignment familiarizes the student with the use of Wireshark. The goal of this assignment is to help the students understand the issues raised in this assignment. It is one of the less challenging assignments.

The students need to do the following:

1. While running packet capture software, ping the webserver and collect packets. Inspect the packets. Create modified packets that could be used to steal traffic from the webserver in a man-in-the -middle exploit.

2. While running packet capture software, perform the ARP poisoning attack and compare the packets captured with the modified DNS packets.

3. Use the packet capture software to inspect the network session of someone else using a web browser and https to view the webpage protected with the certificate.

4. Use sslstrip and the packet capture software to perform a man-in-the-middle attack on an identical session.

5. Compare the packet streams collected with and without the man-in-the-middle exploit.

4.10   Problems

1. List the SSL/TLS flaws presented in the chapter. Sort them in order of severity. Justify your rankings.

2. Briefly explain the good points of the SSL/TLS design. Justify the design decisions made.

3. Mention at least one flaw given in the chapter that is unavoidable. Explain why.

4. Propose a different technique for authenticating users which modifies the role of certificate authorities. The goal of this approach is to remove as many of the current vulnerabilities as possible. Explain how your new approach removes vulnerabilities.

4.11   Glossary

Air gap: A network segment with no physical connection to the larger Internet.

Cache poisoning: An attack where false information is inserted into the system where it is stored locally in order to be exploited later.

Certificate: A cryptographically signed data structure that attests to its owner's identity.

Certificate authority: Entity charged with creating X.509 certificates that attest to the identity of the certificate owner.

Communicating Sequential Processes (CSP): A technique for modeling protocols that allows for logical verification of protocol properties.

DNS: Domain Name Service is a distributed database that is used to translate symbolic names into numeric Internet Protocol addresses.

Man-in-the-middle: An exploit where the attacker violates a protocol connecting two parties by pretending with each party that they are the other legitimate party.

Public key infrastructure (PKI): Network tools used for distributing public keys.

Root certificate: A certificate belonging to an entity that is trusted for identifying network users.

SSL: Secure Socket Layer protocol for encrypting Internet communications.

TLS: Transport Layer Security protocol is the current name for SSL.

X.509: International Telecommunications Union standard for public key distribution.

5

Securing Networks

CONTENTS

5.1 Introduction

In this chapter, we discuss common network security problems and appropriate countermeasures. Where Chapter 2 gave an overview of computer and network security, this chapter provides familiarity with current network security approaches. Many issues discussed, for example virtual private networks, are explored in depth in other chapters. Computers are relatively easy to secure when they are isolated and physically secure, since attackers will have only limited access. But most computers are no longer isolated. They are connected to networks, giving attackers continuous access.

The primary (but flawed) concept behind most network security tools is trying to isolate your machine from potential attackers. The idea is that if your machine was kept within a perimeter that isolates it from potential attacks, then you would be relatively secure. Following this concept, we start by discussing firewalls in Section 5.2. Firewalls limit an attacker's access to the local network. The local network should become a trusted enclave. In Section 5.3, we discuss how virtual private networks (VPNs) connect trusted enclaves to make trust independent of geographic proximity.

Firewalls and VPNs primarily deal with wired networks. Since wireless connections are increasingly important, we discuss wireless security issues in Section 5.4.

The final two sections of this chapter consider violations of trust. Attackers either violate security rules or prevent networks from functioning properly. Intrusion detection systems, discussed in Section 5.5, monitor networks to dynamically detect attackers and attacks violating the rules. Instead of violating our rules, Section 5.6 discusses how attackers use Denial of Service attacks to simply make the network unusable.

5.2 Firewalls

The term firewall comes from construction. It refers to a fireproof barrier meant to halt the spread of fire between or within buildings. A computer firewall is a software or hardware barrier designed to contain security breaches by monitoring and restricting access to sub-networks. A sub-network can be [383, 354]

- **Intranet** – An internal sub-network fully contained within the enterprise,
- **Extranet** – An external sub-network that is trusted in order to allow information sharing, or
- **DMZ** – An internal sub-network that will be neither protected nor trusted. The name is from the military *de-militarized zone*, a buffer region where no military action is permitted.

Typically, a firewall is inserted between security domains. It is common to place the firewall at the network entry point. But additional firewalls can be placed within the network to establish security boundaries. Firewall functionality may include [384]:

- **Packet filtering** – applies a set of rules based on the IP addresses and ports of the packet source and destination to each individual packet. Packets violating rules are dropped.
- **Network address translation (NAT)** – translates the IP addresses of internal hosts to mask them from external monitoring.
- **Proxy service** – has the firewall make high-level application connections with remote systems on behalf of local hosts. This completely divorces network connections between internal and external hosts.

Firewall implementations are generally divided into four classes [116, 383, 440]:

1. **Simple packet filter** – allow or dis-allow access to hosts based on a set of rules using source IP address, destination IP address, and port. Simple packet inspection looks at each packet in isolation. They can inspect only the transport and network layers of the protocol stack. These firewalls have little overhead and are easy to configure. Unfortunately:

   (a) They are vulnerable to source address spoofing,

(b) They do not offer authentication, and

(c) They have trouble with fragmented IP packets, since only the first packet has the port number.

2. **Stateful packet inspection** – monitors each session going through the firewall. The source and destination IP addresses of each packet are matched against a table of open sessions. These firewalls can track TCP session flags and keep a context for UDP traffic. A packet is only allowed through if it matches an expected response for that state. Stateful packet inspection can monitor the packet contents to look for violations of access rules [384, 383]. Stateful packet inspection is also known as *deep packet inspection* [354].

3. **Circuit level gateway** – acts as a user proxy relaying packets to outside hosts. Users usually authenticate themselves to the gateway, which relays packets to the remote host. Circuit level gateways can track traffic up through the session layer.

4. **Application level gateway** – provides a program to work as a user proxy for a given application. Data is entered into the application gateway, which does the interaction with the remote host. Application gateways keep track of all layers of the protocol stack. The application gateway often does extra authentication, format checking, and information logging. Application gateways provide more security, but there is associated overhead. The gateway is subject to denial of service attacks and infection with malware.

Use of firewalls is widespread, but not entirely free of errors. Firewall policies may have unintended consequences, or they can be inconsistent. Policy changes can unintentionally disable legitimate network applications.

Firewalls are subject to a number of attacks. For example, *fragmentation attacks* insert illegal offsets into TCP packets [440]. When the firewall looks at each individual packet, there is no problem. When the fragmented packets are reassembled on the host, the actual packet contents may be quite different.

There are tools that reverse engineer firewall rule bases and determine the structure of the network behind the firewall. The *Firewalk* and *Nmap* tools deserve special notice [440]. A detailed discussion of the structure and use of Firewalk can be found in [355].

5.3 Virtual Private Networks (VPNs)

Firewalls create protected enclaves. However, many organizations are widely distributed and need to connect multiple enclaves into a single trusted network. A virtual private network (VPN) can be used to integrate these isolated enclaves so that they can interact as if they were on a single local network.

This section provides a brief description of what VPNs are. Chapter 6 provides a more in-depth discussion of how to set up and use VPNs.

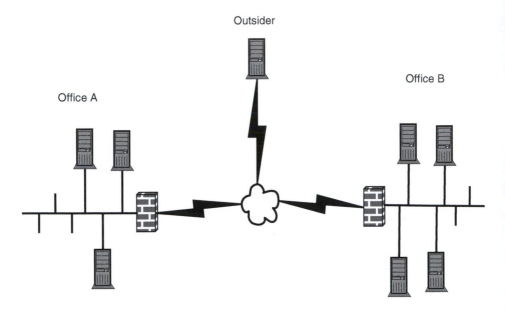

FIGURE 5.1
Offices A and B are both protected by firewalls. They want to share information and resources, without the Outsider having access.

Consider the situation in Figure 5.1. Offices A and B are with the same company, which considers the sub-networks behind the firewalls trustworthy. How can they share resources, without being vulnerable to malicious activities by the Outsider? Firewalls for both offices monitor incoming network traffic. Packets coming from outside the perimeter are monitored. The Outsider can spoof packet source IP addresses using IP addresses from the other office. These packets could be used to stage a denial of service attack, or they could contain malware. The Outsider can also inspect packets as they move through the cloud.

To guard against the attacks, the sub-networks need to:

- verify the original source of the packets they receive,
- guarantee that packets going outside the firewall can not be read while traversing the wide-area network cloud, and
- verify that packets are not tampered with.

A VPN does this by creating virtual connections between sub-networks that can be trusted and do not need to be inspected by the firewall. The VPN provides a private address space for nodes within the VPN, and a secure *tunnel* for communications between trusted enclaves.

Network protocol tunneling is a very useful and common tool. It consists of taking the packets for one protocol and inserting them as data into the payload field of another protocol. For VPNs, it is common to create a software driver that acts like the normal protocol stack. Packets using IP addresses within the range allocated to the VPN are forwarded to the virtual driver. The virtual driver encrypts the VPN traffic and encapsulates it into an IP protocol packet. The destination IP address for the packet encapsulating the VPN data is a host in the other office.

When the destination host receives the packet, it is forwarded to another virtual network protocol stack that removes the encapsulated IP protocol information; decrypts the packet payload; and then processes the tunneled packet as any other network packet.

We note that:

- Tunneling creates an address space that is shared by the two offices and can not be accessed by hosts outside of Offices A and B;
- Assuming that the cryptographic keys are strong and kept private, encryption safeguards the packet contents from being read while traversing the cloud;
- Any attempt by someone without the cryptographic keys to tamper with the VPN traffic will make the data unusable; and
- The use of encryption authenticates the source of the VPN traffic, since it is clear that the system encrypting the VPN packets knows the secret cryptographic keys.

5.4 Wireless Security

While wired and wireless networks are subject to the vulnerabilities and attacks mentioned in Chapter 2, wireless networks are especially vulnerable.[1]

It is extremely easy to intercept packets broadcast over the radio spectrum. The attacker does not even require physical access to the medium. The attacker can simply drive (*war driving*) along streets looking for vulnerable access points. 802.11 signals can transfer data over long distances, ranging from 37 [113] to 382 [231] kilometers. The fact that eavesdropping on wireless communications is passive makes it hard to detect.

---

[1] In this section, we limit the details of our discussion to 802.11 (wifi) wireless connections. Similar issues exist for Global System for Mobile (GSM) cell phone transmissions and 4-G wireless standards (WiMAX and LTE). GSM is not handled, since it is largely out of scope for this book. 4-G standards are not discussed because they are currently in flux and not currently widely deployed.

A number of extensions have been proposed for securing 802.11 wireless communications. These include [255]:

1. *Wireless Equivalent Privacy (WEP)* – was the first 802.11 security extension. Its goal was to make wireless Internet connections as secure as wired connections. WEP has a number of flaws. Tools are available on-line (such as aircrack-ptw) that crack WEP keys within minutes, if not seconds. Among other things are WEP's re-use of initialization vectors (IVs) and incorrect use of the RC-4 stream cipher. WEP should not be used, because of its known weaknesses.

2. *Wi-Fi Protected Access (WPA)* – was the first replacement for WEP. WPA implemented much of the improved 802.11i security standard. WPA improvements over WEP include integrity checking to detect forged packets, improved IV handling, not being vulnerable to replay attacks, and key handling so that can be refreshed. Unfortunately, WPA is subject to dictionary attacks.

3. *Wi-Fi Protected Access II - (WPA2)* – implements the full 802.11i standard. WPA2 has replaced use of the RC-4 stream cipher with AES. It has two classes of authentication: pre-shared key (PSK) or 802.1X. WPA2-PSK relies on using a shared key and is significantly weaker than 802.1X. When the pre-shared key is not used, WPA2 is integrated with the extended authentication protocol (EAP), which includes a number of different authentication options.

Use of WPA2 with EAP is preferred.

Wireless communication has a number of innate weaknesses [440]. DoS attacks are relatively easy by jamming wireless signals, creating duplicate Media Access (MAC) addresses, or duplicating IP addresses. A slightly more difficult DoS attack can be performed by using the wireless protocol with incorrect parameter settings [219]. Traffic monitoring [440] and eavesdropping for wireless communications are relatively easy, since packet headers are sent in clear-text.

Rogue access points are a problem [440]. Insiders can inadvertently add unprotected access points to the network, creating an unprotected path into the network. Outsiders can add access points with artificially high power and the same SSID to hijack sessions, creating an easy man-in-the-middle attack.

Wireless is also vulnerable to packet insertion attacks [178]. During wireless transmissions, some bit flip errors will occur. This gives the attacker the chance to use one valid data communications stream to insert fraudulent communications. Fake packets can be sent as data payloads of legitimate communications. Headers of the real packets will sometimes be corrupted. In which case, nodes receiving the packets will drop the corrupted portions of the packet and accept the encapsulated payload as a legitimate packet. This allows the attacker to insert arbitrary false packets into wireless communications using the same access point.

5.5   Intrusion Detection Systems (IDS)

Intrusion detection is a difficult problem, which many have attempted to solve. Commercial solutions exist, but they have limited utility. A major issue is finding ways to differentiate between normal and abusive system behavior. The taxonomy in [57] provides an overview of intrusion detection. Many IDSs (and most commercial anti-virus software) look for signatures that identify known attacks. These systems are by definition unable to detect and retard new attacks. Other IDSs detect deviations from normal system behavior. Axelsson [57] further divides anomaly detectors into self-learning and programmed. He [57] also divides IDSs into centralized and distributed systems.

5.5.1   Statistical IDS

A major issue in all of these approaches is the inability to find statistical models that can adequately differentiate between normal and aberrant behaviors. Perhaps the most in depth treatment of the use of statistics in computer and network intrusion detection can be found in [280].

   A major reason why the statistical approach has been unsatisfactory is the fact that many network behaviors follow statistical laws with infinite variance (in some cases even infinite means). The modeling in [181] illustrates these issues by exploring the dynamics of worm and virus spreading on computer networks. Promising approaches to intrusion detection use tools closely associated with statistical physics:

- Cellular automata models of the network flow dynamics can be used to characterize network pathologies [94].
- It is possible to consider changing traffic distributions and predict the Hurst parameter by tracking the second moment over time to detect attacks [167]. This approach relies on two essential notions:

   1. traffic before the attack remains self-similar, and
   2. detecting a DoS attack is an *a posteriori* phenomenon.

   This off-line solution does not consider the fact that the Hurst parameter is valid only in a limited range of scales.
- The Therminator project at the Naval Postgraduate School modeled network traffic using entropy equations [143]. The end result was a display of network state, which skilled users were able to use to verify that the network was performing normally.
- Another use of entropy for intrusion detection uses the entropy of packet source addresses to detect the onset of DDoS attacks [248]. Unfortunately, since source addresses are easily spoofed, this concept is of questionable utility.

- Burgess [98] models networks as thermal reservoirs where fluctuations represent the exchange of information.
- Gudonov and Johnson [185] consider information flow as a dynamical system with a phase-space of dimension 10-12.

These research prototypes have not been translated into commercial products, but indicate promising techniques for future network monitors.

5.5.2   Biologically inspired IDS

In nature, immune systems also need to differentiate between normal behaviors and the behaviors of intruders. Multi-cellular organisms maintain themselves through complex distributed interactions. Intruders, including viruses, bacteria, and other infections, take advantage of these interactions to reproduce. The task of immune systems is to identify the intruders from their behaviors, isolate them, and remove them from the system.

Stephanie Forrest and her student Hofmeyr have studied the internals of immune systems, in the hope that these insights could lead to robust IDSs [159]. They used this approach to perform intrusion detection by monitoring network traffic. The features they use are tuples consisting of source address, destination address, and port number [205].

This approach resembles network sniffers like Snort [243], which capture network packets and use rule bases to infer intrusions from packet contents. This approach requires a significant amount of training, and it is not yet clear how well the artificial immune system design can work in operational networks.

5.5.3   IDS testing

As with statistical physics and biology, practical intrusion detection needs to be data driven, and it is in this area that the research community is most lacking. In 1999 DARPA funded an extensive analysis of intrusion detection technologies using a testbed especially created for this purpose [228]. They combined live machines with a simulated network to simulate a larger network in order to derive a realistic system that could be subjected to known attacks. An example packet time series is shown in Figure 5.2. While this was a very useful advance at the time, there are real questions as to how realistic the test data was and how reliable the statistics collected were. A thorough critique can be found in [286].

Lazarevic et al. [34] use data-sets including those in [228] to compare different intrusion detection approaches. The approaches in [34] achieve impressively low false positive rates, but are data mining approaches. They are computationally unsuited for on-line intrusion detection. Possibly the most interesting aspect of [34] is the statistical methods used for evaluating IDS performance.

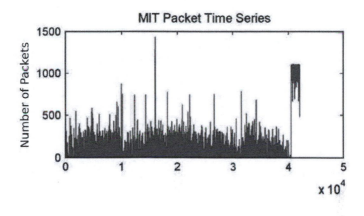

FIGURE 5.2
Example of data collected during the DARPA sponsored MIT Lincoln Labs
intrusion detection trials containing a denial of service incident.

In [90] and other work, we used data from [228] (Figure 5.2), MATLAB
simulations (Figure 5.3), ns-2 simulations (Figure 5.4), collected from the Penn
State network (Figure 5.5), and collected from the Clemson University network (Figure 5.6) to verify IDS concepts. Operational network background
traffic with DDoS attacks are shown in Figures 5.7 and 5.8. This attack traffic was collected by making mirrored copies of campus backbone traffic and
introducing attack traffic to the mirrored traffic.

Our analysis indicated that the background traffic in [228] (Figure 5.2) was
more realistic than ns-2 simulated traffic (Figure 5.4), but was significantly
less bursty than real operational traffic collected from university networks
(Figure 5.5 and Figure 5.6). This indicates that empirical tests on real networks are essential for creating IDS systems. References [105, 90] deal with
issues related to data driven testing of IDS systems in some detail. The use
of honeypot networks to attract network intruders and track their activities
promises to provide information about malware and hacker behavior. Unfortunately, honeypots have no live background traffic. This makes it difficult to
apply their insights to practical systems.

Figures 5.7 and 5.8 show DDoS events on operational networks. Compare
these signals to the time series from simulations in Figures 5.3 and 5.4. The
operational background traffic is very bursty. Approaches tuned to look for
events in the simulations are likely to have unacceptable high positive rates.
Even the MIT Lincoln Labs data designed to have realistic background traffic
is too well-behaved.

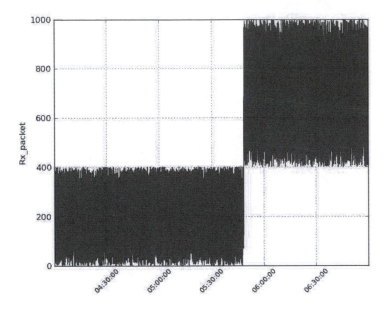

FIGURE 5.3
MATLAB simulated network traffic with a DDoS attack.

5.5.4 IDS products

A comparison of commercially available Intrusion Detection Systems [308] states: "One thing that can be said with certainty about network-based intrusion-detection systems is that they are guaranteed to detect and consume all your available bandwidth. — Because no product distinguished itself, we are not naming a winner." In addition to false positives obscuring the presence of real intrusions, the volume of false positives was enough to crash almost every IDS package during the test. CPU usage by the IDS packages was over 90% in many cases. One IDS froze the system using it on over 30% of the days it was used. These results are typical of user experiences with IDS systems. Based on these reports, we tend to be skeptical as to the utility of current systems.

That said, a new generation of technologies does exist. Intrusion prevention systems (IPS) do in-line processing to analyze information streams, detect attacks, and quarantine or delete suspect packets. They act as a combination firewall, intrusion detection system, and traffic-shaping tool. They typically use dedicated, robust hardware, capable of multi-gigabyte per second throughput. Since they can be installed on internal links, they are not

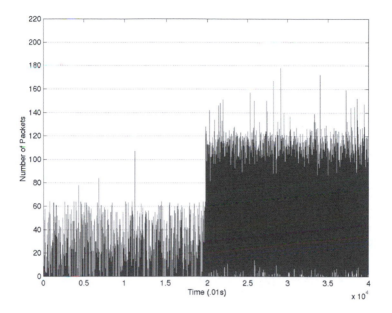

FIGURE 5.4
Network traffic with DDoS attack generated using the ns-2 network simulator.

necessarily perimeter-based security solutions [368]. Their goal is to protect entire networks from attack. There are, however, important issues:

- They perform in-line analysis of data streams in real-time, which limits the amount of analytical processing possible.
- They rely on dedicated hardware. Protection is limited to data paths passing through the IPS, creating potential bottlenecks and single points of failure.

Intrusion detection system, and IPS, acceptance is limited by notoriously high false positive rates [308, 7]. Little or no objective comparison data is available from operational network traffic [106, 105]. There is no reason to believe hardware based intrusion detection will have fewer false positives.

The following citation provides important insights regarding IPS deployment [243]: "an intrusion prevention application is prone to all the problems of intrusion detection, but with potentially damaging consequences. With intrusion prevention, false positives can render your entire network unreachable.

Researchers have found quantitative comparison between IPSs infeasible [368] due to the lack of metrics and test procedures. Published metrics relate mostly to system throughput [368]. Available information on IPS false positive rates comes from marketing sources, and is not credible when compared to detection rates documented by the research community [105].

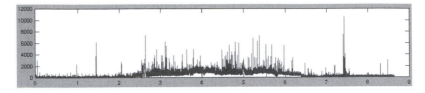

FIGURE 5.5
Network traffic without attack from the Penn State network.

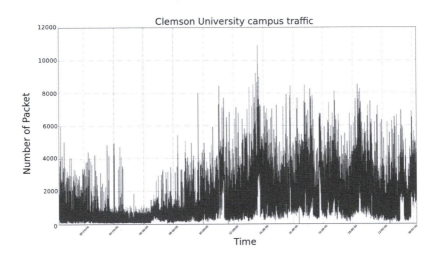

FIGURE 5.6
Network traffic without attack from the Clemson University network.

Of the open source solutions, Snort is the most widely used [243]. Snort is essentially an add-on to the libpcap packet capture library. A sniffer is attached to the system's Ethernet adapter, which is switched to promiscuous mode. Packets are captured as they pass over the Ethernet medium. A number of rule sets have been built that filter packets to detect known threats and signal conditions thought to resemble network intrusions. Anecdotal information states that many universities have Snort installed to check for potential system abuse. Depending on how it is parametrized, Snort can result in network performance degradation and may have very high false alarm rates. Therefore it is frequently set up for multiple levels of performance and the usual settings have a very high alarm threshold.

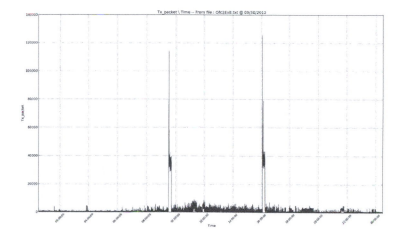

FIGURE 5.7
Network traffic with two DDoS attacks on the Clemson University network.

5.6 Denial of Service

Denial of service (DoS) attacks prevent a system from performing its tasks. DoS attacks are perpetrated either locally or over the network. On a multi-user system, any user consuming an inordinate amount of resources launches a simple DoS attack on other users. This is stopped by attentive system maintenance. Sabotaging equipment is another simple DoS attack, countered by physically protecting devices. Remote DoS attacks using the Internet are of primary interest. DoS attacks have been attempted against the Internet DNS infrastructure, Microsoft, the White House, Amazon.com, and several others.

Two main classes of Internet DoS attacks exist:

1. system exploit attacks, and
2. network attacks.

System exploit attacks use system-specific vulnerabilities. They are used to make systems crash or degrade performance. They can also cause operating systems to lock or reboot. The "Ping of Death" exploit, which used malformed ping packets to crash computers, fits into this category. Another example is the "bonk" attack. Applying patches and bug fixes, as vulnerabilities are discovered, is the typical approach to fixing these attacks [385].

Networking attacks take advantage of vagueness or weakness in protocol specifications. Known Internet networking DoS exploit attacks include:

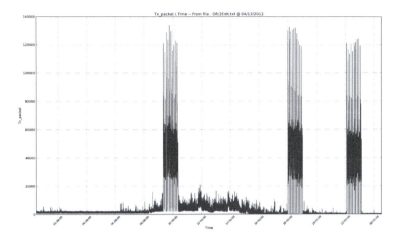

FIGURE 5.8
Network traffic with three attacks from the Clemson University network.

1. attacks on root Internet name-servers,
2. attacks on merchant and media sites, and
3. the Slammer worm.

The network traffic generated by Slammer triggered DoS events for other systems. These attacks can be categorized by the protocol they attack, such as [122]:

- *TCP SYN flooding* – When a client attempts to establish a TCP connection to a server providing a service, the client initiates the connection by sending a SYN message to the listening server. The server then acknowledges the connection by sending SYN-ACK message back to the client. The client then finishes establishing the connection by responding with an ACK message. The connection between the client and the server is then open and the service-specific data can be exchanged between the client and the server. This connection establishment process is called the three-way handshake. A potential problem of the three-way handshake process comes at the point when the connection is half-open, i.e., the server has sent SYN-ACK message to the client, but has not yet received the ACK message from the client. At this state, the server has to keep the half-open connection in a backlog queue that is of limited length until the ACK message is received, or until a connection establishment timer expires (for most TCP implementations, the timer expiration time is set to 75 seconds). Since the Internet Protocol (IP) does not require the source address of a packet to be correct, attackers take advantage of this built-in vagueness of IP to launch the TCP SYN flooding attack by sending the SYN packets with spoofed source IP address to the server. When the server acknowledges the SYN packets with SYN-ACK, it can never reach the client (attacker) and the server has to keep the half-open connection in the backlog queue until the connection establishment timer expires. If attackers send SYN packets with spoofed source IP addresses to the server at a very high rate, the backlog queue can be kept full all the time. In this case, no legitimate users can set up a connection with the server. Any system with TCP/IP can be used to launch TCP SYN flooding attack. Since the TCP SYN packet is small in size, attackers only need a small bandwidth to execute this attack and can cause a very fast network paralyzed [102],

- *UDP packet storm* – Attackers use forged UDP packets to connect a service on one machine to another service on another (or the same) machine. For example, attackers can connect a host's service to the echo service on another (or the same) machine. These two services can produce a very high number of packets that can consume all available network bandwidth between them and can lead to a denial of service on the machine(s) where the services are offered [101],
- *ICMP ping flooding* – Attackers consume all the available bandwidth on a network by generating a large number of packets directed to that network. Normally ICMP Ping/Echo packets are used. This type attack is thus known as ICMP Ping flooding attack [122],
- etc.

These attacks affect all implementations of the protocol [220]. Most networking attacks flood the network with spurious traffic to block legitimate traffic.

In the case of SYN floods, the attacker fills the buffer that keeps track of TCP connections being initiated [380]. This buffer was too small in some operating system versions and it was easy to keep the buffer full, isolating the victim from the network. More brute force attacks are possible, where a large volume of packets fills all of the available bandwidth. Packet queues fill on intermediate machines and legitimate packets get dropped. Packet dropping forces TCP to retransmit packets while flow control slows the packet throughput rate. The network is then unusable for its intended purpose.

A distributed denial of service (DDoS) attack is a networked DoS where nodes work together. The attacker gains access to multiple machines over time and plants zombie processes. A zombie is a daemon that performs the actual attack [171]. At a predetermined time the zombies, located on different computers, launch the attack on the target. Hundreds or thousands of zombies can work together to swamp the bandwidth of the target's network connections. Figures 5.7 and 5.8 show time series of packet arrival rates for distributed denial of service attacks on the Clemson University network.

A DDoS attack is difficult to avoid. The attacker does not need to access any machine on the same sub-network as the target. It is impossible to enforce stringent security on all the Internet Autonomous Systems (ASs). Many systems are not even in the same country as the target. Many IP stack protocols can be used.

Few countermeasures for DDoS attacks exist. They take advantage of the open nature of our computing infrastructure. A DDoS attack is difficult to stop. After it starts, the victim is isolated from the network and has limited ability to act. The victim perceives the attack when the normally chaotic traffic flow suddenly increases. Packets arrive from nodes strewn across the network infrastructure. This set of nodes may vary over time. The zombie processes need to be stopped. Since the packets they send may be spoofed, this is not trivial. Even after the zombies are stopped it is difficult to find the attacker, who may have planted the zombies months in advance.

Note that resources such as network bandwidth, processing ability, and memory, etc. are always limited. Attackers can use any of these limits to launch a DoS attack and deplete the resources available to legitimate users.

5.7   Problems

1. List the classes of attacks handled by technologies described in this chapter.

2. For each security technology discussed in this chapter, explain which attacks it mitigates and how the risk of a successful attack is diminished.

3. Explain the security issues that remain open, in spite of the available security measures.

5.8   Glossary

Denial of service (DoS): Attack that consumes resources so they are not available for legitimate use.

Distributed denial of service (DDoS): A DoS attack using multiple hosts.

DMZ: Internal network that is neither protected nor trusted.

Extranet: An external network that is trusted to allow information sharing.

Firewall: Network appliance for controlling access to a local network.

Fragmentation attack: Illegal offsets in TCP packets allow the attacker to send a set of packets that are innocuous when looked at individually, but malicious when the real data stream is reconstructed.

Intranet: Internal network fully contained in the enterprise.

Intrusion detection system (IDS): Network appliance that monitors network traffic to detect attack traffic.

Network address translation: Replacing local IP addresses with other IP addresses for external communications.

Packet filter: Use of a set of rules by a firewall to allow or deny traffic to transit the firewall on a packet by packet basis.

Proxy: Allowing another node to work as an intermediate for network communications. The friendly equivalent of a man-in-the-middle attack.

Tunnel: Encapsulating the packets of one protocol within the packets of another protocol.

Virtual private network (VPN): A tool for managing a set of nodes located at different geographic locations as if they were all on a local network. A VPN needs to encrypt traffic moving outside the VPN and have a set of private IP addresses for routing.

Zombie: A compromised host used as part of a DDoS attack.

6

Virtual Private Network – Case Study Project

CONTENTS

This chapter presents a case study project. Although this project is significantly less challenging than the other projects in this book, my experience is that this project is essential. Students need to know how to use sniffers to monitor network traffic, to observe how networks operate and understand how vulnerable data packets are on the network.

6.1 Laboratory Preparation

Use a closed network facility for this project. Isolate this laboratory from the campus network by an "air gap."[1] This lets students freely experiment with the sniffer and neither disturb normal network communications nor compromise the privacy of campus Internet traffic.

Have each student use a virtual machine so they can install Linux distributions and necessary software by using administrator or *root* access to their virtual machine. Even though they have root access to their virtual machine, they should not be able to unintentionally compromise the physical host. We recommend either VMWare player [27] or Virtual Box [26]. Both are free and have adequate functionality for this project.

Using the isolated security network, students:

- Learn to use a sniffer,

---

[1]Using an "air gap" means that no cables physically connect the lab network to any outside network, including the campus network.

- Learn to set up a virtual private network (VPN),
- Learn how to use VPNs,
- Explain why VPNs are necessary, and
- Compare the efficiency of two VPNs.

6.2 Assignment

Using a workstation in your laboratory, install a Linux distribution using a virtual machine hypervisor to make your own virtual machine[2].

Make certain that the Linux virtual machine can access the network in the laboratory. Be certain that it allows remote sessions to be initiated using both telnet and ssh[3,4]. Be certain that Wireshark is installed on your virtual machine. Find a partner; have the partner give you access to their virtual machine. You will need to use telnet and/or ssh to remotely access your partner's virtual machine.

Use Wireshark to collect network traffic information for telnet and ssh sessions between the two virtual machines. See how and why ssh is more secure by using network traffic data collected from live sessions.

Install a VPN to connecting the two workstations in the laboratory. Choose one VPN package from the following (note that some of these may not have distributions compatible with the version of Linux you are using):

- CIPE,
- TINC,
- SWAN,
- SSH,
- OPENVPN,
- TUN

In-depth information describing how to install and use these VPNs can be found in [241].

Create scripts that allow the VPN to be started and stopped with minimal effort. You may write the scripts directly as a sequence of shell commands (for example Bash) or use a scripting language like Python or Perl. In demonstrations be prepared to dynamically start, stop, and change VPN packages. Be able to use Wireshark to show that the VPN is active and working correctly.

Have your partner use another VPN. Note that a VPN needs to have

---

[2]The instructor will inform you of the hypervisor to use, as well as any restrictions on the Linux distribution you should use for this project.

[3]Current versions of Linux typically disable telnet; you may need to search for information on-line that describes how to install and/or activate telnet.

[4]Some Linux distributions do not have the ssh-server active by default. It may need to be installed.

a private IP address space in order to be a VPN. Password-less ssh is not sufficient for creating a real VPN. The VPN acts as if it were an IP subnetwork, except that it has restricted access.

In your report:

1. Briefly explain what you did.
2. Explain how Wireshark works.
3. Explain the security differences between telnet and ssh. Include example traces.
4. Give the filter you use in Wireshark to collect the minimal amount of traffic necessary to grab the password from a given insecure application.
5. Explain how your VPN works.
6. Provide startup and shutdown scripts.
7. Contrast the efficiency of the VPN you set up with the VPN your partner set up. Provide data and statistical analysis to support your claim.

Demonstrate your VPN to the instructor. Within 3 to 4 minutes:

1. Demonstrate to the instructor your proficiency in using Wireshark. Collect network traffic data and filter the data to maintain the minimal amount of information needed to compromise telnet or email traffic on the network segment.
2. Use Wireshark to show the security features of your VPN.
3. Start and stop your VPN.

We note that there are many ways to construct Wireshark filters. Your grade will depend in large part on the quality and originality of the filter used to extract password information. Try to collect and display a truly minimal amount of information. If desired, you can use the pcap library instead of Wireshark. If you want to use a script or program to post-process the sniffed network traffic you may.

6.3   Virtual Machine (VM) Use

A virtual machine (VM) is a simulation of a workstation. The simulation includes virtual hardware interfaces that act like the interfaces hardware provides to the operating system. A *hypervisor* is the software that runs the virtual machine workstation simulations. Hypervisor frequently runs on a host operating system, like any other process. Some hypervisors do not require a host operating system; they run on the *bare metal*. The instruction sets of a number of modern processors are designed to allow efficient machine virtualization by hypervisors.

Virtual machines are popular for computer and network security work for many reasons:

- Malicious software activity is *sandboxed*, which means that it is effectively contained within the virtual machine. The host running the hypervisor is not vulnerable to modification.
- Corrupted virtual machines can simply be deleted. Malware analysis can then be restarted on a new virtual machine that is created by copying a few files.
- Some hypervisors allow checkpointing and very invasive analysis of the virtual machine state during execution. In some ways, this lets analysis occur at a level of abstraction lower than the operating system itself.

This lets security researchers work with malicious software with relative ease. This does not imply that hypervisors are perfect. Attacks are possible where the virtual machine can attack the host through the hypervisor, and the host may be able to attack the virtual machine through the hypervisor (known as a *blue pill* attack). Both these attacks are difficult and rare [177].

FIGURE 6.1
The VMWare Player hypervisor running an Ubuntu Linux virtual machine.

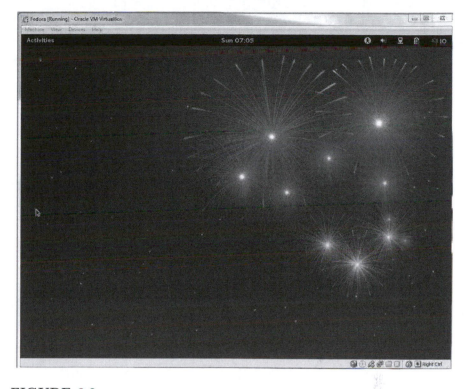

FIGURE 6.2
The Virtual Box hypervisor running a Fedora Linux virtual machine.

In this book, VMs are used to allow students flexible, unfettered access to a virtual system in a manner that is as secure as possible for both students and instructors. Students have administrative access to the virtual machine and can change the system as necessary, without being able to disturb the configuration of the host machine. Modifying the host machine could possibly disrupt other students and the laboratory. Figures 6.1 and 6.2 show recent hypervisor tool versions running recent Linux distributions.

The instructor needs to explain to students which hypervisor is present in the lab. Students will create a virtual machine from a software distribution. The software distribution will be available as a file with the "ISO" extension. The file will either be present on the lab network, or students will download the distribution ISO and copy it to their workstation. The ISO file has the same format as a DVD or CD. Hypervisors and operating systems mount and treat ISO files exactly like DVDs or USB thumb drives.

Virtual machine creation from an ISO is not discussed here. The exact commands to be used depend on:

- Hypervisor used,

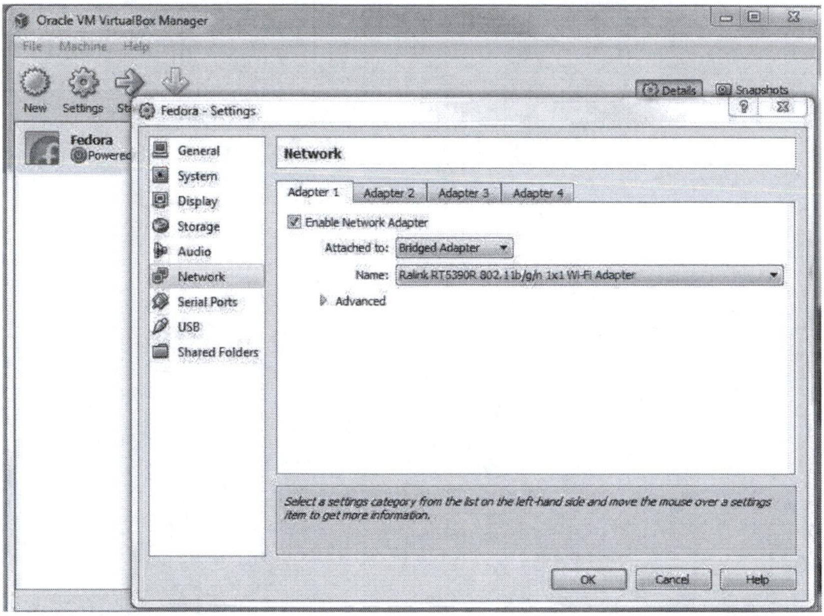

FIGURE 6.3
Defining the virtual Ethernet adapter as bridged.

- Hypervisor version,
- Guest operating system,
- Guest operating system distribution, and
- Guest operating system version.

These commands change regularly, but instructions can easily be found by referring to the on-line documentation for the hypervisor used in the laboratory. Similarly, the steps involved in installing Linux vary from distribution to distribution and version to version. Typically, the process is straightforward. When it is not straightforward, discussions and solutions can usually be found on-line using a search engine.

We suggest making standard Linux distribution ISO files available on a host in the laboratory. Students can then:

- Copy the ISO to the local machine,
- Create a new virtual machine using the hypervisor interface[5],
- When creating the virtual machine, be certain that the network interface is defined as bridged,
- Using the hypervisor tool, assign the virtual DVD device to the ISO file, and

---

[5]We suggest using either VMWare player or VirtualBox.

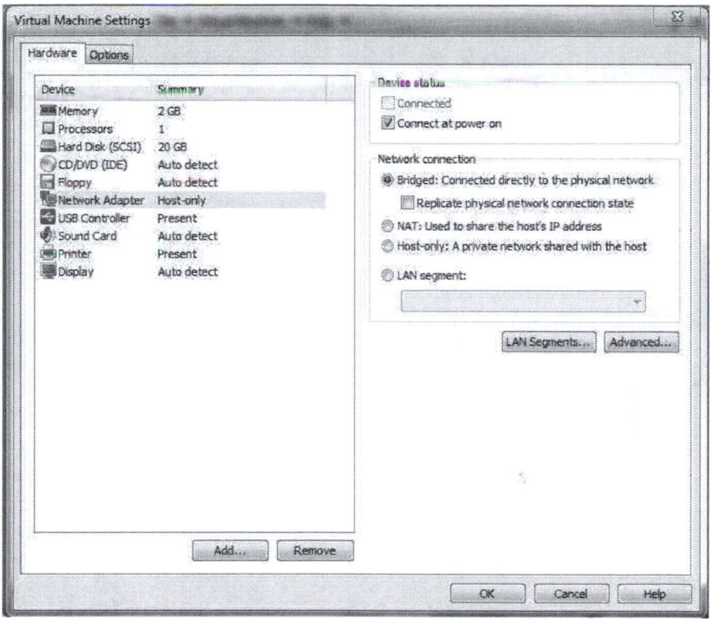

FIGURE 6.4
Defining the virtual Ethernet adapter as bridged using VMWare Player.

- Follow the installation instructions.

It is important for this assignment that the network adapter be defined as a bridged adapter. Figures 6.3 and 6.4 show examples of how to define a bridged Ethernet adapter in recent versions of the hypervisors. This definition lets the virtual machine share the host's physical Ethernet connection while using its own IP address. This means that when the VM is running the VM and the host computer each access the Internet as independent network stacks, even though they share the same physical interface.

Other settings exist that allow the VM to use the same IP address as the host, or even only have access to a virtual network internal to the host computer. The internal network has no direct access to external networks. These settings are useful in other contexts but are not appropriate for this assignment.

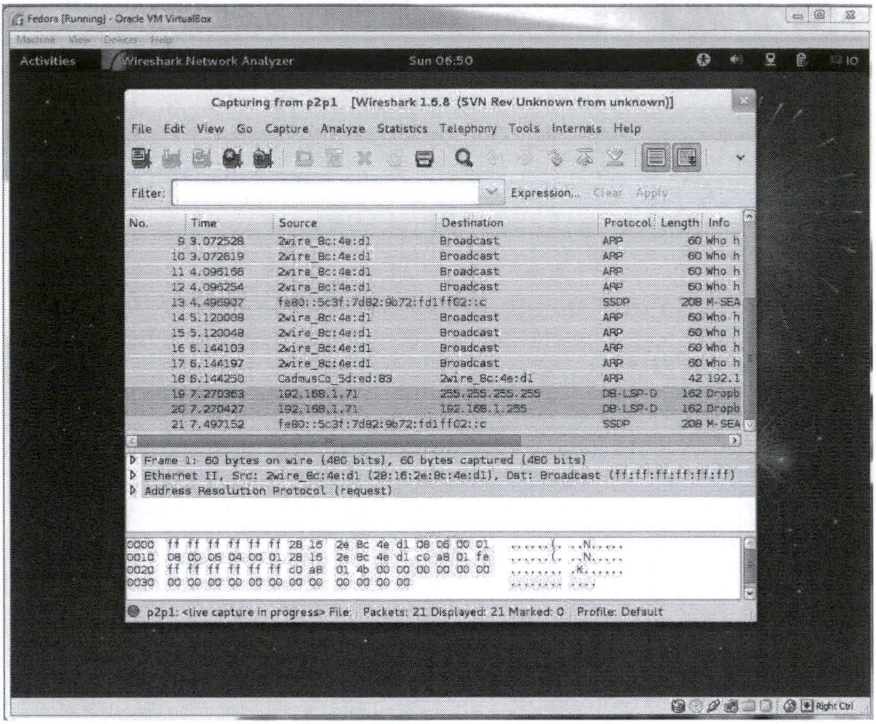

FIGURE 6.5
Example Wireshark session running on a Fedora virtual machine using the
VirtualBox hypervisor.

6.4 Sniffer Use

In this assignment, we will use Wireshark as a *sniffer*. Wireshark is a free,
open source packet analyzer. It uses the *pcap* libraries [355] to display packets captured from the Ethernet interface. A non-GUI version of Wireshark,
Tshark is distributed with Wireshark. Recent versions of Wireshark can also
capture and display packets from wireless network interfaces.[6]

Wireshark can capture, interpret, and display the contents of packets used
by a large number of IP based networking protocols. Figures 6.5 and 6.6 show
example Wireshark sessions. Note that the default display has three sections:

1. **Top** – A list of the most recent packets containing summary information,

---

[6]The student will probably need to run Wireshark as the administrative (root) user on
their VM to have a choice of interfaces to sniff.

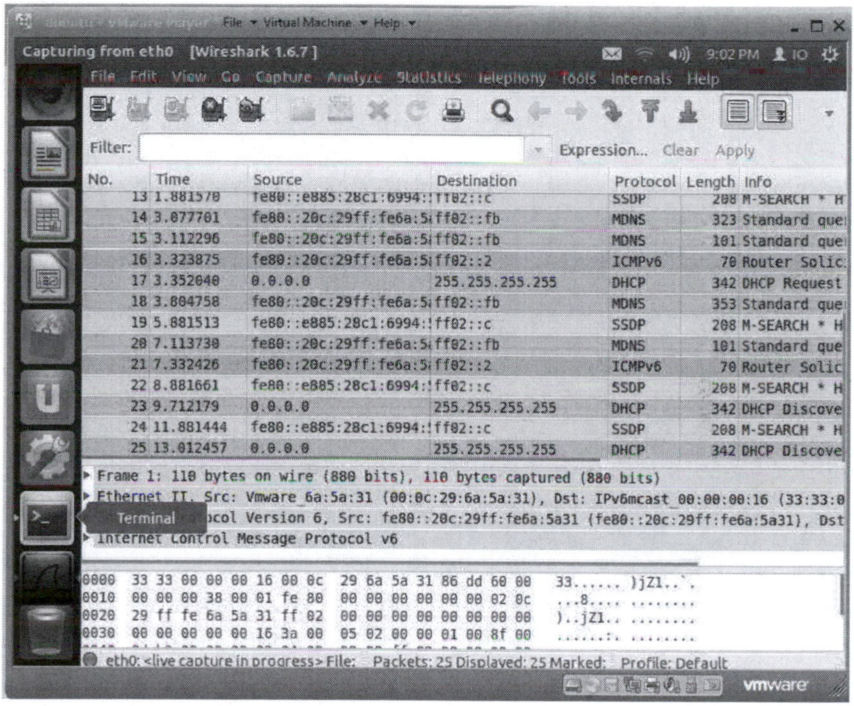

FIGURE 6.6
Example Wireshark session running on an Ubuntu virtual machine using the VMWare Player hypervisor.

2. **Middle** – A detailed interpretation of the packet selected in the top display, and

3. **Bottom** – A hexadecimal and ASCII dump of the contents of the same packet.

If a packet data field is selected in the middle display, the corresponding parts of the packet contents are highlighted in the bottom display.

It is possible to define filters to restrict the classes of packets filtered and/or displayed on the screen. Interfaces exist for defining, storing, and retrieving packet filters. The filter is basically a logical statement continuing logical conditions for different packet fields. For either UDP or TCP sessions, the *follow stream* option isolates and displays the stream of packets associated with a specific network session. You can also store and/or retrieve the packets from a given session.

A network sniffer like Wireshark is a powerful tool for network maintenance and analysis. They are essential for networking research and development. By capturing and analyzing the packet sequences for sessions, it becomes possible to debug protocols and understand how and when errors arise.

Unfortunately, many network protocols are not adequately secured. Frequently, network traffic is not encrypted. For these protocols, the contents is easily read all along the path from the source to the sink. It is slightly more difficult, but not impossible, to change the contents of the packets moving along that same path. In this assignment, Wireshark is used to experience how vulnerable the unencrypted packet streams are to inspection.

6.5   VPN Installation

FIGURE 6.7
The VPN session shown on this Ubuntu virtual machine uses the TUN virtual interface.

Virtual private networks secure protocols that are otherwise insecure. For the basic concepts behind VPNs, please refer to Section 5.3 in this book. Remember that VPNs create a secure virtual network that is overlaid onto the normal wide-area Internet. The VPN shares a hidden address space. Traffic routed through the VPN is encrypted.

Students can either refer to [241] or search on-line for in-depth instructions on configuring and building all the VPNs listed in the assignment given in Section 6.2. While the step-by-step instructions for installing the VPN varies greatly from VPN tool to VPN tool and even from version to version, the concepts are remarkably consistent. Some protocol containing encryption, such as SSH or SSL/TLS, is used to establish a session between two hosts. Normal Internet traffic is *tunneled* through the encrypted protocol.

FIGURE 6.8
The VPN session shown on this Fedora virtual machine uses the TUN virtual interface.

Tunneling consists of creating a stream cypher of the normal Internet traffic and inserting this encrypted stream into the data payloads of the encrypted protocol packets. This is often done by creating a virtual network driver, for example **tun0:**, which the Internet protocol stack can interface with in the same way that it interfaces with the Ethernet interface **eth0:**. Figures 6.7 and 6.8 show virtual machines with an active VPN using interface **tun0:**.

When a virtual interface is used, all normal network protocols can be sent through the VPN with no modification. This simple mechanism can secure all protocols in the TCP/IP protocol suite transparently.

6.6   Problems

1. Follow a UDP or TCP stream for an insecure application that requires a log in on the other side. Compare the amount of information displayed with the volume of information displayed by your filter.

2. Is it possible to create a Wireshark filter that only displays the password? If not, what imposes the limit?

3. Is it possible to use Tshark and a scripting language to create a

filter that only displays the password? If yes, do it. If not, what imposes the limit?

4. Use Wireshark to collect a set of packets from all interfaces while the VPN is active. Use a filter to display only packets collected from interface **eth0:** and another filter to display only packets collected from interface **tun0:** (or the appropriate connection for tunneling if your VPN does not use **tun0:**). Find and explain the differences between the two sets of packets. Does the lack of encryption on the data stream going into **tun0:** mean the data is unprotected?

5. Could a more secure VPN be constructed by tunneling one VPN through another VPN so that the data is encrypted multiple times?

6.7 Glossary

Air gap: To isolate a network segment from the larger Internet, no cable connects the isolated network to the global Internet.

Blue pill: An attack on software in a virtual machine that uses the hypervisor. These attacks come from beneath the operating system. For the virtual machine, it is the same as an attack from the hardware layer of the system.

Hypervisor: Software that is used to execute virtual machines by emulating the underlying hardware.

Sandbox: The logical isolation of programs running inside the virtual machine from programs running on the host computer.

7

Insertion Attacks

CONTENTS

This Chapter considers common attacks that insert an attack vector into data, programs, or memory. Insertion typically corrupts a legitimate process and hijacks it. We present several instances of insertion attacks and then give a general overview of the abstract problem.

Two specific instances of insertion attacks will be treated in more depth in other chapters. Chapter 8 provides a case study project on buffer overflow attacks. In that chapter, students will be provided with a vulnerable program. They then find ways to insert binary code into a running program's memory and trick the system into executing the binary instructions provided. In Chapter 9, students are given an instance of a virus. A virus is a program that inserts its code into valid programs, so that they can execute surreptitiously at a later point of time. The students change the virus to make it polymorphic. Polymorphic code is difficult for current anti-virus products to detect.

In insertion attacks, the adversary either provides input to, or modifies parts of, the system. Carefully constructed attack vectors fool the system. We now consider some specific attacks.

7.1 SQL Injection

In 2010, a data security firm reported [100] that sixty percent of the incidents they investigated in one year were due to SQL injection attacks. For forty percent of their cases, SQL injection was the only vulnerability used. In another twenty percent, SQL injection was combined with another vulnerability to attack their client. Mitre's 2011 *Common Weakness Enumeration (CWE)* report [2] of the most dangerous software errors ranks SQL injection as the worst.

The *Structured Query Language* (SQL) is a standardized language for interacting with relational databases. It was first released in 1979 and is the most widely used database language [14]. In spite of there being ANSI and ISO SQL standards, there are frequently portability issues between different vendor implementations.

SQL injection attacks most frequently occur when queries are constructed from user inputs. These inputs can come from web forms, *uniform resource locators* (URLs), or browser cookies. For example, let's consider a query like [15, 133]:

```
SELECT data FROM table WHERE field = '$INPUT';
```

where $INPUT is user input[1]. The system translates $INPUT and places its contents into the query. Single quote characters delimit a literal value. Let's consider some possible values for $INPUT [133]:

1. `123' or 'x'='x`
2. `;DROP TABLE table--`
3. `;exec(char(0x73687574646f776e)--`
4. `;convert(int,(select top 1 name from sysobjects where xtype='u'))`

which can be embedded into the query. These entries will do the following (in the same order):

1. Since 'x'='x' is a tautology, this clause is true for all entries in the table. This can give an attacker access to the entire database table. For example, an attacker can trick the system into emailing it a list of all passwords for the system.
2. The ";" character signals the end of one statement and the start of a new statement. "Drop TABLE table" will delete the entire TABLE *table* from the database.
3. The command "exec(COMMAND)" sends COMMAND to the shell to be executed. Command "char(HEX)" translates the hexadecimal value HEX into a string of characters. In this example, 0x73687574646f776e translates into "SHUTDOWN," which leads to the database server being taken offline.
4. The system takes the first object of type 'u,' which means the first user table. It tries to convert it into an int, which is illegal. An error message is generated that informs the attacker of the database

---

[1]We will not detail SQL syntax. Interested readers should refer to [161] or any number of SQL references and tutorials.

name. This can be used to discover the types of data stored in the database.

These examples show how SQL injection can corrupt, modify, exfiltrate data from, and/or disable databases. These examples are only the simplest class of SQL injection attacks [133].

SQL injection countermeasures include [133, 324]:

- *Input type checking* – Since the essential problem is that the user introduces malformed input, the programmer filters out characters that can be abused, such as ";". This is not trivial; recent work has considered the correctness of tools for sanitizing inputs and found that most existing input sanitation tools contain errors [207][2].
- *Positive pattern matching* – Check that the input matches the format of a good input,
- *Penetration testing* – Attempt SQL injection attacks on the interface to verify that they are properly detected,
- *Static code checking* – Use of code checking tools to verify program correctness,
- *Limit the amount of database access allowed to remote users* – Make sure user inputs go through an API and that the user has limited rights on the database, or
- *Avoid dynamic SQL use* – Force user inputs to use a static template or bind their inputs to existing tables.

7.2 Buffer Overflow Attack

This section introduces the buffer overflow concept that we explore in depth in Chapter 8. Many languages, most notably C, do not enforce mandatory bounds checking on arrays. A *buffer overflow* occurs when the system tries to store data in an array that is not large enough.

When this occurs in C, the program continues writing beyond the end of the array. The data array is stored at run-time in main memory along with other data, program binary op-codes, and pointers. This means that the data being put into the buffer can overwrite and modify the program being executed in arbitrary ways.

For example, in *stack smashing* an array that is local to a function is overwritten. If the data input is carefully crafted, it inserts *shell code* that is a set of arbitrary binary op-codes onto the stack. The input will also modify a pointer on the stack to point to the shell code. That pointer normally indicates

---

[2]Although the referenced paper looks at cross site scripting and not SQL injection, the data input sanitation issues are essentially the same.

the value the instruction pointer should take on function termination, which should normally allow the routine that called the function to continue execution. This forces the system to execute the shell code once the local function terminates.

In Chapter 8 we explain this in detail together with other buffer overflow variants, such as arc injection and heap smashing.

7.3   Printer Format Vulnerability

Although printer format statements seem innocent, the way that they use C parameter passing can be exploited to produce a number of undesirable outcomes, including [190]:

- Read arbitrary memory locations,
- Write arbitrary memory locations, and
- Get access to a shell program.

In this section, we briefly explain:

- What the vulnerability is,
- How to avoid the vulnerability,
- How to exploit vulnerable programs, and
- How the vulnerability works.

This information is relevant to the Chapter 8 assignment. This vulnerability is present in many programs and programming languages (including C and Perl). Our examples will use C.

For a C program to write text input from the command line to the console, the correct format would be:

```
printf("%s",argv[1]);
```

It is also possible, but inadvisable, to use the following format:

```
printf(argv[1]);
```

In most cases, these two commands have the same functionality. The string given as the first command line parameter is written to the screen.[3]

These two cases differ significantly, however, when

```
argv[1]
```

---

[3]For the sake of simplicity, this section ignores the need for the format string to include \n and stream I/O buffering. The exact time when output appears on the screen is not important.

includes formatting instructions. C library functions process format string statements by manipulating the stack. When programs allow users to input the format string, malicious users can use this stack manipulation to read, write, and modify program memory. In Chapter 8, we will see how dangerous this manipulation can be. The fprintf, printf, sprintf, snprintf, vfprintf, vprintf, vsprintf, and vsnprintf C library functions all share this vulnerability [339].

Consider Program 7.3.1. Compile it with command:

```
gcc -ggdb -pedantic -OO PrintfVulnerable.c -o PrintfVulnerable
```

You can then execute the program using gdb in windowing mode[4]. The format string to be used is either given on the command line, or input using the gdb

```
set args
```

command. If we input format string

```
"%x %x %x %x \n"
```

when the program writes the contents of *buf* to the screen, buf will contain hex integer representations of the first four words on the stack [309]. This occurs because the C library print functions are designed to push the arguments following the print format string onto the stack.

Using gdb, you can observe this phenomenon. Place a break point at the *x=1;* line in Program 7.3.1. With program execution stopped at that point, look at the values of the *esp* and *ebp* registers. These point to the top and bottom of the stack while in the *FormatVulnerable()* function. Note that the *RecursivePrefixLocal()* function serves only to push twenty stack frames onto the stack before *FormatVulnerable()* to help identify the order that items are placed on the stack (more in Chapter 8). By stepping through the *FormatVulnerable()* function, the reader can identify how the values from *argv[1]* are copied to *buf2* and then interpreted and placed into *buf*. By inputting increasing numbers of *"%x"'s*, it becomes possible to traverse the stack and learn the values stored on the stack. Each *"%x"* causes printf to advance one word when it is executed.

We encourage the reader to run this program again and input a command line parameter, like:

```
"%s %s %s %s %s %s %s %s"
```

It is quite likely that this will cause the program to crash with a segmentation fault. The *"%s"* element in a format string tells *printf* to use the word

---

[4]This can be done using Emacs in gdb-many-windows-mode, gdb -w PrintfVulnerable, or insight PrintfVulnerable. The exact command depends on the system being used. Similarly, the exact positions of objects on the stack can vary for many reasons. We describe how this vulnerability works, but do not provide step-by-step instructions. The exact commands depend on many issues that vary from machine to machine, including compiler version, distribution, etc.

```c
#include <stdio.h>
#include <string.h>
#include <stdlib.h>

void FormatVulnerable(int argc, char **argv)
{
  int x;
  char buf [100];
  char buf2[100];
  x = 1;
  strncpy(buf2, argv[1], sizeof buf2);
  snprintf(buf, sizeof buf, buf2);
  printf("Buffer size is: (%d) \nData input: %s \n",strlen (buf),buf);
  printf ("X equals: %d/ in hex: %x\nMemory address for x: (%p) \n",
          x, x, &x) ;
  printf(buf);
  printf("\n");
  printf ("\x25s %p \n",buf,buf);
}
void RecursivePrefixLocal(int i,int argc,char **argv)
{
  printf("In RecursivePrefixLocal(%i)\n",i);

  if(--i) RecursivePrefixLocal(i,argc,argv);
  else FormatVulnerable(argc,argv);
}

int main (int argc, char **argv)
{
  RecursivePrefixLocal(20,argc,argv);
  return 0 ;
}
```

Algorithm Description 7.3.1: Program with print format vulnerability.

currently indicated as a pointer to a string variable. When a large number of
"%s" elements are given, the chances are very good that one of the values on
the stack will redirect the program to a memory location that it is not allowed
to de-reference.

We can overcome this problem by directly writing memory addresses onto
the stack from the command line [309, 393, 335]. This requires inputting binary
values from the command line. One way to do this is to use a hex editor to
write to a file and then using stdin redirection from the command line. It is
also possible to use Perl. To input address 0xbffff3b8 on the command line to
program PrintfVulnerable, the command line would be

```
perl -e 'system "./PrintfVulnerable","\xb8\xf3\xff\xbf" '
```

Alternatively, this is also possible

```
perl -e 'print "\xb8\xf3\xff\xbf" ' | ./PrintfVulnerable
```

The Perl output from the print command could also be redirected to a file.
Since variations in the compiler, compiler command line, and debugger environment will change the order that local variables are put on the stack, the
items stored on the stack, etc., we can not provide exact instructions for redirecting the *%s* directive to output arbitrary strings stored in memory. The
reader will need to use the debugger to find the exact sequences of commands
needed for their environment.

Now that we can read arbitrary locations in memory, the reader should be
interested to learn that using *%n* instead of *%s* lets one overwrite arbitrary
positions in memory. The *%n* directive writes the number of items output thus
far to the memory address stored at the top of printf's stack [309, 393, 335].
By modifying field widths, we can change the value output. For example,
inserting field width directive *%666d* adds 666 to the current number of items.
We refer interested readers to [309], which explains how by writing to different
memory locations it becomes possible to replace arbitrary memory addresses
with arbitrary values. A number of software products have been found to have
this vulnerability.

7.4 SSH Insertion Attacks

Secure shell (ssh) is a very useful program for secure communications between
nodes. Older versions of this tool (1.2.25 and below) were vulnerable to replay
and insertion attacks [291].

In old versions of ssh, crc-32 was used as the hashing technique for verifying
packet integrity. When cbc (cipher block chaining) mode was used, attackers
could identify some command packets in the data stream. Once a packet with
a specific command of interest was identified, the user could execute a known

clear-text attack (see Chapter 3) on the packet. They could then modify the packet and insert arbitrary instructions if desired.

This enables a man-in-the-middle attack, where the attacker intercepts packets, changes the packets, and forwards the modified packets to the victim. This was corrected with *ssh v2*.

7.5   IDS Insertion Attacks

As with ssh insertion attacks, other security tools, such as network intrusion detection systems (IDS's), can be compromised. One common goal of the attacker is simply to find a data sequence that disables the IDS [30]. The IDS can fail in one of two modes:

- Open – leaving the network unprotected, or
- Closed – providing a denial of service attack.

In the first case, an IDS lets all packets through that are not proven to be evil. In the second case, packets are only let through if they are free of malicious content.

There are many ways that attackers can use insertion attacks to hide content from an IDS. The essential vulnerability is that an IDS does not have exactly the same view of the data stream as the host receiving the packets. We recall that TCP/IP works on the sender's end by (roughly) [380]:

- Taking a data stream,
- Slicing it into chunks that become a sequence of packet payloads,
- Adding packet headers to the chunks,
- Sending one packet after the other, and
- Retransmitting packets if acknowledgments are not received in time.

Similarly, the receiving end of the data stream works by (roughly):

- Reading a packet,
- Removing the header, and
- Placing the packet payloads in sequence to reconstruct the input data stream.

An IDS with *deep packet inspection* (DPI) looks at the contents of the data stream and tries to detect malicious items. There are many ways that attackers can insert information to foil DPI.

One issue is TCP's guaranteeing that data streams are correctly delivered to their destination. To do this, TCP has to compensate for packets being lost, delayed, or delivered out of order. It is not uncommon for packets to be retransmitted. This means that the IDS (or the recipient) could see multiple copies of the same packet. When that happens, which packet should be processed? Common solutions are either to ignore packets that are retransmitted, or to process the most recent copy of the packet. A clever attacker would set the maximum number of hops for some packets (TTL - time to live) so that they reach the IDS, but not the destination. In this way, the attacker can overwrite malicious data for the IDS, but not for the victim [189, 30].

Another alternative is to assume that the IDS has limited storage, which forces it to inspect one packet at a time. The packet headers include offset information that describe where each packet payload is placed in the data stream. It is possible to construct a sequence of packets where each packet is innocuous, but the combined packets have an exploit. The offsets are defined incorrectly to have packets overwrite each other. This *packet fragmentation* attack can, once again, cause the data viewed by the IDS and the end host to be two totally different things.

7.6   Viruses

Virus refers to a program that reproduces by copying itself into another program. By the end of 1985, viruses started appearing on personal computers. The origin of most viruses is obscure. Many viruses in the late 1980's are traced to virus factories in the Eastern Block, notably Bulgaria [84], leading to suspicions that some viruses were state sponsored or at least tolerated by hostile foreign governments.

As Internet use and software sharing became more widespread, the number of virus variants and number of machines infected increased. Techniques from epidemiology are used to study the spread of viruses in computer networks [235]. Epidemiology is especially useful for tracking the spread of e-mail viruses [276]. Using the definitions here, the term virus is a misnomer for most e-mail viruses. They are in fact worms as discussed in Section 7.7. We discuss technical details of viruses in Chapter 9.

A virus typically has four components:

1. *Search routine* – look for uninfected files susceptible to infection.
2. *Copy routine* – insert a copy of the virus into the susceptible file.
3. *Payload* – execute logic triggered by the virus, may be a logic bomb.
4. *Profile* – store internal data to aid in detecting uninfected files.

When an infected program is run, the following typically occurs [275, 278]:

- The search routine finds files the virus can infect that do not contain the profile. The profile keeps the virus from infecting the same file repeatedly. Re-infection wastes disk space and processing time. It makes the virus easier to detect.

- The copy routine infects one or more susceptible files. Often the virus is appended to the end of the file and the program start address in the header is modified to point to the virus code. On termination, the virus code jumps to the original program start.
- If the virus has a payload, the payload is run before returning control to the host program. If the payload is a logic bomb, its execution may be conditional on factors external to the virus.

The first viruses infected executable files and/or boot sectors. Boot sector viruses infect computer disks instead of files and run during system initialization. Viruses can be contained in many file types that previously were thought safe. Microsoft Word macro viruses are an example, but postscript and pdf viruses also exist.

Scanners commonly detect known viruses. When detected, the virus is extracted from the infected host file. The virus profile used to detect the virus and the logic used to extract the virus are unique for each virus. Reverse engineering of captured viruses is needed to derive both. This is somewhat effective, but requires reacting to viruses after they spread. Even then, this approach is of limited use against polymorphic viruses that change behavior and internal structure with each execution. We discuss polymorphism in depth in Chapter 9. Another problem is the tendency of attackers to modify existing viruses and re-introduce them into the wild.

Heuristics exist for detecting new viruses before reverse engineering them. Similarly, memory resident programs can block harmful behaviors associated with viruses. Both approaches are plagued by large false positive rates. When the false positive rate is too high, real detections tend to be ignored [39]. The reason for this high false positive rate is that determining whether or not an arbitrary computer program contains a virus is undecidable. It is equivalent to the halting problem [119]. The complexity of detecting computer viruses based on Gödel is discussed in [38].

7.7 Worms

The first use of worm to refer to a malicious network program is in John Brunner's *The Shockwave Rider* [96]. This quote from the book pre-dates both widespread Internet use and computer worm infestations: "a self-perpetuating tapeworm, which would shunt itself from one nexus to another every time his credit-code was punched into a keyboard. It could take days to kill a worm like that, and sometimes weeks."

A worm is an attack that propagates through the network by creating copies of itself. Unlike viruses, worms do not infect other executables. They are independent processes. According to this definition the typical e-mail virus is really a worm, since it does not modify other programs. It merely mails copies of itself. Another definition differentiates between worms and viruses by saying that viruses require a user action to reproduce and worms do not [397]. E-mail viruses would thus be viruses. This differentiation is rather academic now; hybrid attacks like Nimda fit both categories [428].

Worms are interesting, because they are network processes. Epidemiology-based analysis, used for virus propagation, is even more important for studying worm behavior. Important worms to date include:

- The original Morris worm [397] which spread to IP addresses found on the infected host.
- The Code Red I (July 2001) set up multiple threads, where each thread started an exploit on a machine chosen at random from the IP address space. Version 2 (CRv2) infected more than 359,000 out of an estimated 2,000,000 susceptible hosts in less than 14 hours [103, 449]. At its height it infected almost 18 percent of the susceptible machines.
- Code Red II was an entirely new worm, whose propagation improved CRv2 by using more threads and searching a larger space. It used subaddress masking [380] to search for machines in the same subnetwork. Machines on the same subnetwork are:

  - Likely to have similar configurations,
  - Be susceptible to the same infection,
  - Have lower latency between machines, and
  - Be behind the same firewall.

  Code Red II appears to have been primarily a trapdoor allowing access to the infected systems.
- The Slammer attack started on January 25, 2003 and within 10 minutes it had infected over 90 percent of the hosts vulnerable to its attack. It exploited a buffer overflow vulnerability in a Microsoft product. Its rate of spread was over two orders of magnitude faster than Code Red I. As with Code Red I, it chose hosts to infect at random [294]. Slammer propagated quickly by using UDP [380] to send small packets containing the entire exploit. Its propagation rate was limited solely by the network bandwidth on the infected machines. Slammer's code base concentrated entirely on worm propagation and contained no hidden exploits [294]. It caused multiple network outages and was effectively a Denial of Service (DoS) attack.

In addition to random and subnet scanning, other methods can help worms propagate quickly. One could construct a list of vulnerable machines in advance. This lets the worm initially target a small number of machines that it can be certain to infect. Another approach is to have each machine construct a pseudo-random permutation of the addresses in the network. These permutations could be subdivided to avoid simultaneous attempts to infect the same machine [31]. This reduces congestion, speeds propagation, and makes the worm harder to detect. These are referred to as flash worms or Warhol worms.

Worms have secondary effects. Both Code Red II and Nimda caused network outages. Changes in traffic behavior by the worms triggered the Internet's Border Gateway Protocol (BGP). BGP routes messages between Autonomous Systems (AS) along the most efficient path. A number of BGP message storms were concurrent with the height of Code Red II and Nimda propagation [125]. Global disruptions caused by worms could lead to routing table instabilities and perturb traffic beyond problems experienced to date. No adequate worm countermeasures exist as of yet.

7.8 Virus and Worm Propagation

Much of this section is based on work in [181]. This section requires more mathematical background than the rest of the chapter and may be skipped at the instructor's discretion.

Epidemiology is the field of mathematics, medicine, and science that studies the propagation of infections within populations. Typically, epidemiology is used to protect human populations from communicable diseases. Although use of the terms *virus* and *worm* to describe malicious software was originally metaphorical in nature, in many ways the term is more than a metaphor since insights from mathematical epidemiology are useful in analyzing and evaluating methods for securing networks from virus and worm "infestations."

Often, virus and worm infections have two phases. There is an initial epidemic phase, where the disease spreads quickly through the population. After the epidemic phase, the disease either dies out or its scope is reduced to a smaller steady state where the disease is endemic to some regions and may have isolated, smaller flare-ups.

Following [115] when discussing propagation, we define computer worms and viruses synonymously as "a segment of program code that will copy its code into one or more larger 'host' programs when it is activated...that can run independently and travel from machine to machine across network connections."

In epidemiology, populations are made up of individuals with the following *MSEIRZ* states:

- M passive immunity to infection (computer systems without the vulnerability),
- S susceptible to infection (computer systems with the vulnerability, but not yet infected),
- E in a latent period (infected by the pathogen, but not yet infectious),
- I infective and capable of disease transmission,
- R recovered from the infection and immune to reinfection, and
- Z dead.

Individuals transition stochastically[5] from one state to another. It is possible to make the model more complex by creating multiple sub-populations with different characteristics. Not every pathogen has the same set of states, nor do transitions between states always occur in the same order. Models of disease transmission dynamics are named by the order of the state transitions. Common models are *Susceptible-Infected-Susceptible* (SIS) and *Susceptible-Infected-Recovered* (SIR).

The SIS model (Figure 7.1) assumes all members of a population are initially susceptible to infection i.e., upon exposure to a disease any member of the population could become infected. Infected individuals are either removed from the population (by death) or become healthy, at which point they are again susceptible. No one has immunity to the infection. Kephart, Chess, and White first investigated viruses in computer systems from an epidemiological perspective [235]. Their analysis considered PC viruses of that era. At that time, viruses propagated primarily by PC owners exchanging programs via floppy disks or on-line bulletin boards. Email viruses became prevalent in the mid-1990's. Viruses of that era propagated slowly, partly due to the limited network connectivity of that era. They were independently detected, isolated, and eradicated, either on individual machines or in isolated work groups. Virus removal rarely corrected the underlying vulnerability that the virus exploited, leaving machines vulnerable to reinfection. Virus infection and removal rates had approximately the same order of magnitude. This class of infections can be adequately modeled using the SIS model.

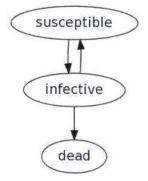

FIGURE 7.1
In the SIS model, the population is either infected, susceptible to infection, or dead.

The SIR model (Figure 7.2) is similar to the SIS model in that all members of a population are initially susceptible to infection and may be eliminated by death; however once an individual has recovered from a disease, he/she enters a

---

[5]The term *stochastic* denotes a non-deterministic, random process.

recovered state with immunity to the disease. This state may be temporary or permanent. Worm removal typically includes patching the basic flaw, making the system immune to reinfection. The SIR model may be appropriate for this class of malware, as long as the infection and recovery rates are of the same order of magnitude.

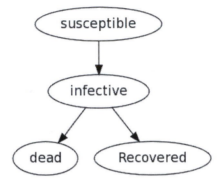

FIGURE 7.2
In the SIR model, the population is either susceptible to infection, infected, recovered from infection and immune, or dead

Computers do not rid themselves of worm and virus infections on their own. An infection is discovered, analyzed, a process is developed to remove the malware, the process is distributed, and executed. See [115] for a detailed treatment.

The first malicious computer worm was the Morris Worm in 1988 [90]. As of the early 2000's, worms started to be written to exploit vulnerabilities that become known by companies distributing patches designed to correct the vulnerability. The patches are reverse engineered. The worm is written and released in the wild, infecting the large number of systems that have yet to install the patch. While the Morris Worm infected 10% of the Internet within a few hours in 1988, the 2003 Slammer worm infected 90% of the susceptible machines within ten minutes. The amount of time required for pathogen removal process is currently much larger than the infection rate. This difference is large enough that the repair rate is not an appreciable factor in determining the size of the outbreak. For example, the Slammer worm was officially reported after 1.5 hours. Countermeasures clearly did not limit the size of its epidemic, which peaked after 10 minutes.

It does not seem valid to include a stochastic transition between states for a repair process in the model for these worms. This makes the SIR model of questionable utility for studying the initial spread of a worm infection. The SIR model would be appropriate for considering some virus infections, or the steady state of the worm infection that occurs later. For example, the Code

Red I worm periodically entered a dormant state and would later restart the propagation process.

Typically, worm removal also patches the vulnerabilities the worm exploits. Since attackers often discover security flaws by reverse engineering security patches, including a patch in the removal software is trivial. The chances of reinfection by a worm are becoming minimal, which makes the SIS model inappropriate for current problems.

Models are solved by creating ordinary differential equations (ODE's) expressing transitions between states. When transition rates are constant, solutions to the ODE's are exponential probability distributions [198]. Techniques for solving sets of differential equations of this type can be found in standard reference works [88, 365]. In particular, the LaPlace transform can be used to convert these problems into sets of linear equations. Equation 7.1 shows a set of differential equations for the SIR model [198].

$$\frac{dS}{dt} = -\beta SI \tag{7.1}$$

$$\frac{dI}{dt} = \beta SI - \alpha I \tag{7.2}$$

$$\frac{dR}{dt} = \alpha I \tag{7.3}$$

For each model, three threshold quantities determine an infection's qualitative behavior: R_0, σ and R. The *basic reproduction number* R_0 is defined as the number of secondary infections that result when one infective is introduced [randomly] into a completely susceptible population [198]. The *contact number* σ is the average number of "adequate" contacts an infected individual has during its infectious period. An *adequate* contact is any contact sufficient for transmitting the infection. For context of a population whose contacts are described by a graph, σ is the average neighborhood size.

The *replacement number* R is the average number of secondary infections produced by an infective during its infectious period. These models are dynamic in nature and hence σ and R are actually functions of time; the parameter R_0 is only defined at the starting time. We have that $R_0 \geq \sigma$ since the number of contacts that can be infected may decrease as time passes. We also have that $R_0 = \sigma(0)$, since the number of secondary infections that results must be at least zero.

During the infection phase, the number of infected individuals will increase in time, making $\sigma \geq R$, as it becomes less and less likely an individual will be in contact with a non-infected individual. Thus we have $R_0 \geq \sigma \geq R$ [198]. Epidemics generally occur in a fully susceptible population if and only if $R_0 > 1$ (i.e., each new infection causes a larger number of secondary infections) [198]. Otherwise, the set I of infectives will decrease over time.

We present a few relevant results from mean-field analysis of the epidemiology problem. Although these results match simulations fairly well, they may overestimate disease spread because of a tacit assumption that the population is fully mixed. In a homogeneous population R_0 is typically proportional to an infection transmission probability p times $\sigma(0)$. If the population is heterogeneous(*e.g.*, different age groups, segments of society with different sexual preferences, or computers with different operating systems), the value of R_0 is less obvious. In this case, a matrix M expresses the infection transmission probabilities for the population classes and the transition rates of individuals between classes. To create an epidemic, it suffices that the effective $R_0 > 1$ for any class in the population. The maximum effective R_0 for any population class can be calculated by finding the *spectral radius* (dominant eigenvalue) of M [137]. If the average number of contacts varies greatly among individuals in a population class, this increases the effective value of R_0 to $R_0(1 + CV^2)$ where CV is the ratio of the second moment and first moment of the distribution of $\sigma(0)$ [269].

To counteract network infections, some type of countermeasure will be required. Consider a patch distribution scheme, or the random immunization strategy of [115]. Centralized patch distribution runs in $O(|G|)$, since the bandwidth at patch distribution centers is limited and the number of such distributions centers is finite and relatively small. For patch distribution using fixed distribution centers to work effectively, the number of distribution centers needs to increase on the same scale as the size of the network. For an infinite network, an infinite number of centers would be required, in which case we are faced with the meta-issue of how to distribute the patch to the distribution centers.

One scalable approach is to use a peer-to-peer distribution system, like bit-torrent. In [115], Chen and Carley argue for a Countermeasure Competing (CMC) strategy for distributing patches. It could be argued that a bit-torrent model would then be a type of CMC.

Details are given in [181] showing that computer worms spreading on graph infrastructures like the Internet will most likely become an epidemic. We also showed that exponential speed of spread for worms such as Slammer is related to the graph structure of the Internet and as a result that the network structure itself may be the cause of its own vulnerabilities.

The structure of large-scale Internet-like networks makes network monocultures inconsequential.[6] An epidemic always occurs within the susceptible sub-population.

Our observations also indicate that exponentially fast spread of the worm through the network should be expected until the network is saturated. Initial infection spreads exponentially quickly because the underlying structure of the network is conducive to explosive growth.

Note that worms can attack the Internet in many ways. If the network is viewed as a flat address space, exponential growth may be unlikely. But, if the worm follows the scale-free connectivity patterns found in many network im-

---

[6]The amount of market share is not really important. When the network size approaches infinity, those nodes running the vulnerable software will have an epidemic.

plementations (i.e., web graph, e-mail traffic flows, autonomous system graph, ... [59]) then exponential growth is likely and should not require excessive skill on the part of the worm designer. On the other hand, should a CMC be found desirable, it is worth considering what types of mechanisms could speed the distribution of the worm countermeasure to give the white worm a natural advantage over infectious agents.

A white worm [7] CMC is more efficient than existing means of transmission. The structure of Internet-like graphs insures saturation and fast spreading of patches just as it does for worms. Although both [181] and [115] support the use of the CMC model of immunization, there are still ethical and practical problems with this approach. Chen and Carley propose the existence of a "safe" network for disseminating countermeasures. However [83] provides a number of arguments against so-called beneficial viruses. Should policy arise from these insights, we must be certain that CMC viruses are controlled and practically applied for the benefit of users and not to their detriment.

7.9   Problems

1. Refer to an SQL manual and create a simple SQL injection attack on a simple query. Explain how the query should be modified to remove the vulnerability.

2. Write a program that has a printer format vulnerability. Show how the vulnerability can be exploited to crash the program.

3. *Advanced* Write differential equations for SIS and SIR models. Use the LaPlace format to solve the models and plot the evolution of the system over time, assuming that the system is 100% vulnerable at the start of the analysis.

7.10   Glossary

Buffer overflow: An insertion attack where the attacker writes past an array boundary.

Deep packet inspection: A network monitoring technology that is capable of analyzing packet payloads.

---

[7]Using a worm to propagate a patch through the network.

Epidemiology: The branch of medicine dealing with the spread and control of contagious diseases.

Insertion attack: An attack that modifies an existing protocol, program, or data structure by inserting additional data or instructions to modify the operation of the system.

Printer format vulnerability: A vulnerability where a format string is input directly by a user. This can be used to execute arbitrary pieces of code.

Shell code: Executable code inserted as a payload by an insertion attack.

SQL injection: This is sometimes pronounced as "sequel injection." An injection attack on databases using SQL.

Stack smashing: A buffer overflow attack on the stack.

White worm: Use of a worm infestation to spread beneficial software.

8

Buffer Overflow – Case Study Project

CONTENTS

This chapter describes how buffer overflows are exploited. A number of different buffer overflow attacks are described and analyzed. In Section 8.6 we present an example program with a number of buffer overflow vulnerabilities. The student assignment will be to exploit these vulnerabilities. By the end of the assignment, the student should know:

- What buffer overflow vulnerabilities are,
- Different classes of buffer overflow exploits,
- How buffer overflow exploits work,
- How buffer overflows can be avoided,
- Basics of software reverse engineering, and
- Details of how the stack works.

For this project, students need access to a virtual machine running Windows XP with Cygwin installed. The Cygwin installation should include the gcc compiler and gdb debugger. It is best for the gdb debugger to run in windowing mode[1]. Windows XP is used because, unlike newer versions of Windows and Linux, its default installation does not include the buffer overflow countermeasures discussed in Section 8.5. Cygwin provides a Linux programming environment under Windows. This combination of tools makes the assignment easier to complete while remaining relevant.

---

[1]To run gdb in windowing mode, input either "gdb -w" or "insight" from the shell. The exact command will vary from system to system.

8.1 Stack Smashing

Stack smashing is the classic buffer overflow exploit. A program is vulnerable to stack smashing when a function allows data to be input into a local array variable without proper array bounds checking. Stack smashing exploits the fact that, in the von Neumann architecture, data input into a program may be interpreted in many ways depending on the context. The same sequence of bits can be data or code, depending entirely on what the processor expects to find in a memory location.

Figure 8.1 shows how computer memory is organized. It is a notional representation. Do not assume any details in the Figure are always true. The positions of any memory segment may vary depending on the processor, operating system, compiler, etc. Do not assume that the text segment (arguments and variables) is always at the low (high) end of memory. Most systems conform to this general model and the model expresses how memory is laid out. Just remember to do simple tests with your code, compiler, and debugger to verify memory layout details when starting to analyze a system.

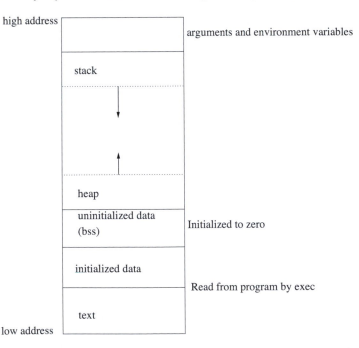

FIGURE 8.1
Notional view of computer logical memory space, based on [379].

The text segment is the program binary. The compiler translates source

```c
/*
  Name - BufferOverflowDemo.C
  Date - 1/1/2010
  Programmer - R. R. Brooks
  Purpose - Show very simple buffer overflow and how to get it working
  using emacs/gdb.
  Input - Input a string.
  Output - Some statements allowing students to see what is going
  wrong.
 */
#include <stdio.h>
#include <stdlib.h>
#include <unistd.h>
#include <fcntl.h>
void InputStringNoCheck(void)
{
  char buffer[]={'@','@','@','@','@','\x00'};
  int   input;
  int   i=0;
  printf("Buffer= %s\n",buffer);
  input=getchar();
  while(input != (int)'\n'){
    printf("input=%c, binary=%x, i=%d\n",input,input,i);
    buffer[i++]=input;
    printf("Buffer= %s\n",buffer);
    input=getchar();
  }
  buffer[i]=0;
  printf("Buffer= %s\n",buffer);
}
void recursion(int i)
{
  if(i>0){
    printf("recurse=%d\n",i);
    recursion(i-1);
    printf("recurse=%d\n",i);
  }else{
    InputStringNoCheck();
  }
}
int main(int argc, char **argv)
{
  int recurse=6;
  printf("Before recursion\n");
  recursion(recurse);
  printf("After recursion\n");
  return(1);
}
```

Algorithm Description 8.1.1: – Program for exploring the stack.

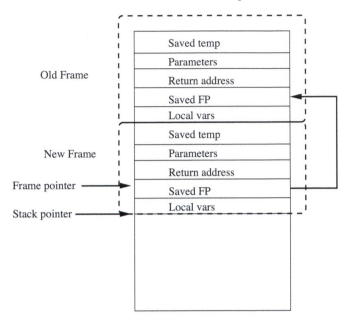

FIGURE 8.2
Notional view of the stack data structure.

code into binary object code. The object code needs to be linked before execution. Linking resolves memory references for objects (variables and functions) stored outside the local object file. Address resolution can be done during the program build (static linking) or at run time (dynamic linking). For Windows (Linux) dynamic linking under uses .dll dynamic link libraries (.so shared objects). The initialized data segment contains data variables where values are specified in the source code. Typically, the text and initialized data segments are the contents of the executable file.

The uninitialized data segment (sometimes referred to as bss) is reserved for global variables whose initial values are not defined at compile time. These values are usually, but not always, set to zero when the program is initially loaded into memory.

The heap and stack are process dynamic memory. The stack size increases (decreases) as function calls are made (terminated). In Figure 8.1, the stack grows downward; moving from high address values to low ones. In the buffer overflow countermeasures section (Section 8.5), we re-examine this assumption. The heap is used to reserve memory using malloc and new calls. In Figure 8.1, the heap grows from low to high addresses. If the heap and stack collide, you get either a stack overflow error (if the stack runs into the heap) or the malloc / new calls return a NULL pointer (if the heap collides with the

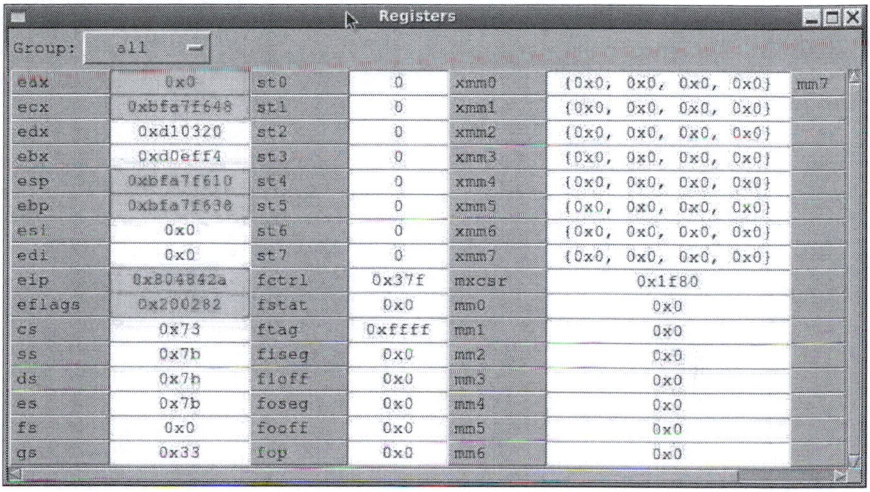

FIGURE 8.3
Register values on the author's machine when Program 8.1.1 is run with input 123 and stopped at a breakpoint set at the first command "char buffer[]=..." of InputStringNoCheck()

stack). In either case, the program has run out of memory. This may cause the program to abort or trigger a "garbage collection" process.

The operating system, command line arguments, and environment variables are located above the stack. Much of this memory is frequently protected against read or write access. Attempts to improperly access protected memory or dereference a NULL pointer will typically terminate the program with a SEGFAULT error.

Figure 8.2 shows a detailed stack format. When a function call is made, a new stack frame is created. This frame contains:

1. *Saved temp* – mainly current register values,
2. *Parameters* – parameter values passed to the function,
3. *Return address* – current instruction pointer for the function calling the new function,
4. *Saved frame pointer* – the address of the frame pointer for the function calling the new function, and
5. *Local variables* – memory space for local vairables used by the new function.

Function initiation also modifies two registers. One register contains the frame pointer, which is set to point to the saved frame pointer in the new stack frame. Another register contains the stack pointer which points to the address where a new frame should be placed when the next function call occurs. This address

```
┌──────────────────────────────── Memory ──────────────────────────── _ □ X
 Addresses
 Address  0xbfa7f610  ⬍                                    Target is LITTLE endian
                0            4            8            c              ASCII
 0xbfa7f610   0x00000001   0x00bf6dc0   0x00d0f4c0   0xbfa7f664   .....m......d...
 0xbfa7f620   0x00000000   0x00000000   0xbfa7f658   0x00d0eff4   .........H.......
 0xbfa7f630   0x00000000   0x00000000   0xbfa7f658   0x08048520   .........X... ...
 0xbfa7f640   0xbfa7f688   0x00be3950   0x00d0f4c0   0x0804864b   ....P9......K...
 0xbfa7f650   0xbfa7f664   0x00d0eff4   0xbfa7f678   0x08048505   d.......x.......
 0xbfa7f660   0x00000000   0x00000001   0x00d0f4c0   0x0804864b   ..............K...
 0xbfa7f670   0xbfa7f684   0x00d0eff4   0xbfa7f698   0x08048505   ................
 0xbfa7f680   0x00000001   0x00000002   0x00d0f4c0   0x0804864b   ..............K...
 0xbfa7f690   0xbfa7f6a4   0x00d0eff4   0xbfa7f6b8   0x08048505   ................
 0xbfa7f6a0   0x00000002   0x00000003   0x00d0f4c0   0x0804864b   ..............K...
 0xbfa7f6b0   0xbfa7f6c4   0x00d0eff4   0xbfa7f6d8   0x08048505   ................
 0xbfa7f6c0   0x00000003   0x00000004   0x00d0f4c0   0x0804864b   ..............K...
 0xbfa7f6d0   0xbfa7f6e4   0x00d0eff4   0xbfa7f6f8   0x08048505   ................
 0xbfa7f6e0   0x00000004   0x00000005   0x00d0f4c0   0x0804864b   ..............K...
 0xbfa7f6f0   0xbfa7f704   0x00d0eff4   0xbfa7f718   0x08048505   ................
 0xbfa7f700   0x00000005   0x00000006   0x00d0f4c0   0x00d0eff4   ................
 0xbfa7f710   0x00000000   0x00000000   0xbfa7f748   0x0804854b   ........H...K...
 0xbfa7f720   0x00000006   0x00000000   0x00d0fcc0   0x00d0eff4   ................
 0xbfa7f730   0x08048570   0x08048370   0x0804857b   0x00000006   p...p...{........
 0xbfa7f740   0x08048570   0x00000000   0xbfa7f7c8   0x00bb0bb6   p...............
└──────────────────────────────────────────────────────────────────────────────┘
```

FIGURE 8.4
Memory contents starting at the address contained in the *esp* register in Figure 8.3.

immediately follows the new stack frame. This process happens every time a function is initiated. This causes the stack to grow. Note: all read/write operations to local variables use a memory addressing mode that calculates positions relative to the current stack pointer.

When a function terminates, the stack shrinks. The current function's return value is usually written to a local variable of the function that called it. The saved frame pointer value is written into the frame pointer register. Saved temp values overwrite the other register values and the instruction pointer is overwritten by the return address value. This lets the calling function continue execution from the point where it was interrupted by the new function call. Use of the stack enables recursion and encourages good programming practices. There is a problem, however, when local array variables have inadequate bounds checking.

Note where local variables are stored on the stack. C and other programming languages use pointer arithmetic when writing to an array. If the base address of array A is X, the address of $A[i]$ will usually be $X + i * s$, where s is the size of an element of A^2. When A is a local variable, it is stored on the stack. If bounds checking is not enforced, then all items stored on the stack can be overwritten and corrupted. Note that in Figure 8.1, the stack grows down and each new stack instance has a lower address value than the previous one. Since array addresses increase with each element and the local variables

---

[2]This uses the C assumption that the first element of A is 0. If the first element is 1, as in FORTRAN, the address of $A[i]$ is $X + (i - 1) * s$.

are at the lowest point on the stack in Figure 8.2, then all the elements in the stack can be replaced with new values by writing beyond the array bounds[3].

Two important facts combine to make stack smashing (a buffer overflow that writes beyond the allocated storage of a local array variable) particularly dangerous:

1. The von Neumann architecture means values written into the buffer can be executable; we discuss this further in Section 8.1.2.
2. Since the return address is stored on the stack, when the current function exits, the program resumes execution by executing the stream of instructions located at the return address.

This makes it straightforward for an attacker to write arbitrary logic into the program's address space and execute it by modifying the return address.

We will now discuss how to reverse engineer the stack (Section 8.1.1) and create *shellcode*, a sequence of binary values that can be inserted onto the stack for execution (Section 8.1.2).

8.1.1   Stack exploration

We will use Program 8.1.1 to observe and reverse engineer the stack. The program is very simple. It recursively executes the *recursion* function 6 times before executing function *InputStringNoCheck*, which prompts the user for text input. The text input is written into a local buffer where there is no bounds checking. We compile the program with command:

```
gcc -ggdb -O0 -Wall -pedantic BufferOverflowDemo.c -o BufferOverflowDemo
```

The flags in the *gcc* command are given to the compiler, because:

- *-ggdb* – Tells the compiler to produce an executable with extra information that allows the *gdb* debugger to be used,
- *-O0* – Tells the compiler to turn off all optimizations[4],
- *-Wall* – Show all warnings, and
- *-pedantic* – Show warnings related to the ANSI standards.

If we run the program with input 123, we see:

---

[3]When this is not stopped by array bounds checking

[4]This is not absolutely necessary, but I suggest students use this option for all assignments in this book. Compiler optimizations can drastically change the logic executed by the program at run time. The logic should normally be semantically identical to the original program, but the sequence of commands executed and intermediate results may be quite different from the sequence of logic given by the source code. This is because the best way for humans to express the ideas may not be the most efficient way for a computer to execute the ideas, especially in a world with multiple cores working in parallel. The complexities of code optimization are not necessary for the assignments given here and are very likely to be an unnecessary source of confusion. Many of the concepts we deal with are based on ambiguities in computer design and implementation; extra sources of confusion need to be avoided at this point.

```
./BufferOverflowDemo
Before recursion
recurse=6
recurse=5
recurse=4
recurse=3
recurse=2
recurse=1
Buffer= @@@@@
123
input=1, binary=31, i=0
Buffer= 1@@@@
input=2, binary=32, i=1
Buffer= 12@@@
input=3, binary=33, i=2
Buffer= 123@@
Buffer= 123
recurse=1
recurse=2
recurse=3
recurse=4
recurse=5
recurse=6
After recursion
```

The output values shown are straightforward. Each entry into recursion outputs the value of its parameter when it starts (decreasing values from 6 to 1) and when it returns (increasing values from 1 to 6). In the middle, we see the buffer changes in response to each getchar() call.

The student should now use gdb with the windowing option[5] and step through the program. Pay attention to memory and register values. For example, if we run this program with input value 123 and a breakpoint set at the first line of function InputStringNoCheck() the register window shows the values in Figure 8.3[6]. The stack pointer register *esp* points to $0xbfa7f610$. We set the Address value in the memory window to that value and see the values in Figure 8.4.

Let's look at the memory values for patterns. We note that memory locations "0xbfa7f65c," "0xbfa7f67c," "0xbfa7f69c," "0xbfa7f6bc," "0xbfa7f6dc," and "0xbfa7f6fc" all contain value "0x8048505." Change the display of the source window from source to mixed, so that we see the source code, its translation into assembler, and the memory locations of the individual instructions. You can then change the scope of the display from "InputStringNoCheck" to

---

[5]To start the debugger, input either "gdb -w *ProgramName Parameters*" or "insight *ProgramName Paramaters*" to the shell. For this example, I input "insight BufferOverflowDemo 123."

[6]These are the values given on a particular Linux machine. It is to be expected that the exact values will vary from machine to machine, but the process followed will provide correct values.

"recursion." Looking at that window in Figure 8.5, we see that memory location "0x8048505" corresponds to the memory location of a "mov" command that is the first assembly instruction for:

```
printf(''recurse=%d\n'' );
```

which is the first instruction after the recursive call to "recursion(i-1)." Since the same function call was made six times from the same code location, it makes sense that the same return address would be stored six times on the stack. If this value is modified at any of the six locations where it is stored on the stack, when one of the recursive function calls exits, the program will start executing instructions at the location indicated by the new value. For example, try enterring the following command into the console window (remember to change the memory locations to fit the values on your machine):

```
(gdb) set *(int *) 0xbfe8577c = 0x80484e3
```

Then use gdb to step through the code. What happens?

The gdb *set *(int *)* command modifies the memory located at position $0xbfe8577c$ to the value after =. Look at the memory display after the command is given. Note that the memory display does not show any change to the memory location. Enter the following command directly to gdb in the console window to examine the contents of the memory:

```
(gdb) x /xw 0xbfe8577c
```

Note the difference between the value displayed using x/xw and the console window. This difference exists because the memory window displays changes made by program execution; it will not respond to changes that you make to memory by your own intervention.

Examine the stack memory in Figure 8.4. Find the positions where local variables and parameters are stored on the stack[7]. Find the locations where frame pointers are stored on the stack[8]. Modify values on the stack using the *gdb set* command. Continue until you can reliably predict how these changes will modify program execution.

Modify Program 8.1.1 by adding local variables of different types to functions. Identify where the variables are stored on the stack.

We note that recompiling the program without the *-ggdb* and/or *-O0* switches will build programs with different stack data structures. The debugger needs to store information on the stack to control program flow.

Finally, run the program, step through routine *InputStringNoCheck()* one command at a time, examine the stack in the memory window, and hold down a key on the keyboard until at least 50 characters are entered. Observe what occurs.

---

[7]Hint – both variables and parameters progress from 6 to 0.
[8]Hint – frame pointer contents point to addresses that you can easily find on the stack.

In essence, this is a very simple stack smashing attack. Data input from the console writes over the stack data structure. For a successful stack smash to occur, there are two remaining steps:

1. Write *shell code* onto the stack, and
2. Modify the *instruction pointer* to contain the address of the shell code.

8.1.2   Shell code

Shell code refers to the payload of an exploit. In this case, it is the code that the buffer overflow injects into process memory.

Remember that, in the von Neumann computer architecture that we use, computer instructions are treated like data. This lets compilers translate source code into executable code. It also lets us copy prgrams to and from disks using the same commands as data files. It is elegant, simple, and useful. We now examine how this idea can be abused.

There are two issues to consider. The first issue is how to find the binary equivalent of the sequence of commands you need to execute. The second issue is how to input that sequence of binary values into the program being executed.

There are a number of techniques for finding the binary values for a sequence of command. Some of the techniques appropriate for this exercise follow:

1. Use the *gcc* compiler and *gdb*. The compiler takes C source code and translates it into binary. If you use the position independent code $-fpic$ switch during compilation, you should be able to place the code anyplace in memory without having addressing problems. In Section 8.1.1, we saw how to find the memory locations associated with a function and how to find the binary values of the words stored at that location, or
2. With *gcc* position independent code, one could insert commands into the program to open a file for binary write and write binary values from memory to the file. You can use *gdb* to find the range of memory to save and then write that range to the file. You would not need to examine memory manually, or
3. One can write a simple assembly language program and examine memory, examine the object file contents, or do something similar to option 2, or
4. Using an assembly language reference, like [425], you can directly translate the assembly code into binary values, or
5. Using a reference like [350] you can find a sequence of ASCII characters that correspond to the binary of an assembly program.

Each of these approaches is fairly straightforward, and tedious in places. I suggest that students use the approach that they feel most comfortable with.

Similarly, there are many different ways of producing a file containing shell code. These include:

1. In Section 7.3, we showed how to use perl to pipe a sequence of binary values into a program on the command line. The student can simply redirect stdout to a file instead of using a pipe,
2. If alphanumeric shell code is used, then the shell code can simply be typed using a text editor. For example, "AAAHHH" is a string of assembly instructions to increment the intel ecx rgister three times and then decrement it three times,
3. A hex editor can be used to input binary values into a file, or
4. A C program with position independent code can be programmed to write the instructions desired into a file.

Any of these ideas are appropriate. For this assignment, the code does not have to be sophisticated. One command is worth noting; the NOP $0x90$ operator does nothing. This makes it very useful for many applications.

8.2   Heap Smashing

Stack smashing attacks exploit the stack data structure. It is also possible to exploit the heap, which is the other type end of dynamic memory in Figure 8.1. Since the heap almost never contains pointers that influence control flow, to exploit the heap buffer overflows typically need to be part of a larger attack. That said, heap vulnerabilities are important and have been responsible for a number of important exploits:

*   The 2010 Aurora exploit was believed to have been used by the Chinese government to compromise companies that include Google, Northrup Grumman, Semantec, Dow Chemical, and Juniper Networks [204]. It used a heap spray exploit to place shell code into Internet Explorer and Adobe Acrobat,
*   In 2012, the VLC multimedia player had a heap overflow in its network streaming protocol allowing arbitrary code execution [414],
*   Heap sprays are a common part of drive-by download attacks on web browsers [212], and
*   A 2012 Adobe Flash zero-day vulnerability used heap spray techniques[367].

We now look at the two main ways of exploiting the heap for buffer overflow. Section 8.2.1 explains the "heap spray," an approach for loading shell code into memory. Section 8.2.2 discusses how overflowing heap buffers can corrupt memory and allow attackers to overwrite arbitrary positions in memory. These two exploits together provide the same capability as the classic stack smashing attack.

8.2.1   Code injection – heap spray

The basic concept behind the heap spray is that the heap provides a large amount of memory where shell code can be stored. To make it easier to modify a pointer value to correctly trigger the shell code, a piece of shell code can be written to the heap multiple times.

The shell code can also have a *NOP sled* prefix. Since the NOP operator (0x90 in hex) does nothing it is common practice to create a NOP sled, which is simply a long sequence of NOP operators. In this case if an instruction pointer points to anywhere in the NOP sled, then the processor continues processing NOPs until it hits and executes the shell code.

Since the heap is dynamic, it is not easy to predict where the shell code will actually be placed in memory. The heap spray makes it relatively easy to find a pointer value that is likely to work correctly. Having multiple copies of the code gives the attacker multiple targets to hit. Using NOP sleds increases the size of each individual target.

8.2.2   Heap corruption

The heap is organized as a pair of doubly linked lists. Each piece of memory (element in the linked lists) is referred to as a chunk. One list keeps track of free memory chunks; the other list keeps track of allocated memory chunks.

Free chunks are stored in bins, which are arranged by the size of the chunks. The last bin is called the wilderness and it is a single chunk situated at the top of the available memory. In almost all cases, the wilderness contains the largest piece of contiguous memory.

When the system is told to release an allocated memory chunk, it uses the two pointers in its doubly linked list. When the free command is called, the status of the heap chunk lists is shown in Figure 8.6. The free command uses the values in the forward and backward pointers to update the pointers in the previous and next chunks as shown in Figure 8.7. The chunk is no longer in the two lists and the integrity of the lists is maintained.

To smash the heap, the attacker requests two very large pieces of memory. Since they both come from the chunk, they will tend to be contiguous. This allows the attacker to write beyond the bounds of the first chunk and overwrite the forward and backward pointers in the chunk. The attacker then frees the corrupted chunk in memory.

When we have smashed the heap and changed the pointer values, the free command can be subverted to change any desired memory location. The value in the backward pointer (which we could replace with a shell code address) is written to the address pointed to by the forward pointer (which we could modify to be the function return address). This allows us to modify the control flow to execute any piece of code we desire [307].

8.3   Arc Injection

Arc injection and pointer clobbering are less complex than heap and stack smashing. Arc injection exploits programs that take advantage of functionality provided by other programs on the system [336]. The C library supports this code reuse (generally a good thing) through the *system()* and *exec()* function calls. For example, the call:

```
system("ls -l ~/Desktop > ./yada-yada.txt");
```

writes a long format listing of the user's Desktop directory into the file yada-yada.txt located in the local working directory.

The functionality provided by the *exec()* family of calls is similar; the difference is *exec()* overwrites current memory space with a new process. The exec call never returns; it replaces the current process with a new one. The other difference is *exec()* refers to a family of calls, each with a different calling convention. Refer to [379] for details about *system()* and *exec()*.

The shell code for arc injection is a simple ASCII string. The attacker finds the address of the string passed to the *system()* function call or the arguments of the *exec()* function call. The attacker then finds a buffer that can be overwritten, where the buffer's address is less than the address of the string or arguments. The attacker can then construct data to be fed into the buffer so that the target string is replaced with the ASCII shell code.

If there is sensitive data between the two addresses, it may be necessary to duplicate the sensitive data in the data constructed to execute the attack. This could occur in the assignment given in Section 8.6.

8.4   Pointer Clobbering

Pointer clobbering [336] is also fairly straightforward. If a program uses a function pointer, such as:

```
void (*FuncPtr)(int,int, char **);
```

an attacker can use a buffer overflow to modify the address pointed to by pointer *FuncPtr*. Note that it is best if the address pointed to has a similar calling frame as the function pointer prototype.

The function pointer can be redirected to shell code that the attacker inserted into the program, another function in the program, or a system routine.

If it points to a system routine, such as a function provided by libc, this can be referred to as return oriented programming [337]. Return oriented programming lets the attacker overcome many safeguards by using system calls directly in ways that were not intended.

8.5   Countermeasures

The buffer overflow vulnerability is widespread. A MITRE Corporation analysis of their Common Vulnerabilities and Exposures (CVE) database found buffer overflows to be the most common operating system vendor advisory [117]. A US Department of Homeland Security analysis of industrial control systems found 47 (42) percent of the vulnerabilities they identified during 2004-2008 (2009-2010) were due to improper input validation, which were frequently buffer overflows [9] [317].

The importance of buffer overflows has led to a number of countermeasures being developed. Of course, the best countermeasure is not having buffer overflows. Careful and correct coding is advisable. This includes using safe string handling functions when appropriate [211]. Careful coding can be augmented by the use of static analysis tools. Static analysis tools analyze computer code directly to look for errors, including a lack of (or incorrect) bounds checking [254]. Of course it is also possible to program using type safe languages, which should not, in theory, be vulnerable to buffer overflows [226]. Type safe languages include Cyclone and Java. We note a famous exploit where Java's type safety has been violated [180] by researchers, but that attack included a physical attack provoking memory errors.

Another easy way of counteracting many buffer overflows is to have the processor specify which parts of the computer memory contain data and which contain code. This feature has long been supported by hardware but was not commonly used by operating systems for many years. Windows calls this data execution prevention where it has been available since 2003. Many other common operating systems have similar features. If executable memory is write protected, it is much more difficult to insert shell code into the system.

Alternatively, many systems have countermeasures that check to see if memory has been corrupted. This is frequently done by writing a randomized value at the end of allocated memory buffers. This value is usually called a *canary* or *stack cookie*. When a buffer is overwritten, this value is modified. When this value is changed, the process is terminated due to memory corruption. Techniques exist for circumventing this in some cases. If the canary/cookie is a static value, the attacker can reverse engineer that value and

---

[9]Improper input validation also included command injection, path traversal, and cross site scripting.

construct an attack that does not disturb the canary value. If it is dynamic, two other attacks have been proposed [267]:

1. The canary value must be stored at two locations in memory, since the system needs a base value for comparision to see that the stack cookie has been modified. The attacker can change both values in memory with the attack, or

2. If the system uses an error handling mechanism, like:

    ```
    try{..}
    catch{e}{...}
    ```

    and the canary is modified within the *try* block, there are opportunities for the attacker to modify either the handler called by the *catch* block or the pointer to the handler routine.

The first method would allow the buffer overflow to occur without being noticed. In the second method memory corruption by the buffer overflow is detected, but the attacker can then use the exception handler to trigger the shell code.

The final countermeasure that we discuss uses the idea of *diversity* to make the attack more difficult [160]. For buffer overflows, diversity is usually implemented as *address space layout randomization* (ASLR) [362]. ASLR makes buffer overflows more difficult to implement, by making it harder to predict where items will be located in memory. Each stack frame can be placed on the stack with a small buffer, whose size it radomly set, between it and the preceding stack frame. Variable positions in memory can be randomized at runtime. The system could randomly choose whether the stack or heap is located at the top of memory and grows down or vice versa. Since memory positions become harder to predict, it is more difficult to craft inputs to the buffer overflow that contain correct pointer values and place them at the right location.

One way to counter ASLR is to use NOP sleds (see Section 8.2.1), by giving the attacker a region of memory to hit, instead of a single memory location.

The only buffer overflow countermeasure that is foolproof is to code carefully and verify data inputs. If data input bounds checking is done correctly, then buffer overflow attacks will not be possible.

8.6   Assignment

Consider the source code of Programs 8.1.2, 8.1.3, 8.1.4, and 8.1.5. Find at least one buffer overflow vulnerability in the program. Be able to subvert the program by making it execute arbitrary instructions that you provide. If you wish, you can modify the program by using the code in Program 8.1 to modify the byte order of the data input.

You should be able to exploit the program from the command line. Implement it in a Windows virtual machine with Cygwin installed. The grade given will depend in part on how challenging the buffer overflow vulnerability was that you exploited.

You should compile the program using this command:

```
gcc -ggdb -O0 -Wall -pedantic VulnerableCode.c -o VulnerableCode
```

Step through the program using a windowing debugger and the following inputs to understand how the program works:

```
./VulnerableCode 7 4 a.exe
./VulnerableCode 7 } a.exe
./VulnerableCode 3 ~ a.exe
./VulnerableCode 5 a.exe
./VulnerableCode 4 a.exe
./VulnerableCode 8 "%s%s%s%s%s%s"
```

Write a report explaining in detail the vulnerability you exploited and how your code worked. In particular, explain how you transfer control from the original program to the code you inserted.

Demonstrate your work with the program with the vulnerability. Compile it. Execute it using gdb. Show exactly how you manage to go from the program as written to the attack code.[10] Section 8.1.2 explains how binary shell code can be created. References [297, 41, 336] are usually useful.

Many students have been able to exploit all the vulnerabilities in the program. At least one has been able to exploit more than three vulnerabilities in one run of the program using a single (long) command line.

8.7 Problems

1. List the buffer overflow exploits given in this chapter in order of increasing difficulty. Justify your ranking.

2. Explain the basic design choices that make buffer overflows possible. Discuss, with the gift of hindsight, whether or not those choices were wise.

3. Explain in detail how dynamic memory (both stack and heap) works. Use screen captures from gdb to illustrate your concepts.

---

[10]Many online tutorials explain how to get a command prompt. That is not very useful for this assignment and more difficult than inserting a small piece of shell code.

8.8   Glossary

Address space layout randomization (ASLR): On the fly randomization of where data and pointers are stored in memory to make buffer flow attacks more difficult to implement.

Arc injection: Buffer overflow that overwrites the command line inputs into a *system()* or *exec()* system call.

Canary: A randomized value inserted at the end of buffers, stack frames, and other memory locations that is used by the system to detect memory corruption.

Diversity: A security technique that makes system operation less predictable in order to make it more difficult to reliably attack the system.

Heap: Dynamic memory that can be allocated and freed by calls to the operating system.

Heap smashing: A buffer overflow exploit that overwrites pointers in the heap, in order to trick free commands into modifying pointers.

Heap spray: Inserting multiple copies of program shell code on the heap, since having multiple targets to aim at increases the likelihood that some target will be hit.

NOP: An instruction that does nothing.

NOP sled: A sequence of NOPs that can be used to make a buffer overflow exploit easier.

Pointer clobbering: Buffer overflow that overwrites the address contained in a function point.

SEGFAULT: System error triggered by an illegal memory access.

Shell code: The payload for a buffer overflow exploit.

Stack: Local data storage for functions that enables recursion.

Stack cookie: A type of canary value used to protect the stack.

Stack smashing: A buffer overflow exploit that overwrites a local data array in a function.

tatic analysis: Verification of computer source code to find flaws.

von Neumann architecture: Basic design of most computers, where instructions can be processed as data.

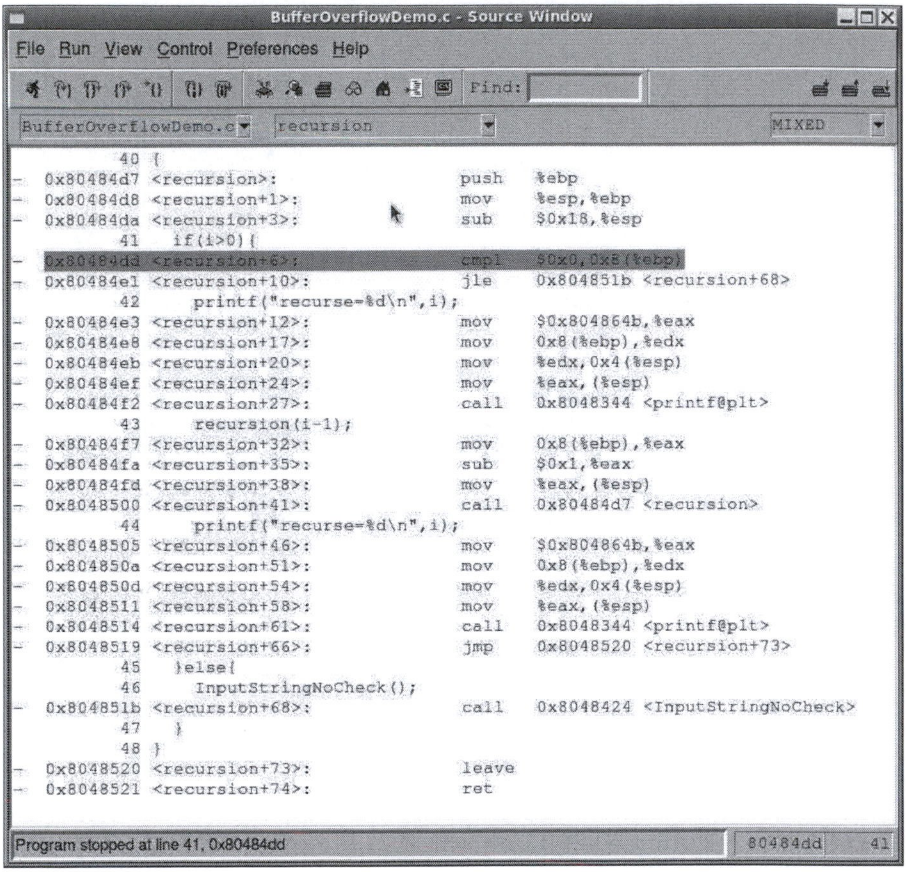
BufferOverflowDemo.c - Source Window
File Run View Control Preferences Help
Find:
BufferOverflowDemo.c
recursion
MIXED
40 {
0x80484d7 <recursion>: push %ebp
0x80484d8 <recursion+1>: mov %esp,%ebp
0x80484da <recursion+3>: sub $0x18,%esp
41 if(i>0){
0x80484dd <recursion+6>: cmpl $0x0,0x8(%ebp)
0x80484e1 <recursion+10>: jle 0x804851b <recursion+68>
42 printf("recurse=%d\n",i);
0x80484e3 <recursion+12>: mov $0x804864b,%eax
0x80484e8 <recursion+17>: mov 0x8(%ebp),%edx
0x80484eb <recursion+20>: mov %edx,0x4(%esp)
0x80484ef <recursion+24>: mov %eax,(%esp)
0x80484f2 <recursion+27>: call 0x8048344 <printf@plt>
43 recursion(i-1);
0x80484f7 <recursion+32>: mov 0x8(%ebp),%eax
0x80484fa <recursion+35>: sub $0x1,%eax
0x80484fd <recursion+38>: mov %eax,(%esp)
0x8048500 <recursion+41>: call 0x80484d7 <recursion>
44 printf("recurse=%d\n",i);
0x8048505 <recursion+46>: mov $0x804864b,%eax
0x804850a <recursion+51>: mov 0x8(%ebp),%edx
0x804850d <recursion+54>: mov %edx,0x4(%esp)
0x8048511 <recursion+58>: mov %eax,(%esp)
0x8048514 <recursion+61>: call 0x8048344 <printf@plt>
0x8048519 <recursion+66>: jmp 0x8048520 <recursion+73>
45 }else{
46 InputStringNoCheck();
0x804851b <recursion+68>: call 0x8048424 <InputStringNoCheck>
47 }
48 }
0x8048520 <recursion+73>: leave
0x8048521 <recursion+74>: ret
Program stopped at line 41, 0x80484dd
80484dd
41

FIGURE 8.5
A display where the program source and binary codes are interleaved. Note that the interleaved code is shown for the recursion() function.

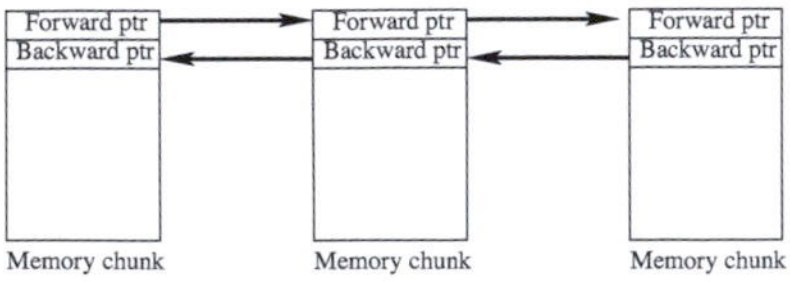
Forward ptr
Backward ptr
Memory chunk
Forward ptr
Backward ptr
Memory chunk
Forward ptr
Backward ptr
Memory chunk

FIGURE 8.6
Normally, the doubly linked list has pointers to both the next (Forward ptr) and previous (Backward ptr) chunk of memory that has been allocated to the process.

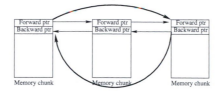

FIGURE 8.7

When memory needs to be freed, the system takes the address stored in the backward (forward) ptr and writes into the backward (forward) pointer of the chunk pointed to by the forward (backward) pointer. This removes the allocated chunk from both lists and maintains their integrity.

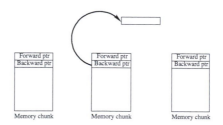

FIGURE 8.8

If the forward and backward pointers of the chunk have been corrupted, the free command allows us to set the value of (almost) any address in memory to any arbitrary value. We can put the shell code address in the backward pointer of the chunk and an address pointing to where the function return address is stored in the forward pointer. When the function exits, the shell code will be executed.

```
/*
  Name - VulnerableCode.C
  Date - 09/22/2005
  Programmer - R. R. Brooks

  Purpose - Illustrate multiple vulnerabilities involving buffer
  overflow attacks. Contains a series of subroutines exhibiting
  poor coding practices.

  Input - A vector of numeric values, followed by a string filename.

  Output - Nothing useful. The program merely serves as a template
  for allowing students to exploit the various coding mistakes made.

 */
#include <stdio.h>
#include <stdlib.h>
#include <unistd.h>
#include <fcntl.h>

int GlobalBuf[42];

void SmashHeap(int argnum, char **argv)
{
  int *DynamicMem;
  int TempChar;
  int i=0;
  int f1;

  printf("In SmashHeap(argc)\n");
  DynamicMem=malloc(24 * sizeof(int));
  if((f1=open(argv[argnum-1],0))==-1)
    printf("Error-can not open file %s \n",argv[argnum-1]);
  while(read(f1,&TempChar,4)>0){
    DynamicMem[i++]=TempChar;
    printf("i=%i ,sizeof(char)=%i,sizeof(int)=%i \n",i,
    sizeof(char),sizeof(int));
  }
}
```

Algorithm Description 8.1.2: First part of program vulnerable to numerous
buffer overflow attacks.

```
void EnterDataToVulnerableBuffer(int *Buffer,int argc,char **argv)
{
  int TempChar;
  int i=0;
  int f1;

  printf("In EnterDataToVulnerableBuffer()\n");
  if((f1=open(argv[argc-1],0))==-1)
    printf("Error-can not open file %s \n",argv[argc-1]);
  while(read(f1,&TempChar,4)>0){
    Buffer[i++]=TempChar;

    printf("i=%i ,sizeof(char)=%i,sizeof(int)=%i \n",i,
    sizeof(char),sizeof(int));
  }
}


void VulnerableLocalData(int argc, char **argv)
{
  int BufOve[14];

  printf("In VulnerableLocalData()\n");

  EnterDataToVulnerableBuffer(BufOve,argc,argv);
}


void RecursivePrefixLocal(int i,int argc,char **argv)
{
  printf("In RecursivePrefixLocal(%i)\n",i);

  if(--i) RecursivePrefixLocal(i,argc,argv);
  else VulnerableLocalData(argc,argv);
}


void AttackGlobal(int argc, char **argv)
{
  int TempChar;
  int i=0;
  int f1;

  printf("In AttackGlobal()\n");
  printf("argc=%i, argv[%i]=%s \n",argc,argc,argv[argc-1]);
  if((f1=open(argv[argc-1],0))==-1)
    printf("Error-can not open file %s \n",argv[argc-1]);
  while(read(f1,&TempChar,4)>0){
    GlobalBuf[i++]=TempChar;
    printf("i=%i ,sizeof(char)=%i,sizeof(int)=%i \n",i,
    sizeof(char),sizeof(int));
  }
}
```

Algorithm Description 8.1.3: Second part of program vulnerable to numerous buffer overflow attacks.

```
void RecursivePrefixGlobal(int i,int argc, char **argv)
{
  printf("In RecursivePrefixGlobal(%i)\n",i);
  printf("argc=%i, argv[%i]=%s \n",argc,argc,argv[argc-1]);
  if(--i) RecursivePrefixGlobal(i,argc,argv);
  else AttackGlobal(argc,argv);
}

void ArcInjection(char *R)
{
  printf("In ArcInjection()\n");
  system(R);
}
void PrintfVulnerability(char *F)
{
  int x;
  char buf [100];
  char buf2[100];
  x = 1;
  strncpy(buf2, F, sizeof buf2);
  snprintf(buf, sizeof buf, buf2);
  printf("Buffer size is: (%d) \nData input: %s \n",strlen (buf),buf);
  printf ("X equals: %d/ in hex: %x\nMemory address for x: (%p) \n",
          x, x, &x) ;
  printf(buf);
  printf("\n");
  printf ("\x25s %p \n",buf,buf);
}

void PrintfVulnerability(char *F)
{
  printf(F);
}
```

Algorithm Description 8.1.4: Third part of program vulnerable to numerous buffer overflow attacks.

```
void (*FuncPtr)(int,int, char **);

int main(int argc, char **argv)
{
  char Command[]="ls >yada.dat                    ";
  int i=1;

  FuncPtr=RecursivePrefixLocal;
  while(i < argc-1){
    printf("main loop i=%d, argv[i]=%s, %d, argv[argc-1]=%s\n",i,
   argv[i],argv[i][0],argv[argc-1]);
    switch(argv[i][0]-48){
    case 1:
      SmashHeap(argc,argv);
      break;
    case 2:
      VulnerableLocalData(argc,argv);
      break;
    case 3:
      RecursivePrefixLocal(argv[++i][0]-48,argc,argv);
      break;
    case 4:
      AttackGlobal(argc,argv);
      break;
    case 5:
      ArcInjection(Command);
      break;
    case 6:
      FuncPtr(argv[++i][0]-48,argc,argv);
      break;
    case 7:
      RecursivePrefixGlobal(argv[++i][0]-48,argc,argv);
      break;
    case 8:
      PrintfVulnerability(argv[++i]);
      break;
    default:
      printf("%s is not recognized by this program",argv[i++]);
      printf(" enter in a sequence of 1 digit numbers \n separated");
      printf(" by spaces.\n");
      printf("Numbers 1-7 refer to functions with buffer overflow");
      printf(" vulnerabilities.\n");
      printf("Number 8 does a format string attack\n.");
    }
    i++;
  }
  return(1);
}
```

Algorithm Description 8.1.5: Final part of program vulnerable to numerous buffer overflow attacks.

```
while(read(f1,&TempChar,4)>0){
   TempChar=((unsigned)(TempChar&0xFF000000)>>24)|
           ((TempChar&0x00FF0000)>>8)|
           ((TempChar&0x0000FF00)<<8)|((TempChar&0x000000FF)<<24);
   DynamicMem[i++]=TempChar;
   printf("i=%i ,sizeof(char)=%i,sizeof(int)=%i \n",i,
   sizeof(char),sizeof(int));
}
```

Algorithm Description 8.1.6: Alternate while loop for reading buffers that swap bytes. Can be used to handle problems due to different memory architectures with different most significant byte locations.

9

Polymorphic Virus – Advanced Case Study Project

CONTENTS

This chapter discusses computer viruses. Section 9.1 discusses how viruses work in general. Section 9.2 explains anti-virus tools and theoretical limits on their effectiveness. We provide notional examples of simple viruses in Sections 9.3, and 9.4. Section 9.5 explains limits on the spread of viruses on a single host. These limits explain why current operating systems are ill-suited for containing viruses.

A common technique for defeating anti-virus programs is to make the virus polymorphic. Sections 9.6 and 9.7 provide background information on polymorphic code. We describe common techniques for detecting polymorphism in Section 9.8 as well as a new research direction that creates *Frankenstein viruses* (Section 9.9) that are difficult to detect.

Section 9.10 concludes this Chapter by providing a case study assignment for students to implement. We suggest students use the same virtual machine (VM) used in Chapter 8. The VM should run Windows XP with Cygwin installed. We need to have both the *gcc* compiler and an NTFS file system on the virtual machine.

I strongly recommend that students refer to the original information sources concerning viruses as much as they can. In particular, Dr. Mark Ludwig's pioneering texts ([275, 277, 278, 276]) are invaluable. They explain how viruses work in detail and are the best descriptions of how to program Windows (MS/DOS) that I have found. Unfortunately, most of these books are out of print. Also the code examples in *The Little Black Book of Computer*

Viruses and *The Giant Black Book of Computer Viruses* use the current programming tools from when they were written (mid-1980's assembler), which makes them awkward for today's students to use. Another important source of virus information is Dr. Fred Cohen's dissertation [119], which is as important today as the day it was published. We discuss his major findings in this chapter.

Read the entire chapter before starting work on viruses. We discuss basic hygiene in Section 9.10. That discussion is essential. Following a few basic rules allows this assignment to be done safely. No student wants to have to reformat their hard drive during the semester.

9.1   Virus Basics

As mentioned in Chapter 1, the idea of self-reproducing programs dates back to Von Neumann's 1966 paper on Cellular Automata [99] and the term "virus" program was used in a science fiction novel in 1972. But the first practical description the security threat posed by viruses was Dr. Fred Cohen's 1986 dissertation [119]. This dissertation predates the appearance of viruses *in the wild*.

We define a computer virus as a program, analogous to biological viruses, that reproduces by inserting itself into existing programs or data structures. The differences between this definition and others[1] is now rather pedantic. Current malware usually integrates ideas from worms, viruses, etc. to create more sophisticated and nuanced attacks.

When the operating system creates a process, it loads a program binary into memory and passes control to the program. Figure 8.1 is a notional view of the computer's logical memory space. Usually, the text and initialized data segments are contained in the executable. Process initiation passes control to some location in the text segment, which contains the program binary.

A virus disrupts this process. It inserts a copy of itself into the program binary. The virus modifies the start address of the program to point to the code inserted into the binary (the virus itself). Once the virus finishes executing, it passes control to the program's original start address. If the virus is relatively small and fast, it is likely to go unnoticed by a victim whose files have been infected.

As mentioned in Section 7.6 when the virus executes, it typically has the following components:

1. *Search routine* – finds new files to infect. Normally, a call to the file system finds programs of the desired type for infection (often *.exe*

---

[1]Another common definition for computer viruses that require human interaction to spread.

or *.com*) where the current program has write access. Care needs to be taken in this step. A call that causes noticeable disk activity may cause the victim to notice something wrong with their computer. Attempts to infect files where the process does not have write access may be written to a security log.

2. *Copy routine* – inserts a copy of the virus into the susceptible file. The virus needs to insert itself into the program binary without disrupting the original program.[2] It also modifies the host program, so that the virus runs before normal processing starts.

3. *Payload* – is logic triggered by the virus some future time. The virus is a tool for propagating the payload logic (which is frequently malicious). We will not discuss payloads. For this book, the payload is an arbitrary piece of code.

4. *Profile* – helps the search routine determine if a file has already been infected. This lets it avoid repeatedly re-infecting the same files. Re-infecting files is senseless, since when files get re-infected they grow. Executable files that steadily increase in size indicate a computer virus infection.

In this chapter, we discuss only executable file viruses. But these are not the only kind of virus. For example, boot sector viruses exist that are triggered whenever the computer boots. They typically look for removable media to infect. Viruses also hide in the file system. One clever place to hide viruses is the bad block list on a disk. Anti-virus programs usually ignore bad blocks, since scanning them potentially harms the disk drive. Interested students are referred to Dr. Ludwig's books [275, 277, 278, 276].

9.2 Anti-virus

It is impossible to infallibly decide whether or not an arbitrary program contains virus code, just as it is impossible to infallibly decide whether an arbitrary program has most non-trivial properties. Why virus detection is undecidable was first presented in Dr. Cohen's dissertation [119]. We reproduce his argument here.

Suppose a function, let's call it *DetectVirus()*, infallibly detects whether or not a program contains a virus. An attacker can then write a virus, let's call it *SneakyVirus()*, that infects files only if *DetectVirus(SneakyVirus())* is false. Consider this pseudo-code:

```
If(DetectVirus(FileInfectedWithSneakyVirus)){
  ExecuteOriginalProgram;
```

---

[2]A successful virus will remain hidden and spread the infection for a long time.

```
}else{
  InfectNewFilesWithVirus;
  ExecuteOriginalProgram;
}
```

If you detect the program as infected with *SneakyVirus()* as a virus, you will have a false positive, since it is not a virus in that case. If you say it is not a virus, then it is in fact a virus and you have a false negative. No matter what decision *DetectVirus(SneakyVirus())* makes, the answer is wrong. We have created a paradox.

Student's familiar with computational theory have probably noticed that this is very simple to Turing's approach [403] to proving that the *entscheidungsproblem* (halting problem) is undecidable (impossible to solve).

Yet, in spite of the fact that it is impossible to solve the general problem as to whether or not an arbitrary program contains a virus, there are a large number of anti-virus products. This does not mean that anti-virus programs are solving an unsolvable problem. Current products do not consider the general problem. Anti-virus tools look for specific known viruses.

To identify viruses, anti-virus vendors gather examples of malware. When a vendor has a large enough set of files that are infected with the same virus, they can analyze the files and find bit patterns that can be used to identify files infected with that virus. These are used as signatures. Files on the computer, files being downloaded, files about to be accessed, etc. are scanned quickly to determine whether or not they contain the signature of an infection. The anti-virus company regularly updates the set of signatures that their software uses to scan client machines for infections.

While this approach is practical and useful, it has the following drawbacks:

- They can not identify new attacks, since they need examples of infected files,
- Over time the number of signatures for known viruses (or malware) can only increase; this gives vendors two alternatives (neither of which is satisfactory):

  1. Let the signature database grow and grow, this consumes disk space on client machines and makes scans slower, or
  2. periodically remove obsolete attacks from the database, which makes it possible for old attacks to be reintroduced and place clients at risk.

- Virus writers can tweak their code to change the part of the program in the signature in order to foil the scanners, and
- False positives can have catastrophic effects on client machines, such as disabling antivirus updates [261], or destroying the operating system [285].

Another approach is to try to identify the types of things malicious software does and have heuristics trigger alarms when those things occur. Unfortunately, this use of heuristics frequently has very high false alarm rates.

9.3 Pseudo-virus with Alternate Data Streams

This section describes a technically unsophisticated pseudo-virus that, while requiring minimal programming, adequately illustrates the concepts behind virus infection and reproduction. It requires a Windows virtual machine with an NTFS file system (Windows XP with Cygwin installed suggested), and a compiler capable of creating *.exe* files (gcc suggested).

This pseudo-virus takes advantage of NTFS support of *Alternate Data Streams* (ADS). ADS is an implementation of the *fork* file system feature. A fork, such as ADS, can be considered as associating a name-space with each file. In the Windows file-systems that support ADS, multiple bit-streams can be associated with a single file. For example if file *host.exe* has 3 forks *fork1*, *fork2*, and *fork3* associated with it, those three forks would be addressed as *host.exe:fork1*, *host.exe:fork2*, and *host.exe:fork3*, respectively. A shell *dir* command, however, will display the original file *host.exe* with its original size. The forks are ignored. As of Windows Vista, *dir* includes options to show forks.

ADS has been used in the past as a simple way of hiding information from casual observers. We note that data forensics experts are well aware of forks, and most data forensics tools will detect any data items hidden in a fork.

For example, the presence of file *virus.exe* could be obscured by creating a fork of file *host.exe* by using the shell command:

```
type virus.exe > host.exe:virus.exe
del virus.exe
```

Give the *dir* command to verify that the file *virus.exe* no longer exists. Now, use this command to verify that you can run the file:

```
start ./host.exe:virus.exe
```

We now have all the information necessary to create our pseudo-virus.

Let's say that we have infected a file *infected.exe*. When *infected.exe* runs, it can discover the name of the *.exe* file being run by inspecting *argv[]*. It then needs to first find a potential victim. We can do this by using the *stat()* function (or equivalent) to find **.exe* executable files. Let's say the file to be infected is named *host.exe*. The pseudo-virus needs only to construct the following shell commands and execute them in turn by using *system()* calls:

```
copy host.exe tmp.exe
copy infected.exe host.exe
type tmp.exe > host.exe:oldprogram.exe
rem tmp.exe
start ./infected.exe:oldprogram.exe
```

This logic replaces *host.exe* with the virus code, and then stores the old *host.exe* as *host.exe:oldprogram.exe*. After having infected the new file and removing any temporary storage the executable *infected.exe* executes the logic of the original *infected.exe*, which is now stored in *infected.exe:oldprogram.exe*.

To complete this implementation, the student can write a C program that does string manipulation and calls to *system()*.

9.4 Simple Virus – Timid

For the sake of simplicity and ease of coding, the assignment will build from the pseudo-virus in Section 9.3. This section will review one of the simplest possible viruses, Timid, which was presented by Dr. Mark Ludwig in *The Little Black Book of Computer Viruses* and *The Giant Black Book of Computer Viruses* [275, 278]. The original Timid source code is available in those two books, which are also the best introductions I have found to DOS and Windows systems programming. It can also be easily found on-line. Unfortunately, Timid is written in 1980's assembler and must be compiled using old versions of Microsoft or Borland Assemblers, which makes working with Timid awkward for many students. In spite of this, it is worth sketching how Timid works. More advanced students may want to download Timid, search deadware sites for obsolete assemblers, and work with a real virus instead of the pseudo-virus.

Timid infects MS-DOS command files, which can be recognized by their ".COM" extension. When a program runs, it is loaded into memory using either a *system()* or *exec* function call. When *system()* is used, the current process is over-written. The *exec()* call creates a new process. MS-DOS command files have only one segment, which means that they can not consume more than 64 kilobytes of memory. This also means that this single segment can be read directly into memory. The binary of the command file is placed into memory directly at position 0x100. The format of the file is not modified. Compare this with the typical C program memory layout in Figure 8.1. Note that because of this MS-DOS command files have neither heap nor stack memory. The ".COM" program execution starts with the binary command located in memory at 0x100.

This allows us to make a very simple virus. Viruses that infect either Linux ELF files or Microsoft EXE files will be more complicated. ELF files can map multiple segments, which may include access to Linux shared objects. The Microsoft portable executable format also allows the program to access multiple segments, which may access dynamic link libraries. Viruses attacking these files need to parse the file header and symbol table. This is not particularly difficult, but can be time consuming and is not absolutely necessary for virus construction.

The logic behind Timid is extremely simple. Timid first searches the disk for a file to infect. It looks for any file in the local directory with a ".COM" extension. To avoid reinfecting files, Timid then checks whether or not the file has been infected. This is done by placing the letters "VI" near the beginning of the file during infection. Once Timid finds an uninfected ".COM" file, it infects it.

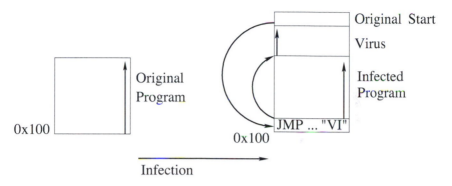

FIGURE 9.1
In a Microsoft command (.COM) file, execution starts at position 0x100. A Timid infection jumps from position 0x100 to Timid. After Timid infects a new file, it replaces the first few words in memory with the original values. It then jumps to position 0x100 and the original file executes as if nothing ever happened.

Infection is simple. Timid makes a copy of the first few words of the file to be infected. These words are replaced with a command to start executing binary commands placed after the existing file followed by the letters "VI." Timid appends itself to the end of the ".COM" file. It appends the first few words of the original file after itself.

Once Timid has finished infecting the new file, it over-writes the first few words of its process in memory with the original values. Finally timid jumps to position 0x100, at which point the original program executes. This process is illustrated in Figure 9.1.

Timid modifies the ".COM" it infects on disk. It also modifies the ".COM" that is currently executing in memory.

9.5 Infection Spreading

Now that we have explored two example viruses, we consider the problem of how a virus propagates. There is a major difference between virus and worm propagation. Worm propagation is based on it finding new hosts on the network that contain the vulnerability that the worm exploits. The virus does not exploit a vulnerability. The virus obeys existing access rules [119]. Both the ADS pseudo-virus and Timid follow existing access rules. In the normal course of events, there is no reason for an alarm to be written into an audit file.

How far can a virus spread? In most modern computer systems, it is rather easy for a virus to spread throughout the entire system. This is because operating systems typically handle access rights in a manner that is friendly to viruses.

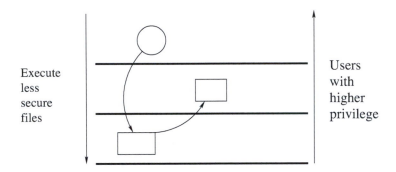

FIGURE 9.2
In most systems, users with high privilege can modify all the files with less privilege. They can also modify those executables. As a result if a superuser ever executes a virus, then the whole system is compromised.

The current security model is presented in Figure 9.2. Superusers have root access to machines. They can read, write, and execute any file on the machine. This means that if a superuser ever executes an infected file, the file can spread throughout the whole system.

A better model is shown in Figure 9.3. If users can only run programs protected from modification by them, infections can only move from more to less secure and infections have a limited range.

One could compare this concept with the separation of powers in the US Constitution. The legislature can write the laws, but they can not execute them. The president executes the laws, but can not modify them. The more power any branch of the government has, the more its actions should be overseen by an independent authority.

Dr. Cohen's thesis proves these ideas by using partially ordered sets (PO-Sets) to find what regions of the system are subject to infection by any given user.

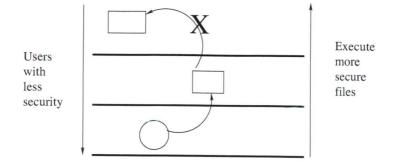

FIGURE 9.3
A better approach would restrict the programs that can be run by superusers. As long as users can only execute files that they are not allowed to modify, infections can only move within a limited part of the system.

9.6   Self-modifying Code

Viruses rely on programs modifying programs surreptitiously. Self-modifying code is generally seen negatively in part because viruses have used this concept maliciously. Many virus and buffer overflow countermeasures include making it illegal to write to executable memory.

Studying the example viruses, though, the student should be able to see that self-modifying code is not absolutely necessary for writing viruses. It is possible to exploit dynamic link libraries (DLLs) or modify function pointers to achieve the same functionality. In fact, many rootkits[3] subvert DLLs and function pointers to subvert secure portions of the operating system that they should not be able to modify [77].

In addition, there are good reasons for self-modifying code. One common reason is using compression to reduce the size of programs. Code can be expanded only when needed for execution. Another good reason is code optimization. Just in time compilation has been widely used in interpreted languages, including LISP, Smalltalk, and Java, to speed up execution.

Self-modifying programs are difficult to write correctly. They involve metaprocessing and it can be difficult to foresee all the consequences of a program that dynamically changes itself.

On the other hand, virus detection relies on finding reliable patterns that the anti-virus software can use to detect infections when they occur. If virus writers can modify their code reliably, then they may be able to foil the anti-virus software companies. But when virus writers modify their code, they still need to recognize infected files. Reinfecting files is bad for many reasons:

---

[3]A rootkit attacks the operating system itself in order to remain hidden.

1. It wastes time and resources for the virus, and
2. Executable files that grow and grow are an obvious indication of a virus infection.

Of course, anti-virus companies can look for programs that change themselves dynamically. They do, however, have to distinguish between viruses that change themselves on the fly and normal optimization, compression, and dynamic linking.

9.7 Simple Polymorphism

There are many ways a virus can modify itself, making itself polymorphic. One common way is to simply add NOP[4] instructions in the middle of code. If all memory addresses are relative and there are no jumps over a piece of code, it is easy to simply add or subtract NOP instructions without modifying program semantics[5].

Another common technique is to re-order the program. A well designed program can possibly be split into chunks that can be shuffled with each infection.

Alternatively, junk code can be inserted into the program. Branch instructions can be constructed that make it impossible for the junk code to be executed, without being obvious.

These approaches all make it difficult to interpret programs and make life more difficult for anti-virus developers. These approaches are all forms of program obfuscation[6] that can be used to modify programs on the fly [120] :

- Replace procedure calls with in-line copies.
- Take two separate code components and merge them into a common procedure.
- Interleave two separate code components.
- Make multiple copies of the same subroutine to hide or change calling patterns.
- Modify loop structures by combining, splitting, or unrolling them.
- Reorder statements, loops, or expressions.
- Insert dead code.
- Replace library calls and standard constructs with non-standard ones, or
- Parallelize code segments.

---

[4]A NOP instruction (literally "no operation") does nothing except advance the program counter. It has a binary value of 0x90 on Intel processors.

[5]Literally, semantics refers to program meaning. In this context, it means that the programs act the same way and produce the same results.

[6]Students may refer to the on-line *International Obfuscated C Code Competition* (http://www.ioccc.org/) for new innovations in this domain.

9.8 Packing and Encryption

By now, students should have realized that obfuscations are pretty weak. More sophisticated tools would encode and decode the virus directly. The two most reasonable ways of doing this would be to either encrypt or compress the virus code.

Encryption could use any of the algorithms mentioned in Chapter 3. This requires the attacker to code encryption and decryption functions that are independent of the virus. The decryption function can not be encrypted, since there would be no decryption routine to translate it into an executable form. The encryption routine also needs access to a key in clear-text that can be used to recover the original virus code. Typically symmetric encryption is used, since the key needs to be available on the host in clear text. The most common form of encryption is to XOR the code with a non-zero randomized bit-stream.

The Dark Avenger is credited with producing the *Mutation Engine* in the early 1990's, which was probably the first widely available tool for making viruses polymorphic. Dr. Ludwig released source code for the Many-hoops virus, which includes the *Visible Mutation Engine (VME)* in [278]. Source code for a program that mutates its own source code can be found in both [276] and many winning entries of the International Obfuscated C Code Contest.

In Chapter 3 we discuss homomorphic encryption, which allows encrypted programs to execute in their encrypted form. This approach is still very much a research topic. Neither practical nor efficient implementations are known, but a practical homomorphic system would have clear applications for developing polymorphic malware.

A number of scripting languages allow programs and data structures to be serialized (written to disk), sometimes in a compressed format. One good example of this would be Java "jar" files, where the Java classes are contained with a zipped archive. In particular for mobile code applications, reducing the volume required to store code can have real advantages. For virus and malware writers, this code "packing" provides ready made primitives for making malware polymorphic and hard to detect. Because this functionality is fairly widely used it can be difficult to differentiate between programs packed for legitimate purposes and obfuscated malware. A discussion of commercial code packers (like UPX), their use in hiding malware, and countermeasures can be found in [436].

We note that both file encryption and file compression will typically create files with higher entropy values than normal programs. One simple technique is to compute the entropy values of binary programs and flag programs with high entropy as suspicious.

9.9   Frankenstein Viruses

Since high entropy values are suspicious, it would be useful for malware writers to create programs that can be polymorphic and difficult to differentiate from their environment. One idea is to develop *Frankenstein viruses* [292].

These viruses are built by combining pieces of code copied directly from the operating system that hosts them. The malware writer creates an outline of the desired logic. This outline is a higher level semantic description of the needed functionality. He then uses ideas from return oriented programming [337], which finds ways of abusing operating system functionality by identifying "gadgets" in the code of the operating system. A gadget is a small piece of code that can be launched by jumping directly into the operating system to accomplish a sub-task. By stitching together a series of gadgets, the Frankenstein virus can be created almost exclusively from parts of the operating system. The idea is that the operating system code will not be suspicious and the malware will not be detected.

9.10   Assignment

For the sake of safety, all work on this assignment needs to be done in the security laboratory. The security laboratory has an isolated network segment, so that rogue programs will be contained within that segment. When writing and modifying your virus, work within your virtual machine. Do not attach removable media to the virtual machine once you have started running the virus. This keeps the virus contained within the virtual environment. Working with viruses is reasonably safe, so long as everyone keeps viruses within the virtual machines in the isolated laboratory.

Use the same virtual machine as with the buffer overflow assignment. The Cygwin environment under Windows XP provides a Linux code development environment and avoids some of the newer security mechanisms.

Using only a virtual machine in the security laboratory, modify a virus. I suggest using either the ADS pseudo-virus or the Timid virus (source code can be easily found on the web).

The initial program finds uninfected executables that it can modify and insert itself into the uninfected program. Insert an innocuous payload that does something non-malicious. A good payload could print a message on the screen, for example. Infected files must be able to further propagate the virus.

You must modify this virus to make it polymorphic. The virus will modify itself each time it is run. This should make the virus as impervious as possible to virus scanning software. The polymorphic virus must be able to recognize infected files and not reinfect them.

Under no conditions should you test these programs on any machine, except a VMWARE virtual machine in the laboratory.

Produce a report that:

- Explains in detail how your virus works,
- Describes how far your virus can propagate if started in a user account, versus in a root account.
- Considers how to predict the rate and breadth of the virus propagation.

Demonstrate the functioning virus to your instructor. Have some way of showing to the instructor that your program infects files that were pristine before execution and does not reinfect infected files. Show that the virus modifies itself enough to foil virus scanners. Explain to the instructor the limitations of your approach.

9.11 Problems

1. How do Microsoft command files (.COM) differ from other executable file formats?

2. Describe a security policy that would contain viruses and not let them spread throughout an entire computer system. Why are policies of this type not currently used?

3. What preconditions must exist for a virus to be able to infect other files?

4. The Ebola virus spreads quickly and kills the people it infects within a few days of infection. The effects of Ebola are obvious and very disturbing. The HIV virus spreads slowly. HIV infections can take years to develop into a disease. The effects of HIV are hidden for decades. Which virus is the greater health risk for society? What lessons does this teach us about computer viruses?

9.12 Glossary

Alternate data stream: A private name space associated with a file in some file systems.

Frankenstein virus: A virus stitched together from small code gadgets copied from the operating system.

NOP: A NOP instruction does nothing except advance the program counter.

Packer: Functions that compress executable code.

PO-Set: A partially ordered set (PO-Set) is a set that includes a less than or equals relation. This relation provides an ordering that is reflexive, antisymmetric, and transitive. In a PO-set there may be some elements where the order is not defined.

Polymorphic: A program that while remaining semantically consistent may be implemented in many ways.

Rootkit: Malware that inserts itself into or below the operating system in order to avoid detection.

Semantics: Where syntax refers to data format, semantics refers to data meaning. For programs, semantics generally means the functionality of a program.

Undecidable: A logic problem where there is no possible way to determine the correct answer.

10

Web Security

CONTENTS

The World Wide Web concept originated with Tim Berners-Lee at CERN, the *Conseil Européene pour la Recherche Nucléaire* in Geneva. The main idea was to create a hyper-text language that took advantage of the Internet. The development of the Mosaic web browser at the National Center for Supercomputing Applications (NCSA) in the early 1990's provided a simple user interface for the web.

Web browsers became the standard user interface for most computer applications. The development of Web 2.0 concepts, that support data integration from many separate entities on the Internet, have made user access to data easier.

In the process, web browsers have become increasingly complex. Browsers include scripting language interpreters and let users open many tabs to simultaneously work with multiple sites. Since the HTML protocol that the web is built on is stateless, developers implemented cookies. Cookies are small pieces of data that are used to create state-like functionality.

It became natural to use the web interface to support commercial and financial applications. To counteract the dangers of sending financial information, such as credit card numbers, in clear-text, the secure http (http-s) protocol was developed. In Chapter 4, we have discussed many issues related to the http-s secure sockets layer technologies. In this Chapter, we discuss web browser security. It provides a very brief introduction to selected web security issues. Browsers are complicated pieces of software; more security issues are found every day.

Section 10.1 explains what cross site scripting (XSS) is and how it works. XSS is a type of simple injection attack. Section 10.2 discusses cross site request forgery (XSRF or CSRF). XSRF attacks allow sessions in one active browser tab to access activity in another tab of the same browser. Instead of discussing a web-specific class of attack, Section 10.3 discusses man-in-the-browser (MITB) attacks. These attacks are a simple adaptation of common attack principles to a very large, complex, and tempting target, the web browser. We finish this chapter with Section 10.4 discussing penetration testing concepts for web applications.

10.1 Cross Site Scripting (XSS)

Cross site scripting (XSS) is in the Open Web Application Security Project (OWASP) list of top ten security vulnerabilities [329]. The basic XSS vulnerability occurs when html code displays input that comes from the user. The user can perform a simple injection attack, like the others listed in Chapter 7. If the user input includes scripting tags, then the browser can be tricked into executing script provided by the user. Simple example inputs could include[1]:

- `<script> alert('XSS');</script>`
- `<a onmouseover="alert('XSS')">xss link</a>`

either one of which could be triggered into displaying an alert box saying "XSS." The XSS attack classes are:

- *Stored XSS* – When user inputs are stored as part of the web page, such as user comments and reviews,
- *Reflected XSS* – When user inputs are echoed by the server, frequently this is information embedded in a URL, or
- *DOM XSS* – When data inputs modify the web page document object model.

XSS can be used in many malicious ways. This includes stealing user credentials or hijacking web sessions. This information can allow attackers to order goods from e-commerce sites, charge items to the user's credit card, or access the user's on-line banking service.

As with SQL injection, a common way of countering this vulnerability is to sanitize inputs. The sanitizer replaces symbols that instruct the browser to interpret inputs as scripting instructions with symbols that the browser ignores. It should be noted that there are many ways of encoding scripting commands that browsers will interpret and execute. Numerous html encoding tools exist. Unfortunately, these tools are not perfect and miss some dangerous inputs [423, 422]. Running the same sanitizer over input twice can even, in some cases, result in re-enabling previously disabled attacks.

---

[1]An example XSS vulnerable website is located at *http://www.insecurelabs.org/Task*. Students are encouraged to visit the site; give scripting inputs; and observe the results.

10.2 Cross Site Request Forgery (XSRF, CSRF)

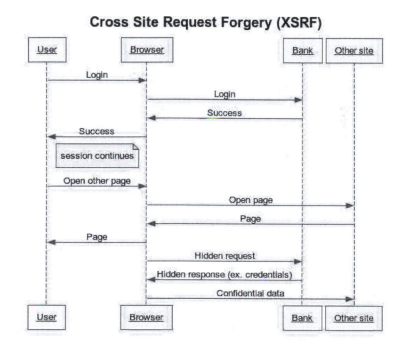

FIGURE 10.1

This sequence diagram shows an example XSRF attack. The user has two sessions open, allowing the "other site" to send requests to scripts at the on-line banking site.

Cross site request forgery (also known as XSRF or CSRF (pronounced C-Surf)) vulnerabilities are also in the OWASP list of top ten web security problems [329]. The problem is that html sessions can send requests to server scripts for any of the sessions currently active in the browser. For example if a user were doing on-line banking and looking at 4-Chan simultaneously, the 4-Chan session could possibly make transactions on the user's bank account. This is invisible to the user. A formal attack tree for XSRF attacks can be found in [265].

Frequently server scripts protect themselves by requiring encrypted cookies that verify that the user is currently logged in. These are ineffective against XSRF, since the browser automatically includes the cookie when sending requests to the server.

For example, in Figure 10.1 the user starts an on-line banking session [131].

While the session is active, the user opens another web-site in the browser. The code in a malicious web page can then activate the bank's server scripts. Since the browser has an active session with the bank, it automatically adds any necessary cookies containing session information when sending the hidden request to the bank. The other site succeeds in getting the same level of access to the bank as the user.

The best defense for a user is to only have one session active at a time, log off sessions when finished, exit the browser, and clear cookies [328]. Other counter-measures require changing current approaches to server-side script implementation [131, 444].

10.3 Man-in-the-Browser

While XSS and XSRF attacks are specific to web technologies, the man-in-the-browser (MITB) attack looks at web browsers to find the same vulnerabilities that we find in all other pieces of software. A MITB attack is simply a Trojan horse.

The attacker finds ways to implant code in a web browser. Web browsers are large, complex and built to be extensible. The attacker implants code in the system that remains hidden and performs a man-in-the-middle attack. The MITB is often a simple browser extension, such as a plug-in [187]. Since the Trojan has access to all the information in the web browser, it can harvest passwords, session id's, etc.

The Torpig botnet [382] made use of a MITB attack. When researchers hijacked Torpig, they found that during a ten day period Torpig grossed between \$83,000 and \$8.3 Million. The more sophisticated MITB attacks remain in the browser. At least one banking MITB attack checked when users tried to view their account on-line and redacted the fraudulent transactions [237].

10.4 Penetration Testing

The idea behind penetration testing [33] is to let a trained professional examine a web application before it is fielded. Penetration testers are frequently ethical hackers who know the vulnerabilities and exploits common to most web applications[2]. Where a real attacker can afford to take a haphazard approach to finding weaknesses in an application, a penetration tester needs to be rigorous, thorough, and systematic. An attacker only needs to find one

---

[2]Penetration testing is not limited to testing web applications, but the theme of this chapter is web security.

error. The penetration tester needs to find and diagnose as many weaknesses in the system as possible.

The penetration tester should start by analyzing the application's architecture and determining the software used to implement each system component. Tools, like the Mitre Corporation's Common Vulnerabilities and Exploits (CVE) database, should be consulted to find known security flaws for the components. The tester then needs to develop a strategy that allows them to test all the system components that a user, or attacker, could possibly access.

For web applications, tools exist that allow penetration testers to record, analyze, modify, and replay sessions. This speeds up testing by letting the penetration tester dynamically create interactive sessions, systematically change inputs, and check for error conditions. There are a large number of common mistakes that need to be checked for, including:

- Ability to handle data inputs that are too large without triggering a buffer overflow,
- Ability to handle zero-length inputs,
- Ability to properly handle special characters (including wildcards, dollar signs, illegal characters, etc.), and
- Ability to sanitize inputs to avoid injection attacks (SQL, XSS, etc.)

Fuzzing [387] is a useful tool for penetration testing. It consists of randomizing the inputs to data fields in order to find error conditions. Fuzzing tools exist that capture protocol sessions and modify them in ways that are both randomized and designed to maximize the likelihood of finding flaws.

10.5   Problems

1. Go to the sample XSS vulnerable website given in Section 10.1 and create a number of successful XSS inputs.

2. Explain why it is possible for a tool that sanitizes html inputs to re-enable vulnerabilities that it removed the last time it was run.

3. One XSRF counter-measure is to insert randomized tokens into server script names. Explain why this works.

4. Find at least five botnets that have used MITB attacks to defraud financial institutions. Try to quantify the amount of money stolen by those botnets.

5. Use a web plugin to record interactive sessions with a web-page. Identfy inputs that a penetration tester should modify to look for errors.

6. Try to reverse engineer the components and software used in a non-trival webpage.

10.6   Glossary

Cross site request forgery (CSRF, XSRF): The submission of a server script request through a browser to an active session from a different active session.

Cross site scripting (XSS): Insertion of executable content into a web page.

Man-in-the-browser: A Trojan horse attack that inserts malicious logic into to a web browser.

Penetration testing: Use of a professional to search for security flaws in an application.

11

Privacy and Anonymity

George Orwell's book *1984* foresaw a future where television surveilled continuously the inhabitants of Oceania. It was a terrifying world where everyone knew they were constantly watched. This chapter[1] explains our current situation where cell phones, automobiles, and computers provide easily accessible information to interested parties. Anonymity is increasingly difficult to maintain, especially on-line. We provide a brief introduction to currently available anonymity tools, followed with a discussion of their vulnerability to traffic analysis attacks. We state known attacks in the current literature and mention the preferred anonymity metric.

George Orwell's *1984* was a terrifying vision of a world with no privacy. Orwell was partly inspired by Yevgeny Zamyatin's *We* [441], a science fiction novel where everyone lived in houses made entirely of glass. In *1984*, everyone's house and workplace has a television transceiver that observes them constantly. The transceiver reminds them continuously that "Big Brother is watching you" [327].

Thankfully, we do not have the problem of constant television surveillance, unless, of course, you live in London (fictional setting of *1984*), where you are expected to be filmed on the average 300 times per day [182]. In the US (with the exception of under-aged school children outfitted with mandatory 24 hour surveillance equipment by their school boards [195], people taking mass transit [23], people whose governments have installed malware on their home computer [359], random pedestrians captured by web cams [386], and renters of computer hardware [72]), government closed circuit television (CCTV) surveillance is less common.

---

[1]Parts of this chapter appeared previously in [126]

Of course, CCTV either requires image processing software or human operators, which is inefficient compared to following people by tracking their cell phones [218]. Alternatively, people can be tracked by leveraging the 2008 federal law requiring mandatory tire pressure monitoring systems on new cars. Cars now continuously broadcast a unique identification code [1, 386]. If simply knowing a person's position is not enough, many people have devices with blue-tooth interfaces. Blue-jacking exploits allow unauthorized users to push data to the device, and blue-snarfing allows surreptitious information (such as voice data stream) collection from devices [386]. Of course, except in London [182], we are not inconvenienced by spies like the fictional Big Brother announcing their presence.

Cell phones are a particularly intimate technology. For cell phones to work, service providers have to be continuously aware of the user's location. For the police, this technology can be used to track large numbers of people continuously and in real time. Many people are not aware this information is available to law enforcement without a warrant [263]. In fact, the entire contents of those cell phones can be accessed and copied by law enforcement within minutes, using mobile data forensic tools like Cellebrite, without a warrant [369].

Social media is widely used for voluntarily sharing private information on-line. Many people are comfortable with this state of affairs. A suggested difference in attitude among age groups led French journalist Jean-Marc Manach to write the provocative book *La vie privée, une problème des vieux cons?* which has a polite English translation of *Privacy, a problem for old farts?*, but research indicates that ideas concerning privacy and data protection do not vary greatly across age groups [206].

The idea of a single point of surveillance that continuously announces its intention to spy seems quaint in our current world. Many Internet users desire anonymity and privacy. Those that are technically literate realize that anonymity is difficult, if not impossible, to achieve. Scott McNealy of Sun Microsystems has the view, "You already have zero privacy. Get over it" [90] and Eric Schmidt of Google told CNBC, "If you have something that you dont want anyone to know, maybe you shouldn't be doing it in the first place" [154]. This implies that people with medical records that they want to be private should just not get sick.

This chapter looks at privacy issues. In Section 11.1 we look at how privacy and anonymity has been measured. We follow this with Section 11.2 giving a brief discussion of some of the more widely used tools for enhancing privacy and anonymity on-line. This is countered with an introduction to computer forensics in Section 11.3. It is worth noting that privacy is not a purely technical problem. In Section 11.4 we discuss legal issues regarding privacy.

The final section (Section 11.5) in this chapter provides information about some recent events. In particular, we present facts concerning Justice Antonin Scalia's views on privacy and an assignment given to law school students to find and document as much about Justice Scalia as possible. These facts lead to some issues for discussion.

11.1 Anonymity Metrics

Privacy and anonymity are related concepts. In this book, we will refer to *privacy* as an individual's ability to restrict access to information about themselves. For example, some professions require that communications with clients be kept private and confidential. The legal, medical, and clerical professions usually have this requirement. Journalists are also expected to keep their sources of information private.

Anonymity is the individual's ability to act without their identity being known. For example, a whistle-blower revealing government corruption would frequently desire to remain anonymous to avoid retribution. A good distinction is that the identity of an individual would be anonymous, while the information being transmitted might be kept private.

One way to measure anonymity is the *anonymity set* first presented in [112]. Given a set of participants, the anonymity set is the subset of participants that may have originated the communication (transaction). Anonymity A is proportional to the size of the anonymity set S:

$$A \propto |S| \tag{11.1}$$

Equation 11.1 is a reasonable metric for logicians and cryptographers. Larger sets provide more anonymity. But this approach assumes that anonymity tools work perfectly and no information is available to the attacker, except for an individual's membership in the set. We discuss side-channels, which often make this assumption unrealistic, in Chapter 12.

In Section 11.2, we explain mix networks, such as Tor and I2P. In part to deal with the realities of these tools, another metric has been proposed [361]. This metric reflects the fact that, although many participants may have originated the message, some may be more likely to have participated than others. In keeping with our Orwellian theme [326], "All animals are equal, but some animals are more equal than others." The new metric is the distribution entropy:

$$A = - \sum_{u \in \Psi} p_u \log_2(P_u) \tag{11.2}$$

where Ψ is the set of users and p_u is the probability user u originated the message. This reflects the reality that analysis typically provides information that correlates users to activities. The correlation may be more or less strong, providing different likelihoods. If one IP address generates 99 percent of the traffic to a web site, adding one or two more users that generate less than $1/10$ of a percent of the traffic to the site will not greatly enhance the privacy of that IP address.

Let's now consider designing an anonymity tool that tries to actively trick the attacker into making the wrong decision. The attacker gets to decide how and when to sample the network, while the anonymity system generates fake traffic to fool the observer. This conflict creates an interesting game theory problem. This problem has been solved. The optimal strategies for both the observer and the intelligent system that wishes not to be observed turn out to be the maximum entropy distribution [183], which is consistent with Equation 11.2.

11.2   Anonymity Tools

Cryptography is commonly used to keep information private from third parties. The ssh tool and ssl/tls protocols use cryptography to tunnel communications without revealing clear-text. Unfortunately, routing information is available in clear-text, so ssh and ssl/tls provide some privacy but no anonymity. We now discuss tools that are used to safeguard user privacy. Unfortunately, they have vulnerabilities.

While protocol tunneling through ssh secures the contents of data transmissions, the IP routing information of the connection is available in clear-text. It is trivial to determine both the source and sink of the secure connection. *Proxy* nodes try to counter this attack. A proxy server works as an intermediate connection. A client node creates a connection to the proxy, which relays packets to the client's intended destination. The proxy similarly forwards response packets back to the client. If the intermediate connection is encrypted, the routing information for packets routed through the proxy are encrypted. Packet sniffing local to the client does not reveal the client's communication patterns, except for frequent communication with the proxy. Packet sniffing at both the client and proxy server will remove all anonymity from this approach. One step proxies include Ultrasurf, which is used by the Falun Gong sect to evade the Great Firewall of China.

Mix networks were designed to extend this concept and allow anonymous network connections over IP networks [25]. A mix network is a large network of cooperating routers. Example mix routing networks include Tor (The Onion Router) and JAP (Java Anon Proxy).

Mix network connections from source to destination take a fixed random route through the network (see Figure 11.1). Each packet is sent into the network with encapsulated tunneling information for each hop taken by the random path through the network. The receiving end of each hop strips off the outer layer of tunneling information, decrypts the contents of the packet, reads the address of the next host on the random path, and forwards the packet. This allows end-to-end secure communication where intermediate hosts can neither:

1. Access the clear text contents of the data, nor
2. Simultaneously know the identity of source and destination.

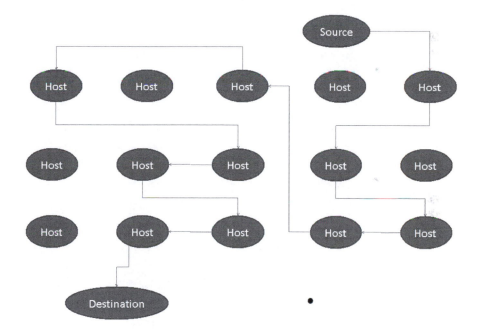

FIGURE 11.1
In mix networks, traffic takes a random path from source to destination. Each hop is chosen from a set of participating nodes. The content for each hop is encrypted with a different key.

This process is called onion routing, since a layer of the onion is peeled away at each hop.

Tor participants run one of three types of services:

1. Relay,
2. Directory server, or
3. Client.

Relays are the backbone of the network. Relays transfer data from clients to other relays, between two relays, or retrieve external resources for a client. By default, relays listen on TCP port 9001 for incoming requests. While they are up, they publish their status to a list of pre-defined directory servers. Directory servers catalog the information they have about relays and vote on which ones to list as running, valid, stable, etc. After servers vote and all agree on a list, they come to a consensus. The consensus is published on a TCP port (9030 by default) where it can be downloaded by clients.

The client service listens for client TCP streams to route through the network. The listener is a SOCKS proxy on port 9050 by default. Before packets arrive to be proxied, the client initializes circuits with relays listed in the downloaded consensus. To create a circuit, the client sends a creation request to the relay it wants to be the first node in its circuit. The client extends this circuit to a second and third node. The client chooses and knows each node in the path for its traffic. The client sets up symmetric key pairs with each node.

When the first data for a TCP stream arrives at the proxy, one of the previously created circuits is selected for the transfer. If no circuits are available, one is created. Before data are transferred, the packet destination is sent through the circuit to the last node to start the connection. The last node is called the exit node. It is where the packets exit Tor and go to their destination. The exit node sends confirmation to the client once it has connected to the destination, allowing the data transfer to begin. Note that data leaving the exit node are in clear text. If there is any personally identifiable information in the stream, all anonymity is lost.

As each data packet is sent, it is split or padded into cells of 512 bytes, which are iteratively encrypted using the key of the circuit relay. The original packet is encrypted with the key for the last node, which is wrapped in another packet and encrypted with the key for the second node, which is encapsulated again and encrypted with the key for the first node. The result is like an onion. As each relay in the circuit receives the onion packet, it decrypts and peels away a layer, forwarding the remaining data structure.

Tor has been funded by both the Naval Research Laboratory and Electric Frontier Foundation. It is an independent project led by Roger Dingledine. Java Anon Proxy was written in Java and originated at technical universities in Germany.

I2P [21] grew from the Freenet community. Freenet was an anonymous distributed data repository with a Peer-to-Peer interface. I2P is an overlay

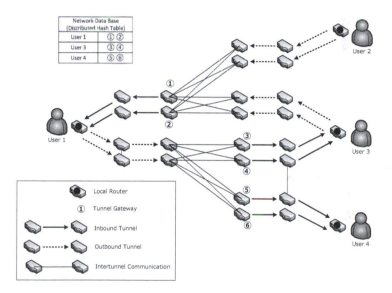

FIGURE 11.2

In I2P each user has incoming and outgoing encrypted pipes. Router nodes make connections between cryptographically identified participants. Participants do not know each other's IP address. "Garlic routing" allows users to encapsulate many "cloves" (independent messages) into a single packet.

network where all participants use cryptographic identifiers as pseudonyms. I2P extends mix network concepts as shown in Figure 11.2. Users create their own encrypted tunnels. Communication occurs by exchanging cryptographic tunnel identifiers. Each tunnel can pass through multiple routers (hops) as defined by the tunnel creator. This is very similar to Tor. In addition, multiple messages (cloves) can be bundled together for "garlic routing." This makes the attacks in Chapter 12 more challenging. I2P also supports medium and high latency modes, which trade off usability for anonymity.

OnionCat creates a VPN within Tor (or I2P) for a closed group of users. OnionCat assigns an IPv6 address to this network making it easy to send any IP based traffic through the network. This allows any application that supports IPv6 to use the Tor network transparently.

Just like any other VPN, OnionCat encapsulates IP packets within IP packets. One difference with VPN's is that OnionCat uses Tor to transmit its data. Since OnionCat's virtual circuits only exist within Tor, each user must run Tor. This also means OnionCat traffic will not have to travel through Tor's high traffic exit nodes. Two users connecting to each other using OnionCat closely resemble a client connecting to a server. One user imitates the client and initializes the connection to the other who accepts it.

In Tor, the server is a hidden service, meaning both server and client cannot determine who or where the other is from the network connection. OnionCat allows each user to be both client and server by requiring each user to set up a hidden service. This allows any OnionCat user to connect to any other OnionCat user, provided the user knows the other's onion-URL. An onion-URL is an 80-bit address assigned by Tor to the user's hidden service. OnionCat combines this onion-URL and a 48-bit prefix to construct the user's IPv6 address. This scheme makes it easy for OnionCat to translate addresses and route traffic into or out of Tor.

11.3 Computer Forensic Tools

On the one hand, there are many users desiring anonymity and privacy. Some of these users are normal citizens that want to protect themselves. Some users that desire anonymity will be malicious intruders, or criminals. We have mentioned some of the access that government and law enforcement have to data. For use in legal proceedings, access to data is not sufficient. For electronic information to be accepted in court, law enforcement needs to make sense of the data and certify that the data have not been tampered with.

By now, anyone reading this book should be aware that there are computer and network security issues that have yet to be fully mastered. They should also be aware that computers and networks are used for criminal activities. This means that digital information has to be analyzed to solve crimes and used as evidence when prosecuting individuals. This domain is referred to as *Digital forensics*. It requires specific skills and diligent execution. *Digital evidence* is data that either establishes that a crime has been committed, provides a link between a crime and its victim, or establishes a link between a crime and its perpetrator [107].

Digital forensics can be problematic for practitioners. For example, a system administrator who discovers evidence of child pornography and deletes it without reporting the problem to law enforcement may be criminally negligent. On the other hand, an administrator that reports the problem to law enforcement without the employer's support may be terminated, forced to hire their own lawyer, testify on their own time, and be unemployed. In some cases, well meaning administrators who attempted to investigate child pornography claims have been prosecuted for downloading and possessing illegal material themselves [107].

Important issues in computer forensics include [107]:

- *Evidence exchange* – traces of digital communications or data transfers help establish the interactions in a criminal case,
- *Evidence characteristics* – categorization and corroboration of evidence is needed to prove charges. For example, many laser printers print a unique sequence of yellow dots that can be used to identify who printed a document [162]. Word documents also contain meta-data that can be used to track the history of a text-processing file.
- *Forensic soundness* – while collecting data changes it, documenting what was done to the digital information, how and why can establish that modifications were either unavoidable or necessary.
- *Authentication* – verifying that the digital information is correct and represents the actual state of the system. Since memory contents and network traffic is dynamic, this can be difficult.
- *Chain of custody* – documentation needs to be preserved that certifies every individual that had access to or control of the evidence. This is essential for data to be permissible as evidence in court.
- *Evidence integrity* – checks need to be performed to certify that data tampering has not occurred. Cryptographic hash values are an essential tool for establishing that evidence is sound.
- *Objectivity* – the analyst needs to be free of bias and provide decision makers with clear views of established facts.

Open source data tools exist [43] that students can use to learn data forensics techniques. Naturally, tools vary according to the operating system present on the computer being analyzed. *The Sleuth Kit (www.sleuthkit.org)* runs on Linux, Mac OS X, and Windows. Data forensic software is typically used to:

- Analyze and securely store file system images, files, partitions, and containers,
- Analyze and securely store system meta-data,

- Create and verify cryptographic hash values,
- *Carve* file systems to search for data formats, magic numbers, file headers, etc. For example, carving can recover image files that are stored with other file names or in regions of the disk that are not included in the directory structure,
- Create forensic images of disks that retain deleted files and slack regions of disks that retain evidence perpetrators have tried to destroy, and
- Analyze browser artifacts that can be used to establish the history of suspect actions on-line.

It is worth mentioning at this point, that on most systems deleting a file simply removes entries from directories and marks positions on the disk free for re-use. File contents remain in place long after the file is deleted. Special purpose *scrubber* programs are needed that overwrite the region on disk where the file was stored multiple times. Similarly, note that scrubbers do not work on most SD-cards. In order to avoid failure, SD-card manufacturers implement a process called *leveling* that changes the physical locations where logical blocks are stored. It is often impossible to actually erase data from an SD-card without physically destroying it.

Similarly, it is worth noting that many electronic devices have unique footprints associated with them. Electronic images can be analyzed to determine the product that produced them. Wireless cards can have identifiable patterns associated with their antenna. Many laser printers write hidden codes on every document they print. This is independent of the meta-data that many systems automatically attach to files they create.

11.4   Privacy Laws

Privacy is an evolving concept. There are cultural, technical, and legal aspects for privacy. We have discussed a number of technical issues related to privacy, but in many respects privacy depends more on the law.

Laws vary greatly internationally. The United States and Europe have quite different laws regarding personal data. In the United States when individuals interact with companies, the data belong to the corporation which is typically free to use that information as they wish[2]. In Europe, individuals usually retain ownership of their data. Corporations are only allowed to use their client's data without permission in ways that are clearly tied to their commercial relationship.

The US Constitution Fourth Amendment protects individuals from "unreasonable search and seizure," which begs the question as to what reasonable

---

[2]There are exceptions to this rule. Medical and student data have legal privacy restrictions

means. The Supreme Court has set this legal standard as a *reasonable expectation of privacy*, which can be interpreted in many ways.

If law enforcement has a warrant, then they have demonstrated the need for specific information to a court, and they have a right to access to anything in the warrant. This may include your computer(s).

If they do not have a warrant, then law enforcement can access:

- Anything revealed to a third party (ex. bank records, records of telephone calls, computer packet routing headers, on-line or off-line conversations with anyone) [165],
- Parts of your business that are open to the public [165],
- Your trash [165],
- Anything in public or in plain view [165], including the contents of your cell phone [369],
- Anything learned by an undercover agent [165],
- Address information on letters [165],
- Anything discovered during a fire inspection or other administrative entry into a private area [165],
- Anything being carried onto an airplane [165],
- Logs of electronic communications, email addresses, IP addresses, and web addresses kept by third parties [165],
- Any item given to a third party (such as a repair shop, friend, relative) [407],
- Anything found by someone who is not acting as a government agent [407],
- Anything agreed to by anyone with access to your computer (ex. roommate with a password, spouse, domestic partner) [407], and
- Anything agreed to by a system administrator [407],

If they do not have a warrant, then law enforcement can not access:

- Items in your residence that are not in plain sight [165],
- Parts of your business that are closed to the public [165],
- Items in opaque containers [165],
- The contents of letters [165],
- Electronic communications, email addresses, IP addresses, and web addresses [165], and
- E-mail and voice-mail [165].

It is worth noting that email from work accounts at public universities are typically subject to *Freedom of Information Act (FOIA)* constraints and are public information. There is some conflict between the FOIA and the *Family Educational Rights and Privacy Act (FERPA)*, which restricts access to student information.

11.5 Privacy Discussion Assignments – Antonin Scalia

Since privacy issues are technical, legal, social, and personal, it is best to consider some anecdotes that raise important issues. Many privacy issues are multi-faceted and have no clear right answer. In this section, we present the facts from real-life cases and provide questions for group discussion.

11.5.1 Dog poop girl

A woman was riding on the subway in Seoul, South Korea with her dog. The dog defecated in the subway car, much to the annoyance of the other passengers. The other passengers loudly demanded that she clean up after her dog. She refused. One woman offered her a tissue. She cleaned her dog but left the feces. She exited the subway train at the next stop and said something rude.

Unfortunately for her, another passenger took photographs of the woman and her dog. These photos were posted on a popular website. The photo became popular as outraged citizens searched for the woman. Within days she had been identified and her personal information posted on-line. She started receiving messages expressing disapproval.

The volume of e-mails sent to her was enough to crash the server of the university she was attending. The humiliation eventually forced the woman to withdraw from her university. The university issued a plea for the e-mail barrage to stop, since the woman was no longer a student.

The woman was inconsiderate and should have cleaned up after her dog, but was the punishment proportional to the crime? Consider and discuss the following questions:

- Was the woman's privacy violated?
- Do you feel that any of the individuals, other than the woman with the dog, acted incorrectly in isolation?
- Are there any measures that could be put in place to stop this type of retribution?
- Should there be measures to control this form of retribution?
- How easy would it be with software like Photoshop to create a fake image of this type?

11.5.2 Antonin Scalia

The Associated Press filed the following report on comments made by Supreme Court Justice Antonin Scalia at a legal conference on privacy issues [200]:

Discussions of privacy rights in the digital era should distinguish between such confidential data as medical records and information that might be per-

sonal but is easy to find out, U.S. Supreme Court Justice Antonin Scalia said Wednesday.

Considering every fact about someone's life private is "extraordinary," he said, noting that data such as addresses have long been discernible, even if technology has made them easier to find. Every single datum about my life is private? Thats silly, Scalia [said].

The report continued [371]

Scalia said he was largely untroubled by such Internet tracking. "I don't find that particularly offensive," he said. "I dont find it a secret what I buy, unless its shameful."

He added there's some information that's private, "but it doesn't include what groceries I buy."

Data such as drug prescriptions probably should be protected, he said, suggesting areas off-limits to data gatherers could simply be listed for legal purposes.

Fordham Law Professor Joel Reidenberg was struck by these comments. He gave an assignment to his students to collect as much publicly available information on Justice Scalia as they could. After four months, the students delivered a 15 page dossier, which included:

- Justice Scalia's home address,
- The value of his house,
- His home phone number,
- His wife's email address, and
- Photos of his grandchildren

The dossier was sent to Justice Scalia, who was not pleased about the incident. When asked for comments, he responded:

I stand by my remark at the Institute of American and Talmudic Law conference that it is silly to think that every single datum about my life is private. I was referring, of course, to whether every single datum about my life deserves privacy protection in law.

It is not a rare phenomenon that what is legal may also be quite irresponsible. That appears in the First Amendment context all the time. What can be said often should not be said. Prof. Reidenberg's exercise is an example of perfectly legal, abominably poor judgment. Since he was not teaching a course in judgment, I presume he felt no responsibility to display any.

Consider and discuss the following questions:

- Do you find Justice Scalia's legal position consistent with his reaction to the dossier?
- Was Professor Reidenberg's assignment ethically correct and/or appropriate?
- Should Professor Reidenberg, or one of his students, be allowed to post the dossier on the web?
- Would posting the dossier on the web be ethical or would it violate Justice Scalia's privacy? Why or why not?

- What classes of purchases made by individual's should be legally protected?
- If purchase information is not private, should the government be able to to collect the names of people that purchase books by Glenn Beck, subscribe to *Mother Jones*, etc.?

11.6 Problems

1. Use search engines to discover as much personal information about yourself as possible.

2. Cardinal Richelieu of France said, "If you give me six lines written by the hand of the most honest of men, I will find something in them which will hang him." Write a brief essay considering this statement in light of the information that you have collected about yourself with the search engine.

3. Compare the lists of items available with and without a warrant to find apparent contradictions.

4. Contrast the functionality of anonymity and forensics tools.

11.7 Glossary

Anonymity: A person's ability to hide their identity.

Carving: Forsenics approach to finding information on disks that ignores file system structure.

Entropy: A function that quantifies the amount of disorder in a system.

Forensics: Data collection and evaluation for use in legal proceedings.

Garlic routing: Routing approach, similar to onion routing, but allows data interleaving.

Onion routing: A method for combining multiple encrypted proxies to provide on-line anonymity.

Privacy: A person's ability to control access to personal data.

Proxy: A computer that acts as a remote copy of the local computer.

Scrubber: Program that over-writes data on disk multiple times to remove information from the disk.

12

Side-Channel Attacks

CONTENTS

The theoretical security of encryption algorithms, ensured by complexity arguments, is rarely beaten. Most encryption systems are defeated by social engineering, implementation flaws, or side-channel attacks [152]. Side-channel attacks take advantage of the fact that computers are physical objects. Even when it can be proved that the only way to derive the input and/or key of a cryptographic algorithm from the observed program output, that does not mean that the information is secure. The act of computation may have measurable physical consequences that can be measured and used to infer the key and/or data input.

Electromagnetic emanations from computer equipment, such as screens, cache memory, and/or keyboards, are a side-channel that can be used to recreate computer sessions. These attacks are generally referred to using the codeword tempest. Information leakage from LED status indicators have also been used [272]. Optical and electrical emanations should therefore be considered as equally sensitive.

Identification and removal of side-channels from computer systems is challenging. Several side-channels are known. Verification of a program's code is not sufficient, the entire hardware/software implementation needs to be analyzed, since some forms of information leakage will not be contained in the system specifications [400]. Even when program verification is done low-level side-channels, such as disk-head positions, may still leak information [400]. Trade-offs can exist between system performance and its ability to mask data transmissions [372].

In this chapter, we concentrate on three important side-channel classes:

- Section 12.1 – *Power analysis* which records power consumption patterns,
- Section 12.2 – *Traffic analysis* inference of communications patterns, and
- Section 12.3 – *Timing attacks* that find timing patterns in data outputs.

We then look at side-channel countermeasures. Section 12.4 describes red-black separation. Other countermeasures are listed in Section 12.5.

12.1   Power Analysis

Power analysis attacks[1] detect variations in power consumption for different operations. Power consumption depends on the inputs (for cryptography: plain-text and secret key). Different operand values cause different switching activities in the memory, buses, datapath units (adders, multipliers, logical units), and pipeline registers of processors (smart cards, BACNET devices, etc.). Among these components, processor datapath and buses exhibit more data-dependent energy variation than memory components [438].

Power analysis attacks have varying degrees of sophistication. Simple Power Analysis (SPA) [239, 240] uses only a single power consumption trace for an operation. From this power trace, an attacker can identify the operations performed (ex. whether or not a branch at point p is taken, or if an exponentiation operation is performed).

Combining power consumption information with knowledge of the underlying algorithm can reveal the secret key. For example, if a branch is taken when a particular bit of a secret key is zero, the attacker can identify this bit by monitoring the power consumption difference between a taken and not taken branch.

Protecting against this type of simple attack can be done by restructuring the code. A restructured algorithm in [123] eliminates branch conditions that reveal secret key information. Randomly introducing noise into power measurement can mislead simple power analysis. Dummy modules can be inserted in the system and activated at random time intervals. These modules consume additional power skewing the original power profile. However, these techniques only provide protection from simplistic approaches. Higher-order power analysis techniques can circumvent these mechanisms.

Differential power analysis (DPA) is a common higher-order power analysis approach. This scheme uses power profiles from several runs and uses the data-dependent power consumption variation to break the key [239]. In [179], the secret key is guessed using 1,000 sample inputs and their corresponding 1,000 power consumption traces. A mean M of the power consumption traces is computed, and then the attacker guesses a particular key and based on the input determines a theoretical value for one of intermediate bit b.

The outcome of bit b is used to separate the 1,000 inputs into two groups (G_1 and G_2) based on $b = 0$ or $b = 1$. If the mean of the power profiles in G_1 is significantly different from M, the guess was correct. The difference

---

[1]A more detailed version of this section can be found in [90]

manifests the downstream computational power differences that used the bit b. Random noise in power measurements is filtered by averaging a large number of samples. The use of random noise to increase the number of samples to an infeasible number could be of theoretical concern, but in practice the cost of adding noise is greater than the cost of doing more analysis runs.

12.2 Traffic Analysis

Traffic analysis can be traced back to World War One [260]. The military has devoted considerable resources to improving their traffic analysis methods and securing their communication methods against them. The growth in popularity of personal computers and the Internet made traffic analysis possible in the civilian sector. Even though an attacker cannot directly see encrypted communications between users, the attacker can analyze:

- Packet headers,
- Packet lengths, and
- Timing between packets

By themselves, these data tell the attacker little. If the attacker pieces this data together from multiple traffic flows, then the attacker can determine [298, 145]:

- Who is talking to whom,
- Where users are located,
- When users communicate,
- What applications or protocols are being used, and
- How much data are being communicated.

When users transmit sensitive information, any of these items could compromise the user.

Traffic analysis can attack any component used in the system. It is possible for web servers to profile browsers accessing web pages. Browsers often have unique profiles that can be unique for a specific user [2]. Web pages can often be uniquely identified, even when sent through an encrypted tunnel using ssl/tls. They can be identified by the sizes of packets sent [202, 76, 262, 197]. Unique signatures can be created for HTTPS websites based on their resources (e.g., HTML, images, CSS, and JavaScript content). If a catalog of SSL-enabled websites could be accessed and profiled beforehand, the timing signatures could be used to detect which websites were being accessed through an encrypting web proxy [202]. The values entered into web-based forms remain secret. A similar concept infers Bayesian nets that detect instances of tunneled protocols [145].

---

[2]Try the Electronic Frontier Foundations "Panopticlick" web page at https://panopticlick.eff.org/ for an example

The encoding scheme used in Voice over IP (VoIP) can identify the language being spoken in encrypted conversations [432]. The attack was successful when a variable bit-rate encoder was used and was tested on conversations between over two thousand native speakers in 21 different languages. The privacy of VoIP users can be further compromised by using hidden Markov models to predict when certain phrases were used during the call [431].

A number of researchers have used traffic analysis techniques to analyze Tor. Tor's position as a widely used anonymity tool makes it attractive for this kind of research.

Traffic analysis has been performed on the Tor network using timing-based congestion [298]. An adversary had to create a single hop circuit with a relay in the global Tor network and flood it with data. Then any time the timing slowed, assuming it was due to the relay and not the link, one could guess that the relay was processing data in a circuit. If enough relays were observed, slow downs in the flows would line up and show the attacker which three relays were used in a circuit. This attack was devised and orchestrated very early in Tors history when there were only 13 nodes on the whole network. Newer research suggests, however, that with a much larger Tor network and heavier traffic that the attack is no longer possible [156].

Pre-compiled catalogs of path round-trip times could be used with a malicious web server to limit Tor's anonymity. To collect round-trip times for comparison, the attacker must connect to servers on various subnets around the Internet and compile a latency map to those subnets. Then, if a user could be directed to the malicious web server using a spear-phishing exploit, they could measure how long the packets took to go round-trip to the client. The client's round-trip time could be compared to the round-trip times on the latency map and a reasonable estimate could be made of 2 to 4 subnets in which the client likely resides [208].

12.3   Time Analysis

One flaw common to both VPNs and mix networks is the ability to extract information about channels by measuring delays between packet transmissions. Researchers have used inter-packet delay information to extract passwords from interactive ssh sessions. Since an interactive ssh session sends one packet per keystroke, the delays between packets over ssh connections reflect the inter-keystroke delays of users typing on their keyboards. The layout of the QWERTY keyboard results in a correlation between keystroke delays and pairs of consecutive keys. The attackers manually constructed a hidden Markov model (HMM) for harvesting passwords from interactive ssh sessions. For non-interactive sessions, timing attacks can exploit the fact that ssh pads only to 8-byte boundaries to infer approximate payload lengths [373].

This attack was generalized in [68]. Statistical data were harvested for native language typists typing in English and Italian. Inter-packet delays were recorded for users typing large documents in English and Italian through ssh secured data connections. Using a data driven HMM inference approach to learn the timing patterns associated with each language, the HMM was able to reliably distinguish the languages being transmitted through the encrypted tunnel.

A similar insight [445] can thwart the anonymity provided by mix networks, like Tor. If attackers can eavesdrop at mix network entry and exit points, they can collect inter-packet timing information. Inter-packet timings of all entry and exit points can be cross-correlated to calculate the mutual information between all entry-exit pairs. This reliably identifies the correct communications paths using sample sizes on the order of seconds to tens of seconds. Surprisingly, this attack works better on larger networks than on smaller ones. This is an example of a larger class of flow correlation attacks [446]. Many of the Tor vulnerabilities detailed in [138] are some type of active or passive flow correlation.

For timing side-channels, it is possible to use hidden Markov models (HMMs) that infer state transitions and infer semantic information directly from timing data, unlike [152, 373] which require prior knowledge of the system being observed. HMM can be inferred directly from observed data. In addition, it is possible to detect interactively whether or not enough training data have been collected to adequately learn the system. This can develop detection tools for arbitrary tunneled protocols that have a known statistical certainty. HMMs have been developed that:

- Detect the language used in interactive ssh sessions [68],
- Detect protocols used in tunneled communications [68, 126], and
- Violate the privacy guarantees of Tor [126].

It was found that the hidden Markov model of an underlying network process could be reconstructed from observations of the inter-packet timings of the packets. Measures were used to validate the models and check to make sure enough data were used for their construction. In cases when not enough data were available, the models could be used after a technique was applied to prune them of any low-probability states and transitions. By calculating confidence intervals and comparing the paths taken by test data through one of these models, a statistical measure is found for how likely it is that two systems are talking through Tor. If two systems are both using Tor, but tunneling different protocols, the confidence intervals will show a rejection. If the two systems are both using Tor and the same protocol, the confidence intervals will accept the data. As an additional step, we find that if the Viterbi paths match, the two systems are using the same instance of the same protocol.

This type of analysis could allow an adversary to defeat the anonymity of Tor without being a global observer. If an adversary is able to observe two systems, these tools can be used to determine if that pair of systems are communicating through the anonymity network.

12.4 Red-black Separation

Red-black separation means that sensitive and non-sensitive data are handled on different machines that are not co-located [90]. These machines use separate cabling and power sources. This guards against power side-channel vulnerabilities. If the cryptographic systems use isolated secure power sources, then power consumption information can not be inferred.

To guard against information leakage due to electromagnetic radiation (tempest) these facilities are usually encased in a Faraday cage. Red and black may signify different levels of information classification, or the difference between cypher-text and plain text.

If the secure devices are in a secure, totally isolated environment, where no emanations can be detected, then power analysis attacks will not be possible. Note that this is expensive and limits the ability to deploy secure systems. Also, note that the ability to disrupt or tamper with power input lines can cause computation errors that may be equally damaging to security.

12.5 Side-channel Countermeasures

There are three general classes of countermeasures to side-channel attacks:

1. Add noise to the channel (this is typically ineffective, since it only increases the volume of information that the attacker needs to collect),
2. Isolate the system physically (red-black separation), or
3. Saturate the channel, so that no data variations exist.

A countermeasure to flow correlation attacks saturates communication channels with dummy traffic [184]. Unfortunately, the existence of steady, large volume packet streams negates most forms of anonymity. The best that could be hoped for is some type of shell game where the attacker can not identify exactly which member of a small set is an active participant. This maximizes the entropy measure for the anonymity set of the group of participants, but the size of this set is likely to be small. The entropy value would be larger for an approach where many non-participants are found to be suspicious.

The reliance of current timing side-channel attacks on point-to-point communications is considered in [36]. The content inference attacks [373, 68] look at timing deltas within sequences of observations. Correlation attacks [445, 446] cross-correlate the packet volume values found within data windows. Both approaches assume packets travel in a fixed path between source and sink. Consider the Bit-Torrent protocol. As the number of peers collaborating in a file transfer grows, the number of potential paths for any portion of the file from a seed to a given user grows exponentially. If one of the collaborating users is the intended sink of the communication originating with the seed (source), the bit torrent protocol provides an efficient communications channel that removes the point-to-point timing vulnerabilities found in Tor/I2P. A collection of paths can protect this network from timing side-channel attacks. This is a type of noise countermeasure that has promise.

To evaluate this approach, we implemented the DES algorithm in software and captured the energy consumption in each cycle using a cycle-accurate energy simulator. We discuss only processor and buses, since memory power consumption is largely data-independent. The simulator uses validated transition-sensitive energy models for both the buses and functional units obtained through detailed circuit simulation and is within 9 percent of actual values [438]. It accurately captures the differences in energy consumption due to data transitions. Working with the simulator lets us monitor the energy consumed in every cycle (along with details of actual instructions executed) and helps quickly identify the benefits of modifying the underlying processor architecture. Current measurement based approaches would be limited by the sampling speed of the measuring devices and it would be more difficult to correlate the operations and sources of energy consumption. The processor modeled for our simulation results is based on 0.25 micron technology using 2.5 V supply voltage.

Power analysis countermeasures can be divided into three classes [179]:

1. Random timing shifts and noise can be added so that computed power consumption means do not correspond to the same instruction. However, it is hard to ensure that randomization is not vulnerable to statistical inference using large samples.
2. Modify the underlying software implementation or algorithm [179]. For instance, the use of non-linear transformations of S-box operations can avoid some DPA attacks. However, software countermeasures are difficult to design.
3. Replace some critical instructions so that energy consumption behavior does not leak information.

12.6   Problems

1. List factors other than timing, and power analysis that could provide possible side-channel attacks, remember that any physical interaction between the machine and its environment could be used.

2. Use a sniffer to collect timing information in your research laboratory to collect data from any automated protocol; for example, create a python script that triggers some tasks on a regular basis. Use the approach in [68] to infer a detection approach.

3. If cryptography creates secure encoding of information, why is it subject to side-channel attacks?

4. Try to make your browser as anonymous as possible for the Panopticlick browser profiler.

12.7   Glossary

Power analysis: A side-channel based on measuring the power consumption of a computer.

Red-black separation: Isolating the secure machines from the rest of the world.

Side-channel: A security vulnerability caused by physical artifacts of the computing process that can be measured by an attacker.

Timing analysis: An attack that recognizes patterns in data stream inter-packet delay time series.

Traffic analysis: An attack that ignores packet payloads and considers packet transmission patterns.

13

Digital Rights Management and Copyright

CONTENTS

13.1 Copyright History

For all practical purposes, copyright was not an issue until Johannes Guten-berg invented the printing press with movable type around 1450. Until then, most people were illiterate and books were copied by hand. Copies had to be made by the few people that were literate. Books were rare and expensive. The laws that existed were from governments and the church to control and censor the distribution of information.

After 1450 printing presses were rare and expensive, but books cheaper to produce and more plentiful. Governments started licensing printers to control their output. The license typically gave printers exclusive rights to print spe-cific titles. Licenses were only valid in the country granting the license, but the import of foreign titles was typically prohibited. The main concern was limiting access to heretical information and the right to a title rested with the printer.

The 1709 *Statute of Anne* is widely recognized as the first copyright statute. It gave the author a monopoly limited to 14 years for their books. If the author were still alive when the copyright expired, then a second 14 year monopoly could be granted. Books no longer under copyright were placed into the *public domain*. Anyone who wants to, can print, distribute, modify, and sell works in the public domain. For the first time, rights to works belonged to the author and those rights expire after a given time.

The basis of copyright in the United States is the Copyright Clause in

239

the U.S. Constitution, which gives Congress the ability to grant limited term monopolies to authors and inventors. This is also the basis of patent law. It is clearly stated that these monopolies must be for a limited time and that the monopolies exist solely to promote progress in arts and sciences. Thomas Jefferson referred to this as the state granting "special privileges" to authors and inventors.

The 1886 Berne convention created an international copyright agreement among member states. Each member state grants citizens of other member states the same rights as its own citizens. Nations may legislate limitations exceptions to copyright as long as:

- limitations and exceptions are for limited special cases,
- reproduction does not interfere with the author's normal exploitation of their rights, and
- limitations do not unreasonably prejudice the legitimate rights of the copyright holder.

Free use of copyrighted material is granted for quotation, teaching, and news reporting. The Berne convention was last revised in 1971.

The US Congress reworked copyright law in 1976. It now covers any tangible medium of expression including pantomime, choreography, audio-visual works, and computer programs. Copyright protection was extended to the life of the author plus 70 years. For anonymous and pseudonymous works protection is for 95 years from first publication or 120 years from the date of the work's creation, whichever is first.

The 1984 *Beta max case* established important principles regarding copyright and technology. Movie studios tried to outlaw the sale of videotaping equipment, since they could be used to make pirate copies of films. The Supreme Court ruled that videotaping equipment could continue being sold, since it had many uses that were not illegal.

In [433], Tim Wu of Columbia Law School argues that there is a noticeable historical pattern with access to media. When new media become available, there are no fixed rules regarding distribution. This leads to freedom, innovation, and complaints from old media. Over time, business consolidates control of the media leading to a loss of freedom and choice in the market place, until a new technical innovation restarts the cycle. Prof. Wu shows how this pattern has worked for music, films, radio, television, cable television, and Internet services. Laws and regulations, like copyright legislation, become a part of this process with entrenched economic interests striving to maintain their position. He specifically mentions Steve Jobs of Apple, who started his career selling devices for making illegal telephone calls and ended by producing "closed garden" devices that were very restrictive in the software that could be used.

13.2 Fair Use

The fair use doctrine expressly permits the moderate use of copyrighted material for many purposes, including:

- education,
- news reporting,
- criticism,
- parody, and
- (in certain contexts) home consumption.

This is allowed, as long as it does not impair the copyright owner's ability to exploit potential markets.

13.3 Creative Commons

In the free software community, the idea of copyleft arose partly in contrast to copyright's common use for commercial exploitation. A number of software authors were interested in sharing code in order to improve the quality of available programs and help advance technology.

If the code that they shared were put into the public domain under copyright law, then others could use the shared code in any way that they desired. This could include packaging and selling the free software. To avoid this, the idea of copyleft was developed. A developer using copyleft could make the code freely available, but retain the rights to place conditions on use. The most common conditions included making derivatives of the free software also freely distributed.

The Creative Commons non-profit corporation[1] was founded by Professor Lawrence Lessig of Harvard. Creative Commons has created and made available for free use a set of copyright licenses that allow content providers to clearly state, in a legally binding way, what rights they do and do not retain. The six major licenses are:

1. Attribution (CC BY) requires attribution to original author,
2. Attribution Share Alike (CC BY-SA) allows derivative works to be distributed under similar licenses,
3. Attribution No Derivatives (CC BY-ND) only the original work can be distributed,
4. Attribution Non-Commercial (CC BY-NC) does not allow the work to be used commercially,

---

[1]http://creativecommons.org/

5. Attribution Non-Commercial Share Alike (CC BY-NC-SA) non-commercial derivative works can be distributed, and
6. Attribution Non-Commercial No Derivatives (CC BY-NC-ND) the work can not be modified and not used commercially.

All of these licenses currently allow unmodified works to be redistributed for non-commercial purposes without modification.

The Creative Commons concept is an attempt to legally codify, and make widely available, many of the ideas related to copyleft and free and open source software. As with all aspects of copyright regulation, the Creative Commons is not without controversy.

13.4   Digital Rights Management

With the increasing availability of electronic media and the ease of content distribution over the Internet, media concerns started researching technical means, in addition to legal means, for restricting distribution of their content.

One of the earlier Digital Rights Management (DRM) technologies was the *Content Scrambling System (CSS)* created by the DVD forum to restrict the copying of DVDs. CSS, which was released in around 1996, used an encryption algorithm to control access to the DVD contents.

In 1999 a Norwegian High School student wanted to create a DVD driver for the Linux operating system. It allegedly took him one afternoon to reverse engineer CSS and develop software, called *DeCSS*, for playing CSS content on Linux. In the resulting legal battle, there were conflicting rulings that the DeCSS program was illegal, but that the DeCSS source code was protected as free speech. This led to many different versions of DeCSS being made available, including T-shirts, implementations in multiple languages, gif representations, plain English dramatic readings, and even haiku form[2].

Multiple DRM systems have been developed and deployed since CSS. There are some major problems with almost every system. These include:

1. Any media sold containing DRM is developed to deliver the contents of the system to the consumer. If anyone wants to pirate media, nothing stops them from recording the output of the system and re-recording it without DRM,
2. For this system to be effective, it has to stop all attacks. If any single attacker is successful then the media can be easily distributed, and
3. To deliver content to the consumer, the DRM system has to be able to decode the content. If encryption is used, that means that the

---

[2]see http://www.cs.cmu.edu/ dst/DeCSS/Gallery/

key for the encryption will be read into memory at some point and be readily accessible to the system.

Numerous DRM approaches have been fielded and almost always they are cracked shortly thereafter. It may be possible for an approach applying principles from the trusted computing group [289] to be successful. In that approach, there is a hardened *Trusted Platform Module (TPM)* which serves as a root of trust. The TPM is tamper proof and contains cryptographic keys. These keys are used by the TPM to verify hardware and software signatures before they are used by the computer. In theory, an approach like this could produce a closed system that can not be compromised. This would severely limit the ability of users to program or modify their systems, creating a very strong "closed garden."

As with all computer systems, it is difficult to make devices that work in physically uncontrolled spaces without being compromised.

13.5 Digital Millennium Copyright Act

The 1996 *Digital Millennium Copyright Act (DMCA)* was passed in 1998. It made criminal the act of circumventing DRM technologies. It also forbid production and distribution of tools designed to aid in DRM circumvention. It exempted Internet service providers from prosecution if their networks were used for distributing pirated materials. Exemptions exist for security researchers in order to allow analysis of security techniques and advance the art, although there have been attempts based on the DMCA to stifle publication of academic articles on computer security [9].

There are concerns about the consequences of the DMCA. Some manufacturers have installed electronics on equipment parts or supplies that serve only to verify that the parts are produced and delivered by the manufacturer. If electronics contain a DRM technology, it is illegal to reverse engineer the DRM to create compatible equipment. This has effectively removed competition and innovation in many parts of the spare parts market. Companies can make it legally impossible for others to interface with their devices.

13.6 The Darknet

One interesting argument against the use of DRM referring to *The Darknet* was made in [69]. The authors, who were employees of Microsoft Corporation, made three basic assumptions from [69]:

1. Any widely distributed object will be available to some users in a form that can be copied,
2. Users will copy objects if it is possible and in their interest,
3. Users are connected by high bandwidth channels that allow copying.

The simple conclusion of these three assumptions is that DRM will not work.

The first assumption may be the weakest, but history has shown that in most systems some highly skilled users have found ways around copy protection in the past. The other two assumptions are easily satisfied on today's network.

The authors posit that, if these assumptions are satisfied, there will be one or more *Darknets* that allow covert sharing of digital media. Darknets need:

- Facilities for inputting media,
- Means for transferring media,
- Interfaces for reading media,
- Databases for finding media, and
- Data storage.

They trace the evolution of Darknets from people copying floppy disks to Napster and beyond. These networks evolve, become increasingly secretive, and increasingly easy to use.

The business implication of this work is that DRM makes media increasingly unattractive by being difficult to access, subject to arbitrary restrictions, etc. This makes the Darknet more attractive. As users become accustomed to using the Darknets, they are more likely to use those systems than the commercial distribution networks.

13.7 Patent Trolls

A related problem with intellectual property law is the emergence of a phenomenon called *patent trolls*. Patent trolls buy and accumulate patents, but do no original innovation. Their purpose is to actively seek litigation in order to force technology firms to pay money for alleged patent infringements. Sometimes the threatened litigation is accompanied by very vague descriptions of the patents the victim is allegedly using. Some of the patents used in litigation are of doubtful legitimacy; a number of overly broad (or lacking real innovation) patents have been granted over the years.

The patent trolls may have large resources and litigation may be very expensive. This threat of litigation has made it more difficult to start small technology companies. The seriousness of this problem is evidenced by Google purchasing Motorola for $13 billion in 2012, solely to own its patents in order to ward off this type of litigation [1].

13.8   Discussion Assignment – Business Case for DRM

- Consider yourself as a content provider. Use the information provided in this chapter to make the business case for or against investing in a DRM solution for your product.
- Read the first chapter of Cory Doctorow's book *Content* [141][3] and debate his attitude towards the business case for or against DRM.
- Is the current practice with copyright and patents consistent with the justification for granting these forms of intellectual property protection?

13.9   Discussion Assignment – Technical Case for DRM

- When recorded audio was first introduced, musicians argued that the new technology would destroy music by making musicians obsolete. Was this argument valid? How is it different from the use of audio on the Internet?
- When radio was first introduced, audio recording companies argued that the new technology would destroy music by making audio recordings obsolete. Was this argument valid? How is it different from the use of audio on the Internet?
- Propose a DRM technology that is technically sound.
- Describe ways of circumventing any DRM technology.
- Discuss whether or not technical evolution should be limited in order to safeguard existing business models.
- Discuss whether or not DMCA limits technical evolution.

13.10   Glossary

Closed garden: An information system with extremely restricted access for media and programs.

Copyright: Law governing the rights that authors and other media creators have on their works.

Creative Commons: A nonprofit organization that maintains a free set of copyright licenses that give less restrictive access to content.

---

[3]Can be downloaded for free from URL in index.

CSS: Content Scrambling System was a DRM system for DVDs.

Darknet: Argument positing that DRM approaches will be broken. Attempts to stop sharing will create progressively more difficult to track and easier to use networks.

DeCSS: Algorithm for breaking CSS.

Digital millennium copyright act: Law making it illegal to break DRM.

Digital rights management (DRM): Software used to limit access to digital content for intellectual property protection.

Fair use: Limited use that is allowed for copyrighted material for specific purposes.

Patent: A form of intellectual property protection that gives inventors exclusive rights for a limited period of time in exchange for invention disclosure.

Patent troll: A company that purchases and uses patents solely for litigation.

Public domain: Works not covered by a copyright license are in the public domain and free for use by anyone.

14

Security Economics

CONTENTS

There is a growing body of research involving interactions between information security and economics [46]. Current market incentives reward behaviors that do not safeguard the well-being of the public.

The consequences of poor software quality for consumers and the economy as a whole are immense. Dr. David Rice cites NIST studies showing the annual cost of insecure software to the United States as conservatively $180 billion[1] [348]. He also cites a market research survey, which finds 75 percent of computers connected to the Internet have been infected and used to distribute spam. In addition, numerous cases exist where software errors have proved fatal [314, 79, 288]. The case of the Therac-25 radiation therapy machine where a faulty user interface resulted in patients being fatally irradiated is a frequently cited case of a fatal computer software bug [288]. The long term consequences of this trend to our profession are not difficult to foresee. If products are unreliable, they are undesirable.

The rest of this Chapter is organized as follows. Section 14.1 discusses software liability laws and end user license agreements. This is followed by Section 14.2 giving a brief description of how network externalities influence the economics of computer systems. The software reliability problems are aggravated by code bloat Section 14.3 and the economics of *lemon markets* Section 14.4. Section 14.5 looks at how system quality is assured by software engineering. We end the chapter with Section 14.6 explaining how macroeconomics and game theory can be applied to determine and modify the consequences of market regulations on computer systems products.

---

[1]The same source estimates losses from Hurricane Katrina to be approximately $100 billion.

14.1   Liability and EULAs

The current software development philosophy of "we'll ship it on Tuesday and get it right by version 3" [48] is exacerbated by the ease of distributing patches over the Internet. There is little financial incentive to test rigorously. It is common to use clients as unpaid software testers to gradually find errors in programs [348].

This is enabled by End User License Agreements (EULAs) that tend to deny liability for damages due to software failures. This lack of liability is codified in the Uniform Computer Information Transactions Act (UCITA) which is law in both Virginia and Maryland. The Computer Fraud and Abuse Act (CFAA) passed by Congress in 1984 states "No action may be brought ... for the negligent design or manufacture of computer hardware, computer software or firmware." [121].

If there is no financial incentive for testing systems pre-release to avoid harming clients, then one should expect products to have low quality in general.

14.2   Network Externalities

In addition to there being no incentives for testing, there are real incentives to avoid testing. Hardware and software markets have *network externalities*: the value of an investment depends in large part on whether or not other parties make the same purchase decision [234]. These markets are "tippy," i.e., minuscule differences in quality or perception result in major differences in profitability.

In our industry, network externalities often result in markets where one product dominates the market. This explains the historically dominant market positions of the IBM PC, Microsoft Windows, and Intel processor architecture [67].

The need to be the dominant player induces pressure to be "first to market" with new applications. Arriving early usually tips the market enough to dominate it. In this "winner take all" [132] context, actions that improve product quality and security, but delay delivery, can be fatal to an enterprise. Ross Anderson of Cambridge says: "If (Bill) Gates had put proper access controls in (Microsoft) Windows ... from day one... then Steve Jobs would be a very much richer man..." [50].

14.3 Code Bloat

Another reason for shoddy products is *code bloat*. Software becomes larger and more complex over time. New versions are released to increase the number of features instead of reducing the number of errors. Since industry perceives that this matches user demand [172], this trend continues in spite of a survey by the Standish Group indicating that 45 percent of computer program features are *never used* [377]. If users buy products with more features, it makes sense to add as many features as possible to a system. But if the users never use those features, testing and quality assurance is a waste of money.

14.4 Lemon Markets

These economics factors driving the production of shoddy systems are exacerbated by software being a "lemon market" [40] with information asymmetry between buyer and seller. The buyer can not reliably distinguish between quality goods and shoddy products. Under these conditions, buyers choose the lower priced product. Shoddy products can be produced more cheaply. This drives quality products from the market.

14.5 Software Engineering

Software engineering analyzes current practices to improve system design, implementation, and test [334]. The Software Engineering Institute of Carnegie Mellon University has developed a standardized approach for evaluating development processes. The Capability Maturity Model Integration (CMMI) [251, 334] uses the following levels of organizational maturity:

1. *Initial* - Minimal *ad hoc* management,
2. *Managed* - Reasonable planning using realistic estimates,
3. *Defined* - Management rules are documented, standardized, and integrated into the process,
4. *Quantitatively managed* - The development process is measured and quantified, and
5. *Optimizing* - Measurement values are used to constantly improve the process.

Although most software development teams remain at levels one through three of CMMI, quantitative metrics exist for levels four and five. Quantitative management and optimization of the development process is enabled by a number of tools for measuring software [251, 70, 398].

14.6 Macroeconomics and Game Theory Introduction

Microeconomics tools exist that can be used to design market mechanisms that enforce a *social choice*. Game theory is the mathematics of conflict. It has been an essential part of economics since the seminal work by von Neumann and Morgenstern [418]. Nash won the Nobel prize in economics by extending [418] to show equilibrium solutions exist when players have finite sets of strategies with well-defined payoff values [246].

Mechanism design is a sub-field of microeconomics that aggregates user preferences to find a joint decision, called the *social choice* [311]. Typical applications of mechanism design include defining auction and voting systems. This approach is also used to design computer networks [415, 330] and distributed algorithms [157]. Mechanism design can analyze competitions among multiple players with hidden information and find the system's externalities. Of particular interest is studying how public policies regulating a market influence the social choice.

14.7 Problems

- Explain which business decisions currently have the strongest economic incentives.
- Suggest changes to the legal framework that you would expect to increase the quality of computer systems.
- Discuss how changes to increase system quality may modify the cost of those systems. How would you determine whether or not those changes would be worthwhile?

14.8 Glossary

Code bloat: The tendency of software packages to become increasingly large and complex over time.

Computer Fraud and Abuse Act: Law that protects manufacturers of faulty computer products.

EULA: End user license agreement is the license that users must agree to before using a product. They typically deny any liability for their product.

Game theory: The mathematics of conflict, also used to analyze economics problems.

Lemon market: A market where consumers can not differentiate between low and high quality products will tend to be dominated by low quality merchandise.

Network externalities: The value of a product dependent on the use by others of the same product.

15

Conclusions

This presents a course of study for computer and network security. This course has multiple goals. We want students to understand technical aspects of computer security. This includes realizing that security works simultaneously across multiple levels. Software needs to be written correctly. Data need to be protected cryptographically as appropriate. But these actions are all implemented on physical machines. The physical machines can also leak information. A proper security architecture can not ignore any of these factors.

We also hope that this course motivates students to better understand the design and implementation of computers and networks. There is a natural fascination with how tools can be misused. This analysis can help provide an in depth understanding of the logical and physical mechanisms used by modern technology.

Another important lesson is that computers and networks are part of society. They were created to answer pressing needs of the countries that created them. In many ways, those needs were military. Security flaws are now being exploited by criminal elements, like any weakness in the social fabric is exploited. Also, weaknesses exist for a reason. There will always be flaws due to carelessness, but systematic flaws usually are not based on carelessness or stupidity. Sometimes the wrong decision can be lucrative.

Bibliography

[1] "WSJ: Regulators to issue final rule requiring pressure monitors by 2008 model year," CNN, April 2005 ,`http://money.cnn.com/2005/04/06/Autos/tires.dj/index.htm`, (last visited Feb. 2010).

[2] 2011 cwe/sans top 25 most dangerous software errors `http://cwe.mitre.org/top25/`.

[3] Basic socket interface extensions for ipv6, `http://tools.ietf.org/html/rfc3493`.

[4] "Bin Laden: Steganography Master?", Feb. 7, 2001, `http://www.wired.com/news/politics/0,1283,41658,00.html?tw=wn\_story\_page\_prev2`.

[5] Casper Manual. `http://www.comlab.ox.ac.uk/people/gavin.lowe/Security/Casper/manual.pdf`. (last visited Jan. 2012).

[6] Internet x.509 public key infrastructure certificate and certificate revocation list (crl) profile, `http://www.ietf.org/rfc/rfc3280.txt`.

[7] "Intrusion detection should be a function, not a product", `http://www.csoonline.com/article/218447/intrusion-detection-should-be-a-function-not-a-product`, (last visited 2012).

[8] Phlashing, `http://www.boingboing.net/2008/05/20/phlashing-attack-per.html` (last visited July 2011).

[9] Princeton student sued over cd copying paper, `http://www.billboard.com/articles/news/68692/princeton-student-sued-over-cd-copying-paper` (last visited March 2013).

[10] RFC 4033, DNS Security Introduction and Requirements, March 2005, `http://tools.ietf.org/html/rfc4033` (last visited April 2012).

[11] RFC 4034, Resource Records for the DNS Security Extensions, March 2005, `http://tools.ietf.org/html/rfc4034` (last visited April 2012).

[12] RFC 4035, Protocol Modifications for the DNS Security Extensions, March 2005, `http://tools.ietf.org/html/rfc4035` (last visited April 2012).

[13] Shibboleth: General Info, `http://shibboleth.internet2.edu/about.html` (last visited 5/2011).

[14] Sql history, `http://www.faircom.com/ace/enl_22_s12_t.php` (last visited Sept. 2012).

[15] Sql injection attacks by example.

[16] Steganography: Hidden Data, Computerworld, June 10, 2002, `http://www.computerworld.com/securitytopics/security/story/0,10801,71726,00.html`.

[17] The International Obfuscated C Code Contest, http://www.ioccc.org, (last visited Jan. 2012).

[18] `http://dewy.fem.tu-ilmenau.de/CCC/CCCamp07/video/m4v/cccamp07-en-2050-Estonia\_and\_information\_warfare.m4v`.

[19] `http://www.cryptool.org` (last visited Oct. 2011).

[20] `http://www.fsel.com` (last visited Jan. 2012).

[21] `http://www.i2p2.de/index.html` (last checked Feb. 2010).

[22] `http://www.openssl.org` (last visited Dec. 2011).

[23] `http://www.safetyvision.com/client-testimonials/` (last visited Feb. 2010).

[24] `http://www.tcpdump.org/` (last visited May 2012).

[25] `http://www.torproject.org` (last checked April 2008).

[26] Virtualbox, `https://www.virtualbox.org/wiki/Downloads` (last visited July 2012).

[27] Vmware player download center, `https://my.vmware.com/web/vmware/evalcenter?p=player` (last visited July 2012).

[28] www.wireshark.org (last visited May 2012).

[29] *American Heritage Dictionary of the English Language, Electronic Version*. Microsoft Corporation, Redmond, WA, 1992.

[30] Insertion, evasion, and denial of service: Eluding network intrusion detection, `http://insecure.org/stf/secnet_ids/secnet_ids.html`, 1998.

[31] S. Staniford, V. Paxson, N. Weaver, et al. How to own the internet in your spare time. In *Proceedings of the 11th USENIX Security symposium*, volume 8, pages 149–167, 2002.

[32] 24C3. http://dewy.fem.tu-ilmenau.de/CCC/24C3/mpeg4/ 24c3-2279-en-deconstructing_xbox_360_security.mp4 (last visited May 2008).

[33] Andreu A. *Pen Testing for Web Applications*. Wiley, Indianapolis, Indiana, 2006.

[34] J. Srivastava A. Lazarevic and V. Kumar. Cyber threat analysis a key enabling technology for the objective force (a case study in network intrusion detection), army science conference, http://minds.cs.umn. edu/papers/asc2002.pdf, 2002.

[35] Martin Abadi and Andrew D. Gordon. A calculus for cryptographic protocols: The spi calculus. In *4th ACM Conference on Computer and Communications Security*, pages 36–47. ACM Press, 1997.

[36] C. Abott. Strengthening the Anonymity of Anonymous Communications Systems. Master's thesis, Clemson University, 2011.

[37] S. Adair, R. Deibert, R. Rohonzinski, N. Villeneuve, and G. Walton. JR032010 Shadows in the Cloud: Investigating Cyber Espionage 2.0, http://shadows\-in\-the\-cloud.net.

[38] L. Adleman. An abstract theory of computer viruses. In *Advances in CryptologyCRYPTO88*, pages 354–374. Springer, 1990.

[39] Aesop. *Aesop's Fables*. Seastar Books, NY, 2000.

[40] George A. Akerlof. The market for "lemons": Quality uncertainty and the market mechanism. *The Quarterly Journal of Economics*, 84:488–500, 1970.

[41] aleph1@underground.org Aleph One. Smashing the stack for fun and profit, *Phrack*, http://insecure.org/stf/smashstack.html.

[42] A.I. Alrabady and S.M. Mahmud. Analysis of attacks against the security of keyless-entry systems for vehicles and suggestions for improved designs. *Vehicular Technology, IEEE Transactions on*, 54(1):41–50, Jan. 2005.

[43] Cory Altheide and Harlan Carvey. *Digital Forensics with Open Source Tools: Using Open Source Platform Tools for Performing Computer Forensics on Target Systems: Windows, Mac, Linux, Unix, etc.* Syngress, 2011.

[44] James P. Anderson. Computer Security Technology Planning Study, ESD-TR-73-51, Vol. 1, Vol. II, 1972.

[45] R. H. Anderson, S. Feldman, P. M. andGerwehr, B. H. Houghton, R. Mesic, J. Pinder, J. Rothenberg, and J. R. Chiesa. Securing the U.S. Defense Information Infrastructure: A Proposed Approach, Rand Corporation, Santa Monica, CA, 1999, http://www.rand.org/publications/MR/MR993/.

[46] Ross Anderson. Talk at DeMonfort, http://www.tech.dmu.ac.uk/STRL/news/annual-seminar/STRL-ADS-2009.m4v.

[47] Ross Anderson. Why cryptosystems fail. In *Proceedings of the 1st ACM Conference on Computer and Communications security*, CCS '93, pages 215–227, New York, NY, 1993. ACM.

[48] Ross Anderson. Why information security is hard - an economic perspective. In *17th Annual Computer Security Applications Conference*, page 358, December 2001.

[49] Ross Anderson. *Security Engineering: A Guide to Building Dependable Distributed Systems*. Wiley, 2 edition, 2008.

[50] Ross Anderson. Information security - where computer science, economics and psychology meet, http://www.tech.dmu.ac.uk/STRL/news/annual-seminar/STRL-ADS-2009.m4v, 2009. Video of technical seminar.

[51] ARD. plusminus: Einzelhandel - Fingerprint-System überlistet, http://www.youtube.com/watch?v=aBm\-WsJ2U1c\&feature=player_embedded (last accessed May 2011).

[52] Arjen K. Lenstra, James P. Hughes, Maxime Augier, Joppe W. Bos, Thorsten Kleinjung and Christophe Wachter. Ron was wrong, Whit is right, http://eprint.iacr.org/. Cryptology ePrint Archive, Report 2012/064, 2012.

[53] K. J. Arrow. Classificatory notes on the production and transmission of technological knowledge. *The American Economic Review*, 59(2):29–35, 1969.

[54] W. Aspray, A. G. Bromley, M. Campbell-Kelly, P.E. Ceruzzi, and M. R. Williams. *Computing Before Computers*. Iowa State University Press, Ames, Iowa, 1990.

[55] William Aspray. The Institute for Advanced Study Computer: A Case Study in the Application of Concepts from the History of Technology. In Rojas and Hashagen, editors, *The First Computers – History and Architectures*, pages 179–193. MIT Press, 2000.

[56] Aspray, William. Oral history interview with Nicholoas Metropolis 1987: http://www.cbi.umn.edu/oh/display.phtml?id=81.

[57] S. Axelsson. Intrusion detection systems: A survey and taxonomy, `http://www.ce.chalmers.se/staff/sax/taxonomy.ps`.

[58] L. Cavallaro B. Gilbert M. Szydlowski R. Kemmerer, C. Kruegel B. Stone-Gross, M. Cova and G. Vigna. Your botnet is my botnet: Analysis of a botnet takeover. In *Proceedings of the ACM CCS*. ACM, 2010.

[59] A.L. Barabási and R. Albert. Emergence of scaling in random networks. *Science*, 286(5439):509–512, 1999.

[60] M. Barborak, M. Malek and A. Dahbura. The Consensus Problem in Fault Tolerant Computing. *ACM Computing Surveys*, 25(2):171–220, 1993.

[61] Gregory V. Bard. A challenging but feasible blockwise-adaptive chosen-plaintext attack on ssl. In *Secrypt 2006, Proccedings of the Internaitonal Conference on Security and Cryptography*, pages 7–10. INSTICC Press, 2006.

[62] M. Barreno, B. Nelson, R. Sears, A.D. Joseph, and J. D. Tygar. Can machine learning be secure? In *ASIA CCS '06*, 2006.

[63] Lejla Batina, Sddka Berna rs, Bart Preneel, and Joos Vandewalle. Hardware architectures for public key cryptography. *Integration, the VLSI Journal*, 34(1-2):1 – 64, 2003.

[64] Friedrich L. Bauer. The plankalkül of konrad zuse –revisited. In Rojas and Hashagen, editors, *The First Computers – History and Architectures*, pages 277–294. MIT Press, 2000.

[65] D. E. Bell and L. J. La Padula. Secure Computer System: Unified Exposition and MULTICS Interpretation, MTR-2997 Rev. 1, 1976.

[66] H. Berghel. Malware month. *Communications of the ACM*, 46:15–19, 2003.

[67] Stanley M. Besen and Joseph Farrell. Choosing how to compete: Strategies and tactics in standardization. *Journal of Economic Perspectives*, 8:117–131, 1994.

[68] H. Bhanu. Timing Side-channel Attacks on SSH. Master's thesis, Clemson University, 2010.

[69] Peter Biddle, Paul England, Marcus Peinado, and Bryan Willman. The darknet and the future of content distribution. In *ACM Workshop on Digital Rights Management*, volume 6, page 54, 2002.

[70] Stefan Biffl, Aybueke Aurum, Barry Boehm, Hakan Erdogmus, and Paul Gruenbacher, editors. *Value-based Software Engineering*. Springer Verlag, Berlin, 2006.

[71] Eli Biham and Adi Shamir. Differential cryptanalysis of the full 16-round des. In Ernest Brickell, editor, *Advances in Cryptology CRYPTO 92*, volume 740 of *Lecture Notes in Computer Science*, pages 487–496. Springer, Berlin / Heidelberg, 1993. 10.1007/3-540-48071-4_34.

[72] Nick Bilton. Rented computers captured customers having sex, F.T.C. says, http://bits.blogs.nytimes.com/2012/09/26/rented-computers-captured-customers-having-sex-f-t-c-says/.

[73] B. E. Binde, R. Mcreem, and T. J. O'Connor. Assessing outbound traffic to uncover advanced persistent threat, sans technology institute.

[74] J.-Y. Birrien. *Histoire De L'Informatique.* Que sais-je? Presses Universitaire De France, Paris, France, 1990.

[75] Alex Biryukov and Dmitry Khovratovich. Related-key cryptanalysis of the full aes-192 and aes-256. In Mitsuru Matsui, editor, *Advances in Cryptology ASIACRYPT 2009*, volume 5912 of *Lecture Notes in Computer Science*, pages 1–18. Springer, Berlin / Heidelberg, 2009. 10.1007/978-3-642-10366-7_1.

[76] George Bissias, Marc Liberatore, David Jensen, and Brian Levine. Privacy vulnerabilities in encrypted http streams. In *Privacy Enhancing Technologies*, pages 1–11. Springer, 2006.

[77] Bill Blunden. *The Rootkit Arsenal: Escape and Evasion in the Dark Corners of the System.* Jones & Bartlett Publishers, 2012.

[78] Johannes Blmer and Jean-Pierre Seifert. Fault based cryptanalysis of the advanced encryption standard (aes). In Rebecca Wright, editor, *Financial Cryptography*, volume 2742 of *Lecture Notes in Computer Science*, pages 162–181. Springer, Berlin / Heidelberg, 2003. 10.1007/978-3-540-45126-6_12.

[79] Walt Bogdanich. "Radiation offers new cures, and ways to do harm," http://www.nytimes.com/2010/01/24/health/24radiation.html?pagewanted=1. *New York Times*, January 2010.

[80] Andrey Bogdanov. Linear slide attacks on the keeloq block cipher. In Dingyi Pei, Moti Yung, Dongdai Lin, and Chuankun Wu, editors, *Information Security and Cryptology*, volume 4990 of *Lecture Notes in Computer Science*, pages 66–80. Springer, Berlin / Heidelberg, 2008. 10.1007/978-3-540-79499-8_7.

[81] N. B. Bolyard. "All About Certificate Extensions," NSS TEchnical Note: 3, http://www.mozilla.org/projects/security/pki/nss/tech-notes/tn3.html (last visited May 2012).

[82] Stephen C. Bono, Matthew Green, Adam Stubblefield, Ari Juels, Aviel D. Rubin, and Michael Szydlo. Security analysis of a cryptographically-enabled rfid device. In *Proceedings of the 14th conference on USENIX Security Symposium - Volume 14*, pages 1–1, Berkeley, CA, 2005. USENIX Association.

[83] V. Bontchev. Are "Good" Computer Viruses Still a Bad Idea? `http://vx.netlux.org/lib/avb02.html`.

[84] V. Bontchev. The Bulgarian and Soviet Virus Factories, `http://vx.netlux.org/lib/avb05.html`.

[85] P. Bright. Spearpphishing + zero-day: RSA hack not "extremely sophisticated," `http://arstechnica.com/security/news/2011/04/spearphishing-0-day-rsa-hack-not-extremely-sophisticated.ars` (last accessed May 2011).

[86] P. Bright. Comodo hacker: I hacked DigiNotar too; other CAs breached, `http://arstechnica.com/security/2011/09/comodo-hacker-i-hacked-diginotar-too-other-cas-breached/` (last visited May 2012), 2011.

[87] R.G. Brody, E. Mulig, and V. Kimball. Phishing, Pharming, and Identity Theft. *Academy of Accounting and Financial Studies Journal*, 11(3):43–56, 2007.

[88] W. L. Brogan. *Modern Control Theory, 3rd ed.* Prentice-Hall, Inc, Englewood Cliffs, NJ, 1991.

[89] R. R. Brooks. Mobile code paradigms and security issues. *Internet Computing, IEEE*, 8(3):54 – 59, May-Jun 2004.

[90] R. R. Brooks. *Disruptive Security Technologies with Mobile Code and Peer-to-Peer Networks*. CRC Press, Boca Raton, FL, 2005.

[91] R. R. Brooks and Juan Deng. Lies and the lying liars that tell them: A fair and balanced look at TLS. In *Proceedings of the Sixth Annual Workshop on Cyber Security and Information Intelligence Research*, CSIIRW '10, pages 59:1–59:3, New York, NY, 2010. ACM.

[92] R. R. Brooks and S. S. Iyengar. Robust Distributed Computing and Sensing Algorithm. *IEEE Computer*, 29(6):53–60, 1996.

[93] R. R. Brooks and S. S. Iyengar. *Multisensor Fusion: Fundamentals and Applications with Software*. Prentice Hall PTR, Upper Saddle River, NJ, 1998.

[94] R. R. Brooks and N. Orr. A model for mobile code using interacting automata. *Mobile Computing, IEEE Transactions on*, 1(4):313 – 326, Oct-Dec 2002.

[95] R. R. Brooks, S. Sander, Juan Deng, and J. Taiber. Automobile security concerns. *Vehicular Technology Magazine, IEEE*, 4(2):52 –64, june 2009.

[96] J. Brunner. *The Shockwave Rider*. Ballantine Books, NY, 1975.

[97] M. Brunner, H. Hofinger, C. Krauss, C. Roblee, P. Schoo, and S. Todt. Infiltrating critical infrastructures with next-generation attacks w32. stuxnet as a showcase threat, Fraunhofer-Institute for Secure Information Technology SIT Munich.

[98] M. Burgess. Thermal, non-equilibrium phase space for networked computers. *Physical Review E*, 62:1738, 2000.

[99] A.W. Burks and J. Von Neumann. *Theory of Self-Reproducing Automata*. University of Illinois Press, Urbana, 1966.

[100] C. Maple, and A. Phillips, and 7Safe. UK security breach investigations report, an analysis of state compromise cases, http://7safe.com/breach_report/Breach_report_2010.pdf.

[101] CERT Advisory CA-1996-01. Udp port denial-of-service attack, 1996.

[102] CERT Advisory CA-1996-21. Tcp syn flooding and ip spoofing attacks, 1996.

[103] CAIDA. The spread of the code-red worm crv2 http://www.caida.org/analysis/security/code-red/coderedv2_analysis.xml.

[104] Brice Canvel, Alain Hiltgen, Serge Vaudenay, and Martin Vuagnoux. Password interception in a SSL/TLS channel. In *Advances in Cryptology - CRYPTO 2003*, pages 583–599. 2003.

[105] G. Carl, G. Kesidis, R. R. Brooks, and Suresh Rai. Denial-of-service attack-detection techniques. *Internet Computing, IEEE*, 10(1):82 – 89, Jan.-Feb. 2006.

[106] Glenn Carl, Richard R. Brooks, and Suresh Rai. Wavelet based denial-of-service detection. *Computers & Security*, 25(8):600 – 615, 2006.

[107] Eoghan Casey. *Digital Evidence and Computer Crime*. Academic, San Diego, 2011.

[108] C. Castillo, D. Donato, L. Bechetti, P. Boldi, S. Leonardi, M. Santini, and S. Vigna. A reference collection for web spam. In *ACM SIGIR Forum*, volume 40, 2006.

[109] P.E. Ceruzzi. *A History of Modern Computing*. MIT Press, Cambridge, MA, 1998.

[110] E. Chabrow. RSA's Post-Breach Security, http://www.govinfosecurity.com/podcasts.php?podcastID=1178, (last visited July 2011).

[111] D. W. Chadwick and A. Otenko. The PERMIS X.509 role based privilege management infrastructure. *Future Generation Computer Systems*, 19(2):277–289, 2003.

[112] David Chaum. The dining cryptographers problem: Unconditional sender and recipient untraceability. *Journal of Cryptology*, 1:65–75.

[113] Kameswari Chebrolu, Bhaskaran Raman, and Sayandeep Sen. Long-distance 802.11b links: performance measurements and experience. In *Proceedings of the 12th Annual International Conference on Mobile Computing and Networking*, MobiCom '06, pages 74–85, New York, NY, 2006. ACM.

[114] K. Chellapilla and D. M. Chickering. Improving cloaking detection using search query popularity and monetizability. In *AIRWeb '06*, 2006.

[115] Li-Chiou Chen and Kathleen M. Carley. The impact of countermeasure propagation on the prevalence of computer viruses. *IEEE Transactions on Systems, Man and Cybernetics-Part B*, 34(2):823–833, April 2004.

[116] W. R. Cheswick and S. M. Bellovin. *Firewalls and Internet Security*. Addison-Wesley, Reading, MA, 1994.

[117] S. Christey and R.A. Martin. Vulnerability type distributions in cve. *Mitre report, May*, 2007.

[118] Soon Ae Chun and Vijayalakshmi Atluri. Geospatial database security. In Michael Gertz and Sushil Jajodia, editors, *Handbook of Database Security*, pages 247–266. Springer US, 2008. 10.1007/978038748533111.

[119] F Cohen. *Computer Viruses*. PhD thesis, University of Southern California, 1986.

[120] Christian Collberg, Clark Thomborson, and Douglas Low. A taxonomy of obfuscating transformations, 1997.

[121] Congress. Title 18, part 1, chapter 47, url-http://www.law.cornell.edu/uscode/18/1030.html, (last visited January 2010) 1984.

[122] CERT coordination center. Denial of service attack, 2001.

[123] Jean-Sébastien Coron. Resistance against differential power analysis for elliptic curve cryptosystems. In *Cryptographic Hardware and Embedded Systems*, pages 725–725. Springer, 1999.

[124] The National Research Council. *Technology, Policy, Law, and Ethics Regarding U.S. Acquisition and Use of Cyberattack Capabilities.* National Academy Press, Washington, DC, 2009.

[125] J. Cowie, A. Ogielski, B. J. Premore, and Y. Yuan. Global routing instabilities triggered by code red ii and nimda worm attacks. Technical report, Tech. Rep., Renesys Corporation, 2001.

[126] R. Craven. Traffic Analysis of Anonymity Systems. Master's thesis, Clemson University, 2010.

[127] W. L. Cukier, E. J. Nesselroth, and S. Cody. Genre, Narrative and the "Nigerian Letter" in Electronic Mail. In *Proceedings of the 40th Hawaii International Conference on System Sciences*, 2007.

[128] D. Kennedy, J. O'Gorman, D. Kearns, and M. Aharoni. *Metasploit: The Penetration Tester's Guide*. No Starch Press, San Francisco, CA, 2011.

[129] B. Dang. Methods for Understanding Targeted Attacks with Office Documents, `http://dewy.fem.tu-ilmenau.de/CCC/25C3/video\_h264\_720x576/25c3\-2938\-en\-methods\_for\_understanding\_targeted\_attacks\_with\_office\_documents.mp4`.

[130] P. Davern and M. Scott. *Steganography: its history and its application to computer based data files*. Dublin City University, 2002.

[131] Philippe De Ryck, Lieven Desmet, Wouter Joosen, and Frank Piessens. Automatic and precise client-side protection against csrf attacks. *Computer Security–ESORICS 2011*, pages 100–116, 2011.

[132] Eddie Dekel and Suzanne Scotchmer. On the evolution of attitudes towards risk in winner-take-all games. *Journal of Economic Theory*, 87:125–143, 1999.

[133] Krassen Deltchev. *New Web 2.0 Attacks*. Bachelor's thesis, Ruhr University, Bochum, Deutschland`http://www.nds.ruhr-uni-bochum.de/teaching/theses/Web20/`, February 2010.

[134] Juan Deng, R. Brooks, and J. Taiber. Security automata integrated xacml and security validation. In *IEEE SoutheastCon 2010 (SoutheastCon), Proceedings of the*, pages 338–343, March 2010.

[135] Department of Defense. Department of Defense Trusted Computer System Evaluation Criteria, DoD 5200.28-STD, CSC-STD-001-83, 1985.

[136] T. Deshpande, P. Katsaros, S. Basagiannis, and S.A. Smolka. Formal analysis of the dns bandwidth amplification attack and its countermeasures using probabilistic model checking. In *High-Assurance Systems Engineering (HASE), 2011 IEEE 13th International Symposium on*, pages 360 –367, Nov. 2011.

[137] O. Diekmann and J.A.P. Heesterbeek. *Mathematical Epidemiology of Infectious Diseases: Model Building, Analysis and Interpretation*, volume 5. Wiley, 2000.

[138] R. Dingledyne. "Security and anonymity vulnerabilities in Tor Past, present, and future," 25th Chaos Computer Congress, Berlin, 2008, http://media.ccc.de/browse/congress/2008/25c3-2977-en-security_and_anonymity_vulnerabilities_in_tor.html (last visited Feb 2010).

[139] Hans Dobbertin, Lars Knudsen, and Matt Robshaw. The cryptanalysis of the AES—a brief survey. In Hans Dobbertin, Vincent Rijmen, and Aleksandra Sowa, editors, *Advanced Encryption Standard AES*, volume 3373 of *Lecture Notes in Computer Science*, pages 571–572. Springer, Berlin / Heidelberg, 2005. 10.1007/11506447_1.

[140] C. Doctorow. *Overclocked: Stories of the Future Present http://craphound.com/overclocked/download/*. Running Press, 2007.

[141] Cory Doctorow. *Content: Selected Essays on Technology, Creativity, Copyright, and the Future of the Future*. Tachyon Publications, 2008.

[142] A. Dolan. Social Engineering, SANS Institute, http://www.sans.org/reading_room/whitepapers/engineering/social\-engineering_1365.

[143] S.D. Donald, R.V. McMillen, D.K. Ford, and J.C. McEachen. Therminator 2: A thermodynamics-based method for real-time patternless intrusion detection. In *MILCOM 2002. Proceedings*, volume 2, pages 1498 – 1502 vol.2, Oct. 2002.

[144] Bret Dunbar. *A Detailed Look at Steganographic Techniques and Their Use in an Open-Systems Environment*. SANS Institute, 2002.

[145] M. Dusi, M. Crotti, F. Gringoli, and L. Salgarelli. Tunnel hunter: Detecting application-layer tunnels with statistical fingerprinting. *Computer Networks*, 53(1):81–97, 2009.

[146] M. A. Dyrud. "I brought you a good news"': An analysis of Nigerian 419 letters. In *Proceedings of the 2005 Association for Business Communication Annual Convention*, 2005.

[147] E. Rescorla, A. Langley, B. Smith, S. Schultze, and S. Kent. SSL/TLS Certificates: Threat or Menace?, Usenix Security 2011, https://www.usenix.org/conference/usenix-security-11/ssltls-certificates-threat-or-menace (last visited May 2012).

[148] P. Eckersley and J. Burns. "Is the SSLiverse a safe place?" Talk at 27C3, https://www.eff.org/files/ccc2010.pdf, year=2010, (last retrieved in May 2012).

[149] P. Eckersley and J. Burns. "An observatory for the SSLiverse," Talk at Defcon 18., July 2010, `https://www.eff.org/files/DefconSSLiverse.pdf`, (last retrieved in May 2012), 2010.

[150] Benjamin Edelman. Adverse selection in online "trust" certifications. In *Proceedings of the 11th International Conference on Electronic Commerce*, ICEC '09, pages 205–212, New York, NY, 2009. ACM.

[151] Serge Egelman, Lorrie Faith Cranor, and Jason Hong. You've been warned: an empirical study of the effectiveness of web browser phishing warnings. In *Proceeding of the twenty-sixth Annual SIGCHI Conference on Human Factors in Computing Systems*, CHI '08, pages 1065–1074, New York, NY, 2008. ACM.

[152] E. English and S. Hamilton. Network security under siege: The timing attack. *Computer*, pages 95–97.

[153] M. Erdos and S. Cantor. Shibboleth Architecture DRAFT v05, `http://shibboleth.internet2.edu/docs/draft\-internet2\-shibboleth\-arch\-v05.pdf` (last visited 11/2010).

[154] Richard Esguerra. Google CEO Eric Schmidt Dismisses the Importance of Privacy, `https://www.eff.org/deeplinks/2009/12/google-ceo-eric-schmidt-dismisses-privacy`.

[155] D. Molnar et al. "MD5 considered harmful today," 25th Chaos Computer Congress, Berlin, January 2009, `http://dewy.fem.tuimenau.de/CCC/25C3/video\_h264\_720x756/25c3-3023-enmaking\_the\_theoretical\_possible.mp4.torrent`, 2009.

[156] Nathan S. Evans, Roger Dingledine, and Christian Grothoff. A practical congestion attack on tor using long paths. In *Proceedings of the 18th Conference on USENIX Security Symposium*, SSYM'09, pages 33–50, Berkeley, CA, 2009. USENIX Association.

[157] Joan Feigenbaum, Michael Schapira, and Scott Shenker. *Algorithmic Game Theory*, chapter 14 - Distributed Algorithmic Mechanism Design, pages 363–384. Cambridge University Press, Cambridge, UK, 2007.

[158] D. Fetterly, M. Manasse, and M. Najork. Spam, damn spam, and statistics. In *Seventh International Workshop on the Web and Databases*, 2004.

[159] S. Forrest and S. A. Hofmeyr. Immunology as information processing. In A. Segel and I. R. Cohen, editors, *Design Principles for Immune Systems and Other Distributed Autonomous Systems*, pages 361–387. Oxford University Press, Oxford, UK, 2000.

[160] S. Forrest, A. Somayaji, and D.H. Ackley. Building diverse computer systems. In *Operating Systems, 1997, The Sixth Workshop on Hot Topics in*, pages 67–72. IEEE, 1997.

[161] B. Forta. *SAMS Teach Yourself SQL in 10 Minutes*. SAMS Publishing, Indianapolis, IN, 2000.

[162] Electronic Frontier Foundation. List of printers which do or do not display tracking dots, `https://www.eff.org/pages/list-printers-which-do-or-do-not-display-tracking-dots`, (last visited March 2013).

[163] Electronic Frontier Foundation and J. Gilmore. *Cracking DES: Secrets of Encryption Research, Wiretap Politics and Chip Design*. O'Reilly, San Francisco, CA, 1998.

[164] Barbara Fox and Brian LaMacchia. Certificate revocation: Mechanics and meaning. In Rafael Hirchfeld, editor, *Financial Cryptography*, volume 1465 of *Lecture Notes in Computer Science*, pages 158–164. Springer, Berlin / Heidelberg, 1998. 10.1007/BFb0055479.

[165] Electronic Frontier Foundation. Surveillance self defense, `https://ssd.eff.org/your-computer/govt/privacy` (last visited March 2013).

[166] Frontline. Cyber war, `http://www.pbs.org/wgbh/pages/frontline/shows/cyberwar/warnings/`.

[167] W. Allen, G. A. Marin, and S. Luo. Network monitoring for computer intrusion detection.

[168] F. C. Gaertner. Fundamentals of Fault-Tolerant Distributed Computing in Asynchronous Environments. *ACM Computing Surveys*, 31(1):1–26, 1999.

[169] David Galula. *Counterinsurgency Warfare: Theory and Practice*. PSI Classics of the Counterinsurgency Era. Praeger Security International, Westport, CT, 1964.

[170] T. Gamble. Implementing execution controls in unix. In *Seventh System Administration Conference (LISA '93)*, 1993.

[171] L. Garber. Denial-of-service attacks rip the internet. *Computer*, 33(4):12 –17, Apr 2000.

[172] Bill Gates. Interview with Bill Gates, October 1995.

[173] C. Gentry. *A Fully Homomrphic Encryption Scheme*. PhD thesis, Stanford University, 2009.

[174] D. Gerrold. *When H.A.R.L.I.E. was One*. Ballantine Books, 1972.

[175] Christophe Giraud. Dfa on aes. In Hans Dobbertin, Vincent Rijmen, and
       Aleksandra Sowa, editors, *Advanced Encryption Standard AES*, volume
       3373 of *Lecture Notes in Computer Science*, pages 571–571. Springer,
       Berlin / Heidelberg, 2005. 10.1007/11506447_4.

[176] Philippe Golle, Dan Greene, and Jessica Staddon. Detecting and cor-
       recting malicious data in VANETs. In *Proceedings of the 1st ACM
       International Workshop on Vehicular Ad Hoc Networks*, VANET '04,
       pages 29–37, New York, NY, 2004. ACM.

[177] N. Gonzalez, C. Miers, F. Redigolo, T. Carvalho, M. Simplicio,
       M. Naslund, and M. Pourzandi. A quantitative analysis of current se-
       curity concerns and solutions for cloud computing. In *Cloud Computing
       Technology and Science (CloudCom), 2011 IEEE Third International
       Conference on*, pages 231 –238, Dec. 2011.

[178] T. Goodspeed and S. Bratus. Packets in packets, http://dewy.fem.
       tu-ilmenau.de/CCC/28C3/mp4-h264-LQ/28c3-4766-en-802_11_
       packets_in_packets_h264-iprod.mp4.

[179] Louis Goubin and Jacques Patarin. Des and differential power analy-
       sis the duplication method. In *Cryptographic Hardware and Embedded
       Systems*, pages 728–728. Springer, 1999.

[180] S. Govindavajhala and A.W. Appel. Using memory errors to attack
       a virtual machine. In *Security and Privacy, 2003. Proceedings. 2003
       Symposium on*, pages 154–165. IEEE, 2003.

[181] C. Griffin and R. Brooks. A note on the spread of worms in scale-free
       networks. *Systems, Man, and Cybernetics, Part B: Cybernetics, IEEE
       Transactions on*, 36(1):198 –202, Feb. 2006.

[182] T. K. Grose. "When Surveillance Cameras Talk," *Time*,
       Feb. 2008 ,http://www.time.com/time/printout/0,8816,1711972,
       00.html (last visited Feb. 2010).

[183] Peter Gruenwald. Strong entropy concentration, game theory, and al-
       gorithmic randomness. In David Helmbold and Bob Williamson, edi-
       tors, *Computational Learning Theory*, volume 2111 of *Lecture Notes in
       Computer Science*, pages 320–336. Springer, Berlin / Heidelberg, 2001.
       10.1007/3-540-44581-1_21.

[184] Yong Guan, Xinwen Fu, Dong Xuan, Prashanth U Shenoy, Riccardo
       Bettati, and Wei Zhao. Netcamo: Camouflaging network traffic for qos-
       guaranteed mission critical applications. *Systems, Man and Cybernetics,
       Part A: Systems and Humans, IEEE Transactions on*, 31(4):253–265,
       2001.

[185] V. Gudonov and J. Johnson. Network as a complex system: Information flow analysis, `http://arxiv.org/abs/nlin/0110008v1`, 2001.

[186] G. Guette and B. Ducourthial. On the sybil attack detection in vanet. In *Mobile Adhoc and Sensor Systems, 2007. MASS 2007. IEEE Internatonal Conference on*, pages 1 –6, Oct. 2007.

[187] Philipp Gühring. Concepts against man-in-the-browser attacks. *Update*, 2006:09–12, 2006.

[188] Peter Gutmann. *Engineering Security*. `http://www.cs.aukland.ac.nz/~pgut001/pubs/book.pdf`, 2012.

[189] H. Haas. IDS Insertion and Evasion Techniques, `http://www.perihel.at/sec/docs/evasion.pdf` (last viewed Nov. 2012), 2009.

[190] P. Haas. Advanced format string attacks, `https://www.defcon.org/images/defcon-18/dc-18-presentations/Haas/DEFCON-18-Haas-Adv-Format-String-Attacks.pdf`, 2010.

[191] S. Hada and M. Kudo. XML Access Control Language: Provisional Authorization for XML Documents, `http://www.trl.ibm.com/projects/xml/xacl/xacl\-spec.html`, 2000.

[192] C.T. Hager and S.F. Midkiff. An analysis of bluetooth security vulnerabilities. In *Wireless Communications and Networking, 2003. WCNC 2003. 2003 IEEE*, volume 3, pages 1825 –1831 vol.3, March 2003.

[193] R. A. Haldane. *The Hidden World*. St. Martin's Press, NY, 1976.

[194] D. R. Hankerson, D. G. Hoffman, D. A. Leonard, C. C. Lindner, K. T. Phelps, C. A. Rodger, and J. R. Wall. *Coding Theory and Cryptography: The Essentials*. Marcel Dekker, Inc., NY, 2 edition, 2000.

[195] D. Hardy, L. Woolever, and J. Tanfani. "Subpoena issued in L. Merion webcam case," Philadelphia Inquirer, Feb. 2010, `http://www.philly.com/philly/news/homepage/84835492.html` (last visited Feb. 2010).

[196] C. Herley and D. Florencio. A profitless endeavor: Phishing as tragedy of the commons. In *NSPW '08*, 2008.

[197] Jan Herrmann. Interoperable access control for geo web services in disaster management. In R Allan, U. Frstner, W. Salomons, Shailesh Nayak, and Sisi Zlatanova, editors, *Remote Sensing and GIS Technologies for Monitoring and Prediction of Disasters*, Environmental Science, pages 167–178. Springer, Berlin Heidelberg, 2008. 10.1007/9783540792598_10.

[198] Herbert W. Hethcote. The mathematics of infectious diseases. 42(4):599–653, 2000.

[199] P. Heymann, G. Koutrika, and H. Garcia-Molina. Fighting spam on social web sites: A survey of approaches and future challenges. *IEEE Internet Computing*, pages 36–45, November-December 2007.

[200] Kashmir Hill. What Fordham knows about Justice Scalia, `http://abovethelaw.com/2009/04/what-fordham-knows-about-justice-scalia/` (last visited March 2013).

[201] M. J. Hinek. *Cryptanalysis of RSA and Its Variants*. CRC Press, Boca Raton, FL, 2010.

[202] Andrew Hintz. Fingerprinting websites using traffic analysis. In Roger Dingledine and Paul Syverson, editors, *Privacy Enhancing Technologies*, volume 2482 of *Lecture Notes in Computer Science*, pages 229–233. Springer, Berlin / Heidelberg, 2003. 10.1007/3-540-36467-6_13.

[203] C. A. R. Hoare. *Communicating Sequential Processes*. Prentice Hall, `http://www.usingcsp.com/cspbook.pdf`, (last visited Dec. 2011), 1985.

[204] C. H. Hochstaetter. Aurora: Angriff mit ie-exploit aus china auf google und den rest der welt, `http://www.zdnet.de/41525729/aurora-angriff-mit-ie-exploit-aus-china-auf-google-und-den-rest-der-welt/2/` (last visited Jan 2013).

[205] S. Hofmeyr and S. Forrest. Architecture for an artificial immune system. *Evolutionary Computation*, 7:1289–1296, 2000.

[206] Chris Hoofnagle, Jennifer King, Su Li, and Joseph Turow. How different are young adults from older adults when it comes to information privacy attitudes and policies? *Available at SSRN 1589864*, 2010.

[207] Pieter Hooimeijer, Benjamin Livshits, David Molnar, Prateek Saxena, and Margus Veanes. Fast and precise sanitizer analysis with bek. In *Proceedings of the 20th USENIX conference on Security*, SEC'11, pages 1–1, Berkeley, CA, 2011. USENIX Association.

[208] Nicholas Hopper, Eugene Y. Vasserman, and Eric Chan-Tin. How much anonymity does network latency leak? *ACM Trans. Inf. Syst. Secur.*, 13:13:1–13:28, March 2010.

[209] R. Housley. RFC3280: Internet X.509 Public Key Infrastructure Certificate and Certificate Revocation List (CRL) Profile, `http://www.faqs.org/rfcs/rfc3280.html` (last visited 5/2011).

[210] J. D. Howard and T. A. Longstaff. A Common Language for Computer Security Incidents, Sandia Report, SAND98-8867.

[211] M. Howard and D. LeBlanc. *Writing Secure Code.* Microsoft Press, Redmond, WA, 2003.

[212] F.H. Hsu, C.K. Tso, Y.C. Yeh, W.J. Wang, and L.H. Chen. Browser-guard: A behavior-based solution to drive-by-download attacks. *Selected Areas in Communications, IEEE Journal on,* 29(7):1461–1468, 2011.

[213] D. J. Icove. Collaring the cybercrook: An investigator's view. *IEEE Spectrum,* (6):31–36, 1997.

[214] C. N. Igwe. Socio-economic developments and the rise of 419 advance-fee fraud in Nigeria. *European Journal of Social Sciences,* 20(1):184–193, 2011.

[215] Sebastiaan Indesteege, Nathan Keller, Orr Dunkelman, Eli Biham, and Bart Preneel. A practical attack on keeloq. In *Proceedings of the Theory and Applications of Cryptographic Techniques 27th Annual International Conference on Advances in Cryptology,* EUROCRYPT'08, pages 1–18, Berlin, Heidelberg, 2008. Springer-Verlag.

[216] Philip G. Inglesant and M. Angela Sasse. The true cost of unusable password policies: password use in the wild. In *Proceedings of the 28th International Conference on Human Factors in Computing Systems,* CHI '10, pages 383–392, New York, NY, 2010. ACM.

[217] Jesus Tellez Isaac, Jose Sierra Camara, Sherali Zeadally, and Joaquin Torres Marquez. A secure vehicle-to-roadside communication payment protocol in vehicular ad hoc networks. *Computer Communications,* 31(10):2478 – 2484, 2008.

[218] M. Isikoff. "The Snitch in your Pocket," *Newsweek,* Feb. 2010, `http://www.newsweek.com/id/233916` (last visited Feb. 2010).

[219] R. R. Brooks, J. Deng, and J. Martin. Assessing the effect of wimax system parameter settings on mac-level local dos vulnerability. *International Journal of Performability Engineering,* 8:183–198, 2012.

[220] J. Kevin, G. M. Weaver, N. Long, and R. Thomas. Trends in Denial of Service Attack Technology, Tech. Report, CERT Coordination Center, Carnegie Mellon University, 2001.

[221] Tom N. Jagatic, Nathaniel A. Johnson, Markus Jakobsson, and Filippo Menczer. Social phishing. *Commun. ACM,* 50:94–100, October 2007.

[222] Markus Jakobsson. Modeling and preventing phishing attacks. In Andrew Patrick and Moti Yung, editors, *Financial Cryptography and Data Security,* volume 3570 of *Lecture Notes in Computer Science,* pages 578–578. Springer, Berlin / Heidelberg, 2005. 10.1007/11507840_9.

[223] B. J. Jansen. Adversarial information retrieval aspects of sponsored search. In *AIRWeb '06*, 2006.

[224] W. Jansen and T. Karygiannis. Mobile Agent Security, NIST Special Publication 800-19, http://csrc.nist.gov/mobileagents/publication/sp800-19.pdf, August 1999.

[225] W. Jie, J. Arshad, R. Sinnott, P Townend, and Z. Lei. A Review of Grid Authentication and Authorization Technologies and Support for Federated Access Control. *ACM Computing Surveys*, 43(2):12:1–12:26, 2011.

[226] T. Jim, G. Morrisett, D. Grossman, M. Hicks, J. Cheney, and Y. Wang. Cyclone: A safe dialect of c. In *USENIX Annual Technical Conference*, volume 90, 2002.

[227] C. Jones. Social Engineering: Understanding and Auditing, SANS Institute, http://www.sans.org/reading_room/whitepapers/engineering/understanding\-auditing_1332.

[228] J.W.Haines, et al. 1999 DARPA Intrusion Detection Evaluation Design and Procedures, Technical Report 1062, MIT Lincoln Laboratories, 2001.

[229] Dan Kaminsky. "Something About Network Security," Blackhat 2009, http://www.blackhat.com/presentations/bh\-usa\-09/KAMINSKY/BHUSA09\-Kaminsky\-BlackOpsPKI\-VIDEO.MOV (last visited August 2009).

[230] Dan Kaminsky. Why we were so vulnerable to the DNS vulnerability, http://dewy.fem.tu-ilmenau.de/CCC/25C3/video_h264_720x576/25c3-2906-en-why_were_we_so_vulnerable_to_the_dns_vulnerability.mp4.

[231] M. Kanellos. Ermanno pietrosemoli has set a new record for the longest communication wi-fi link, http://interred.wordpress.com/2007/06/18/ermanno-pietrosemoli-has-set-a-new-record-for-the-longest-communication-wi-fi-link/, (last visited July 2012), 2007.

[232] P.A. Karger and R. R. Schell. Multics security evaluation: Vulnerability analysis, http://csrc.nist.gov/publications/history/karg74.pdf.

[233] P.A. Karger and R. R. Schell. Thirty Years Later: Lessons Learned from the Multics Security Evaluation, http://www.acsac.org/2002/papers/classic-multics.pdf.

[234] Michael L. Katz and Carl Shapiro. Network externalities, competition, and compatibility. *The American Economic Review*, 75:424–440, 1985.

[235] J.O. Kephart, S.R. White, and D.M. Chess. Computers and epidemiology. *Spectrum, IEEE*, 30(5):20–26, 1993.

[236] Rudolf Kippenhahn. *Code Breaking*. The Overlook Press, Woodstock, NY, 1999.

[237] Amit Klein. Gift wrapped attacks concealed online banking fraud during 2011 holiday season, http://www.trusteer.com/blog/gift-wrapped-attacks-concealed-online-banking-fraud-during-2011-holiday-season.

[238] Paul Kocher. Timing attacks on implementations of Diffie-Hellman, rsa, dss, and other systems. In Neal Koblitz, editor, *Advances in Cryptology CRYPTO 96*, volume 1109 of *Lecture Notes in Computer Science*, pages 104–113. Springer, Berlin / Heidelberg, 1996. 10.1007/3-540-68697-5_9.

[239] Paul Kocher. Introduction to Differential Power Analysis and Related Attacks, http://www.cryptography.com/dpa/technical/index.html. 1998.

[240] Paul Kocher, Joshua Jaffe, and Benjamin Jun. Differential power analysis. In *Advances in Cryptology – CRYPTO'99*, pages 789–789. Springer, 1999.

[241] O. Kolesnikov and B. Hatch. *Building Linux Virtual Private Networks (VPNs)*. NewRiders, Indianapolis, IN, 2002.

[242] Vladimir Kolovski. Formalizing xacml using defeasible description logics. Technical report, 2006.

[243] J. Koziol. *Intrusion Detection with Snort*. SAMS Publishing, Indianapolis, IN, 2003.

[244] B. Krebs. Malware Silently Alters Wireless Router Settings, 06/11/2008, http://voices.washingtonpost.com/securityfix/2008/06/malware_silently_alters_wirele_1.html (last visited April 2012).

[245] D. R. Kuhn, V. C. Hu, W. T. Polk, and S.-J. Chang. Introduction to Public Key Technology and the Federal PKI Infrastructure, NIST Special Publication 800-32, February 2001.

[246] Harold W. Kuhn, editor. *Classics in Game Theory*. Princeton University Press, Princeton, 1997.

[247] Markus G. Kuhn. Compromising emanations: Eavesdropping risks of computer displays, Technical Report UCAM-CL-TR-577 ISSN 1476-2986, University of Cambridge Computer Laboratory.

[248] R. Balupari L. Feinstein, D. Schnackenberg and D. Kindred. Statistical approaches to ddos detection and response. *Advanced Security Research Journal, McAfee Security Research*, VI:41–52, 2004.

[249] RSA Laboratories. 3.1.5 How large a key should be used in the RSA cryptosystem?, `http://www.rsa.com/rsalabs/node.asp?id=2218` (last visited Dec, 2011).

[250] Qualsys SSL labs.

[251] Linda M. Laird and M. Carol Brennan. *Software Measurement and Estimation: A Practical Approach*. Wiley-Interscience, Hoboken, NJ, 2006.

[252] L. Lamport, R. Shostak, and M. Pease. The Byzantine Generals Problem. *ACM Trans. Prog. Lang. Syst.*, 4(3):382–401, 1982.

[253] C. E. Landwehr, A. R. Bull, J. P. McDermott, and W. S. Choi. A Taxonomy of Computer Program Security Flaws, with Examples, NRL/FR.5542939591, Naval Research Laboratory, Nov. 19, 1993.

[254] D. Larochelle, D. Evans, et al. Statically detecting likely buffer overflow vulnerabilities. In *Proceedings of the 10th USENIX Security Symposium*, volume 10, 2001.

[255] A.H. Lashkari, M.M.S. Danesh, and B. Samadi. A survey on wireless security protocols (wep, wpa and wpa2/802.11i). In *Computer Science and Information Technology, 2009. ICCSIT 2009. 2nd IEEE International Conference on*, pages 48 –52, Aug. 2009.

[256] J. Leffers. Hacker-Club veröffentlicht Schäuble Fingerabdruck, Spiegel On-line Netzwelt, `http://www.spiegel.de/netzwelt/web/0,1518, 544203,00.html` (last accessed May 2011).

[257] A. Leinwand and K. F. Conroy. *Network Management: A Practical Perspective*. Addison-Wesley, Reading, MA, 1996.

[258] K. Lemke, C. Paar, and M. Wolf. *Embedded Security in Cars*. Springer-Verlag, Berlin, 2006.

[259] R. Lemos. Microsoft Warns of Hijacked Certificates, `http://news.cnet.com/2100-1001-254586.html`.

[260] Ronald Lewin. A signal-intelligence war. *Journal of Contemporary History*, 16(3):501–512, 1981.

[261] J. Leyden. Sophos antivirus classifies its own update kit as malware, the register, `http://www.theregister.co.uk/2012/09/20/sophos_auto_immune_update_chaos/` (last visited Jan. 2013).

[262] Marc Liberatore and Brian Neil Levine. Inferring the source of encrypted http connections. In *Proceedings of the 13th ACM Conference on Computer and Communications Security*, pages 255–263. ACM, 2006.

[263] Arthur Lichtblau. Police are using phone tracking as a routine tool, http://www.nytimes.com/2012/04/01/us/police-tracking-of-cellphones-raises-privacy-fears.html?pagewanted=all,.

[264] Limnios. *Arbres de Defaillance*. Hermes Editions, Paris, 2000.

[265] Xiaoli Lin, Pavol Zavarsky, Ron Ruhl, and Dale Lindskog. Threat modeling for csrf attacks. In *Computational Science and Engineering, 2009. CSE'09. International Conference on*, volume 3, pages 486–491. IEEE, 2009.

[266] William S. Lind. *Maneuver Warfare Handbook*. Westview Press, Boulder, CO, 1985.

[267] D. Litchfield. Defeating the stack based buffer overflow prevention mechanism of Microsoft Windows 2003 server. *Blackhat Asia.(Dec. 2003)*, 2003.

[268] Xiaonan Liu, Zhiyi Fang, and Lijun Shi. Securing vehicular ad hoc networks. In *Pervasive Computing and Applications, 2007. ICPCA 2007. 2nd International Conference on*, pages 424 –429, July 2007.

[269] A.L. Lloyd and R.M. May. How viruses spread among computers and people. *Science*, 292(5520):1316–1317, 2001.

[270] Gabriel Lopez, Oscar Canovas, Antonio Gomez-Skarmeta, Sassa Otenko, and David Chadwick. A heterogeneous network access service based on permis and saml. In David Chadwick and Gansen Zhao, editors, *Public Key Infrastructure*, volume 3545 of *Lecture Notes in Computer Science*, pages 55–72. Springer, Berlin / Heidelberg, 2005. 10.1007/11533733_4.

[271] C. Lorenz. The Death of E-Mail, slate.com (last visited April 2011).

[272] Joe Loughry and David A Umphress. Information leakage from optical emanations. *ACM Transactions on Information and System Security (TISSEC)*, 5(3):262–289, 2002.

[273] S. Loureiro. *Mobile Code Protection*. PhD thesis, Institut Eurecom, 2001.

[274] G. Lowe. Casper: A compiler for the analysis of security protocols. In *Computer Security Foundations Workshop, 1997. Proceedings., 10th*, pages 18 –30, Jun 1997.

[275] M. Ludwig. *The Little Black Book of Viruses.* American Eagle Publications, Tucson, 1991.

[276] M. Ludwig. *The Little Black Book of Email Viruses: How to Protect Yourself from Internet-based Attack.* CreateSpace, 2009.

[277] M.A. Ludwig. *Computer Viruses, Artificial Life, and Evolution,* volume 2. American Eagle Publications Inc, 1993.

[278] M.A. Ludwig. *The Giant Black Book of Computer Viruses.* American Eagle Publications, 1998.

[279] S. E. Madnick and J. J. Donovan. *Operating Systems.* McGraw-Hill, Auckland, NZ, 1978.

[280] D. J. Marchette. *Computer Intrusion Detection and Network Monitoring.* Springer – Verlag, New York, NY, 2001.

[281] Moxie Marlinspike. "New Tricks for Defeating SSL in Practice", Blackhat DC 2009, `http://www.blackhat.com/presentations/bh\-dc\ -09/Marlinspike/BlackHat\-DC\-09\-Marlinspike\-Defeating\ -SSL.pdf` (last visited May 2012).

[282] Moxie Marlinspike. "Null Prefix Attacks Against SSL/TLS Certificates," Blackhat 2009, `http://www.blackhat.com/presentations/ bh\-usa\-09/MARLINSPIKE/BHUSA09\-Marlinspike\-DefeatSSL\ -PAPER1.pdf` (last visited August 2009).

[283] Moxie Marlinspike. `http://www.thoughtcrime.org/software.html` (last visited May 2012).

[284] Mitsuru Matsui. Linear cryptanalysis method for des cipher. In Tor Helleseth, editor, *Advances in Cryptology EUROCRYPT 93*, volume 765 of *Lecture Notes in Computer Science*, pages 386–397. Springer, Berlin / Heidelberg, 1994. 10.1007/3-540-48285-7_33.

[285] D. McCullagh. Buggy McAfee update whacks Windows XP PCs, CNET, `http://news.cnet.com/8301-1009_3-20003074-83.html` (last visited Jan 2013).

[286] J. McHugh. Testing intrusion detection systems: A critique of the 1998 and 1999 DARPA intrusion detection system evaluations as performed by Lincoln Laboratory. *ACM Trans. Inf. Syst. Secur.*, 3(4):262–294, November 2000.

[287] A. J. Menezes, P. C. van Oorschot, and S. A. Vanstone. *Handbook of Applied Cryptography.* CRC Press, Boca Raton, FL, 1997.

[288] Keith Miller, Tracy Camp, Laurie Smith, King Deborah Johnson, and Barbara Moskal. "a history of the introduction and shut down of therac-25," `http://computingcases.org/case_materials/therac/case_history/CaseHistory.html`. (last visited January 2010), 2010.

[289] Chris Mitchell. Trusted computing. Institution of Electrical Engineers, 2005.

[290] K. Mitnick. *The Art of Deception*. Wiley Publishing, Indianapolis, IN, 2002.

[291] Mitre. Cve-1999-1085 `http://cve.mitre.org/cgi-bin/cvename.cgi?name=1999-1085` (last visited November 2012).

[292] Vishwath Mohan and Kevin W Hamlen. Frankenstein: Stitching malware from benign binaries. In *Proceedings of the 6th USENIX Conference on Offensive Technologies*, pages 8–8. USENIX Association, 2012.

[293] R. C. Molander, A. S. Riddile, and P.A. Wilson. Strategic Information Warfare: A New Face of War, Rand Corporation, Santa Monica, CA, 1996, `http://www.rand.org/publications/MR/MR661/MR661.html`.

[294] D. Moore, V. Paxson, S. Savage, C. Shannon, S. Staniford, and N. Weaver. Inside the slammer worm. *Security & Privacy, IEEE*, 1(4):33–39, 2003.

[295] Robert Morris and Ken Thompson. Password security: A case history. *Communications of the ACM*, 22:594–597, 1979.

[296] R. Munroe. XKCD Security, `http://xkcd.com/538/` (last visited Oct 2011).

[297] murat@enderunix.org. Buffer overflows demystified, `http://www.enderunix.org/documents/eng/bof-eng.txt`.

[298] S.J. Murdoch and G. Danezis. Low-cost traffic analysis of Tor. In *Security and Privacy, 2005 IEEE Symposium on*, pages 183 – 195, May 2005.

[299] M. Naedele. Standards for XML and Web Services Security. *IEEE Computer*, 36(4):96–98, 2003.

[300] John A. Nagl. *Learning to Eat Soup with a Knife: Counterinsurgency Lessons from Malaya and Vietnam*. The University of Chicago Press, Chicago, Ill, 2002.

[301] R. M. Needham and M. D. Schroeder. Using encryption for authentication in large networks of computers. *Communications of the ACM*, 21(12):993–999, 1978.

[302] M. Needleman. The Shibboleth Authentication/Authorization System. *Serials Review*, 30(3):252–253, 2004.

[303] M. Nekovee. Modeling the spread of worm epidemics in vehicular ad hoc networks. In *Vehicular Technology Conference, 2006. VTC 2006-Spring. IEEE 63rd*, volume 2, pages 841–845, May 2006.

[304] B. Nelson, A. Phillips, F. Enfinger, and C. Steuart. *Guide to Computer Forensics and Investigations*. Thoomson Course Technology, 2006.

[305] E. Nemeth, G. Snyder, S. Seebass, and T. R. Hein. *Unix System Administration Handbook*. Prentice Hall PTR, Upper Saddle River, NJ, 2 edition, 1995.

[306] B. C. Neuman and T. Ts'o. Kerberos: An authentication service for computer networks. *IEEE Communications*, 2(9):33–38, 1994.

[307] J.P. Neumann. Programmiersprachenwahl bei der entwicklung sicherheitsrelevanter software, hochschule darmstadt–fachbereich informatik–. 2008.

[308] Newman, D., Snyder, J., and Thayer, R. Crying Wolf: False alarms hide attacks, http://www.nwfusion.com/techinsider/2002/0624security1/html.

[309] T. Newsham. Format string attacks, http://seclists.org/bugtraq/2000/Sep/0214.html (last visited nov. 2012), 2000.

[310] R. K. Nichols and P. C. Lekkas. *Wireless Security: Models, Threats, and Solutions*. McGraw-Hill Telecom, NY, 2002.

[311] Noam Nisan. *Algorithmic Game Theory*, chapter 9 - Introduction to Mechanism Design (for Computer Scientists), pages 209–241. Cambridge University Press, Cambridge, UK, 2007.

[312] Rishab Nithyanand, Gene Tsudik, and Ersin Uzun. Readers behaving badly. In Dimitris Gritzalis, Bart Preneel, and Marianthi Theoharidou, editors, *Computer Security ESORICS 2010*, volume 6345 of *Lecture Notes in Computer Science*, pages 19–36. Springer, Berlin / Heidelberg, 2010. 10.1007/978-3-642-15497-3_2.

[313] Bruce Norman. *Secret Warfare*. David & Charles, Newton, Abbot, Devon, UK, 1973.

[314] Richard Norton-Taylor. MoD knew of chinook flaws before fatal crash, says father, http://www.guardian.co.uk/uk/2010/jan/04/chinook-death-crash-new-evidence. *guardian.co.uk*, January 4 2010.

[315] OASIS. eXtensible Access Control Markup Language (XACML) Version 3.0, Committee Specification 01 10 August 2010.

[316] OASIS. OASIS Service Provisioning Markup Language (SPML) v2 - SAML 2.0 Profile, OASIS Standard 2006.

[317] US Dept. of Homeland Security. Common cybersecurity vulnerabilities in industrial control systems, `http://www.us-cert.gov/control_ systems/pdf/DHS_Common_Cybersecurity_Vulnerabilities_ICS_ 2010.pdf` (last visited Jan 2013).

[318] National Institute of Standards and Technology. Federal Information Processing Standards Publication 197, `http://csrc.nist.gov/ publications/fips/fips197/fips-197.pdf`.

[319] The Parliament of the Commmonwealth of Australia. *Hackers, Fraudsters and Botnets: Tackling the Problem of Cyber Crime, The Report of the Inquiry into Cyber Crime.* Commonwealth of Australia, 2010.

[320] G. Ollmann. The Pharming Guide, `http://www.ngssoftware.com/ papers/ThePharmingGuide.pdf`.

[321] G. Ollmann. The Phishing Guide: Understanding and Preventing Phishing Attacks, IBM Corporation.

[322] CNN Online. "Computer worm grounds flights, blocks ATMs," `http: //www.cnn.com/2003/TECH/internet/01/25/internet.attack/`.

[323] OpenSSL. X509v3_config(5), `http://www.openssl.org/docs/apps/ x509v3\_config.html\#Basic\_Constraints\_` (last visited May 2012).

[324] Oracle. Tutorial on defending against sql injection attacks, `http:// apex.oracle.com/pls/apex/f?p=44785:29:0:RP:NO:::`, 2009.

[325] N. Orr. A Message-Based Taxonomy of Mobile Code for Quantifying Network Communication. Master's thesis, Penn State, 2002.

[326] G. Orwell. *Animal Farm.* Secker and Warburg, London, 1945.

[327] G. Orwell. *Nineteen Eighty-Four.* Secker and Warburg, London, 1949.

[328] The Open Web Application Security Project (OWASP). Cross-site request forgery (csrf), `https://www.owasp.org/index.php/ Cross-Site_Request_Forgery_(CSRF)`.

[329] The Open Web Application Security Project (OWASP). OWASP top ten project, `https://www.owasp.org/index.php/Top_10`.

[330] Asuman Ozdaglar and R. Srikant. *Algorithmic Game Theory*, chapter 22 - Incentives and Pricing in Communications Networks, pages 571–592. Cambridge University Press, Cambridge, UK, 2007.

[331] Donn B. Parker. The dark side of computing: Sri international and the study of computer crime. *IEEE Annals of the History of Computing*, pages 3–15, 2007.

[332] Bryan Parno and Adrian Perrig. Challenges in securing vehicular networks, 2005.

[333] Pevny, T., Fridrich, J., and Ker A. From blind to quantitative steganalysis. *IEEE Trans. on Info. Forensics and Security (in press)*, 2011.

[334] Shari Lawrence Pfleeger and Joanne M. Atlee. *Software Engineering: Theory and Practice*. Prentice Hall, Upper Saddle River, NJ, 2010.

[335] Phrack. Format string exploits, http://www.epanastasi.com/?page_id=60, 1996.

[336] J. Pincus and B. Baker. Beyond stack smashing: Recent advances in exploiting buffer overruns. *Security & Privacy, IEEE*, 2(4):20–27, 2004.

[337] M. Prandini and M. Ramilli. Return-oriented programming. *Security & Privacy, IEEE*, 10(6):84–87, 2012.

[338] Fletcher Pratt. *Secret and Urgent*. Blue Ribbon Books, Garden City, NY, 1942.

[339] The Open Web Application Security Project. Format string attack, https://www.owasp.org/index.php/Format_string_attack (last visited November, 2012).

[340] R. Russell, et al. *Stealing the Network: How to Own the Box*. Syngress, Rickland, MA, 2003.

[341] S. Rai and D. P. Agrawal. *Advances in Distributed System Reliability*. IEEE Computer Society Press, Los Alamitos, CA, 1990.

[342] S. Rai and D. P. Agrawal. *Distributed Computing Network Reliability*. IEEE Computer Society Press, Los Alamitos, CA, 1990.

[343] Sriram Ranganathan. *Key and Certificate Management in Public Key Infrastructure Technology*. SANS Institute, 2001.

[344] Maxim Raya, Daniel Jungels, Panos Papadimitratos, Imad Aad, and Jean-Pierre Hubaux. Certificate revocation in vehicular networks. Technical report, 2006.

[345] Kent C. Redmond and Thomas M.. Smith. *From Whirlwind to MITRE*. The MIT Press, Cambridge, MA, 2000.

[346] Eric Rescorla. Security holes... Who cares? In *SSYM'03: Proceedings of the 12th Conference on USENIX Security Symposium*, pages 75–90, Berkeley, CA, 2003. USENIX Association.

[347] B. Rexroad. Stopping DNSChanger Trojans, 03/22/2012, http://notworkingexchangeblog.att.com/enterprise-business/ stopping-dnschanger-trojans/ (last visited April 2012).

[348] David Rice. *Geekonomics*. Addison-Wesley, Upper Saddle River, NJ, 2 edition, 2008.

[349] M. Riley and S. Rastello. IMF State-Backed Cyber-Attack Follows Hacks of Lab, G-20, http://www.businessweek.com/news/2011-06-13/ imf-state-backed-cyber-attack-follows-hacks-of-lab-g-20. html (last visited July 2011).

[350] rix@hert.org. Writing ia32 alphanumeric shellcodes, http://www. phrack.org/issues.html?issue=57&id=15#article, (last visited Jan 2013).

[351] P. Ryan and S. Schneider. *Modelling and Analysis of Security Protocols*. Addison-Wesley, Harlow, UK, 2001.

[352] Anthony E. Sale. The Colossus of Bletchley Park. In Rojas and Hashagen, editors, *The First Computers – History and Architectures*, pages 351–364. MIT Press, 2000.

[353] K. Sampigethaya, Mingyan Li, Leping Huang, and R. Poovendran. Amoeba: Robust location privacy scheme for VANET. *Selected Areas in Communications, IEEE Journal on*, 25(8):1569–1589, Oct. 2007.

[354] K. Scarfone and P. Hoffman. Guidelines on Firewalls and Firewall Policy, NIST Special Publication 800-41, http://csrc.nist.gov/ publications/nistpubs/800-41-Rev1/sp800-41-rev1.pdf, September 2009.

[355] Mike D. Schiffman. *Building Open Source Network Security Tools*. Wiley, Indianapolis, 2003.

[356] A. U. Schmidt, N. Kuntze, and R. El Khayari. Spam over Internet Telephony and How to Deal With It, arXiv 0806.1610v1: http://arxiv. org/abs/0806.1610v1.

[357] M. Schneider. Self-Stabilization. *ACM Computing Surveys*, 25(1):45–67, 1993.

[358] B. Schneier. *Applied Cryptography*. Wiley, Indianapolis, 1996.

[359] Benjamin Schorn and Philipp Schneider. *Überwachungsstaat Deutschland 2.0? Der "Bundestrojaner,"*. GRIN Verlag, 2007.

[360] Logical Security. History of cryptography, http:\\www. logicalsecurity.com/resources/whitepapers/Cryptography.pdf.

[361] Andrei Serjantov and George Danezis. Towards an information theoretic metric for anonymity. In Roger Dingledine and Paul Syverson, editors, *Privacy Enhancing Technologies*, volume 2482 of *Lecture Notes in Computer Science*, pages 259–263. Springer, Berlin / Heidelberg, 2003. 10.1007/3-540-36467-6_4.

[362] H. Shacham, M. Page, B. Pfaff, E.J. Goh, N. Modadugu, and D. Boneh. On the effectiveness of address-space randomization. In *Proceedings of the 11th ACM Conference on Computer and Communications Security*, pages 298–307. ACM, 2004.

[363] D. P. Siewiorek and R. S. Swarz. *The Theory and Practice of Reliable System Design*. Digital Press, Maynard, MA, 1982.

[364] A. Silberschatz, P. Galvin, and G. Gagne. *Applied Operating System Concepts*. Wiley, NY, 200o.

[365] G. F. Simmons. *Differential Equations with Applications and Historical Notes*. McGraw-Hill, New York, 1972.

[366] Simon Singh. *The Code Book*. Doubleday, NY, 1999.

[367] snort.org. Cve-2012-1535:flash 0-day in the wild, `http://vrt-blog.snort.org/2012/08/cve-2012-1535-flash-0-day-in-wild.html` (last visited Jan 2013).

[368] J. Snyder. Inflated image, `http://www.opus1.com/o/completed/inflate_image.html` (last visited 2004), 2004.

[369] Chris Soghoian and Naomi Gilens. New document sheds light on government's ability to search iPhones, `http://www.aclu.org/blog/technology-and-liberty-criminal-law-reform-immigrants-rights/`.

[370] Christopher Soghoian and Sid Stamm. Certified lies: Detecting and defeating government interception attacks against ssl. Technical report, 2010.

[371] Daniel Solove. Justice Scalia's conception of privacy, `http://www.concurringopinions.com/archives/2009/01/justice_Scalias_1.html`, (last visited March, 2013).

[372] Sang Hyuk Son, Ravi Mukkamala, and Rasikan David. Integrating security and real-time requirements using covert channel capacity. *Knowledge and Data Engineering, IEEE Transactions on*, 12(6):865–879, 2000.

[373] Dawn Xiaodong Song, David Wagner, and Xuqing Tian. Timing analysis of keystrokes and timing attacks on ssh. In *Proceedings of the 10th conference on USENIX Security Symposium - Volume 10*, pages 25–25, Berkeley, CA, 2001. USENIX Association.

[374] A. Stabek, P. Watters, and R. Layton. The seven scam types: Mapping the terrain of cybercrime. In *2010 Second Cybercrime and Trustworthy Computing Workshop*, 2010.

[375] William Stallings. *Network and Internetwork Security*. Prentice Hall, Englewood Cliffs, NJ, 1995.

[376] Sid Stamm, Zulfikar Ramzan, and Markus Jakobsson. Drive-by pharming. In Sihan Qing, Hideki Imai, and Guilin Wang, editors, *Information and Communications Security*, volume 4861 of *Lecture Notes in Computer Science*, pages 495–506. Springer, Berlin / Heidelberg, 2007. 10.1007/978354077048038.

[377] Standish Group. Requirements - the budgeting syndrome, http://www.featuredrivendevelopment.com/node/614, last visited January 2010 2002.

[378] W. R. Stevens. *UNIX Network Programming*. PTR Prentice – Hall, Englewood Cliffs, NJ, 1990.

[379] W. R. Stevens. *Advanced Programming in the UNIX Environment*. Addison-Wesley, Reading, MA, 1993.

[380] W. R. Stevens. *TCP/IP Illustrated, Vol. 1-3*. Addison-Wesley, Reading, MA, 1993.

[381] Clifford Stoll. *The Cuckoo's Egg: Tracking a Spy Through the Maze of Computer Espionage*. Doubleday, 1989.

[382] Brett Stone-Gross, Marco Cova, Lorenzo Cavallaro, Bob Gilbert, Martin Szydlowski, Richard Kemmerer, Christopher Kruegel, and Giovanni Vigna. Your botnet is my botnet: analysis of a botnet takeover. In *Proceedings of the 16th ACM Conference on Computer and Communications Security*, CCS '09, pages 635–647, New York, NY, 2009. ACM.

[383] K. E. Strassberg, R. J. Gondek, and G. Rollie. *Firewalls: The Complete Reference*. McGraw-Hill, Osborne, NY, 2002.

[384] M. Strebe and C. Perkins. *Firewalls 24seven*. Sybex, San Francisco, 2002.

[385] E. Strother. Denial of service protection the nozzle. In *Proceedings of the 16th Annual Computer Security Applications Conference*, ACSAC '00, pages 32–, Washington, DC, 2000. IEEE Computer Society.

[386] D. Suarez. "Daemon: Bot-Mediated Reality," Presentation to the Long Now Foundation, Aug. 2008 http://fora.tv/2008/08/08/Daniel_Suarez_Daemon_Bot-Mediated_Reality (last visited Feb. 2010).

[387] Michael Sutton, Adam Greene, and Pedram Amini. *Fuzzing: brute force vulnerabilty discovery.* Addison-Wesley Professional, 2007.

[388] C. Swenson. *Modern Cryptanalysis, Techniques for Advanced Code Breaking.* Wiley, Indianapolis, 2008.

[389] Symantec.cloud. Symantec.cloud MessageLabs Intelligence, February 2011 Intelligence Report.

[390] H. Tayler. Schlock Mercenary, `http://www.schlockmercenary.com/` `2006-03-29` (last visited Oct. 2011).

[391] H. Tayler. Schlock Mercenary, `http://www.schlockmercenary.com/` `2009-10-19` (last visited Oct. 2011).

[392] Computer Emergency Response Team. Understanding and Protecting Yourself Against Money Mule Schemes, `http://www.us\-cert.gov/` `reading\_room/money\_mules.pdf`.

[393] team teso. Exploiting format string vulnerabilities, `http:` `//crypto.stanford.edu/cs155old/cs155-spring08/papers/` `formatstring-1.2.pdf`, 2001.

[394] S. Thomas. *SSL and TLS Essentials: Securing the Web.* John Wiley and Sons, New York, 2000.

[395] K. Thompson. Reflections on trusting trust. *Communications of the ACM*, 27(8):761–763, 1984.

[396] T. Thornburgh. Social engineering: The "dark art". In *InfoSecCD Conference '04* , 2004.

[397] H.F. Tipton and M. Krause. *Information Security Handbook.* CRC Press, Boca Raton, FL, 2003.

[398] Steve Tockey, editor. *Return on Software.* Addison-Wesley, Boston, 2005.

[399] B. Toxen. *Real World Linux Security.* Prentice Hall PTR, Upper Saddle River, NJ, 2003.

[400] C-R Tsai, Virgil D. Gligor, and C. Sekar Chandersekaran. On the identification of covert storage channels in secure systems. *Software Engineering, IEEE Transactions on*, 16(6):569–580, 1990.

[401] Mao Tse-Tung. *On Guerrilla Warfare.* University of Illinois Press, Urbana, 1961.

[402] A. Tsotsis. ComScores Says you Don't Got Mail: Web Email Usage Declines, 59% Among Teens!, `http://techcrunch.com/2011/02/07/` `comscore-says-you-dont-got-mail-web-email-usage-declines-` `59-among-teens/` (last visited April 2011).

[403] A. Turing. On computable numbers, with an application to the entscheidungsproblem (1936). *B. Jack Copeland*, page 58, 2004.

[404] M. Turino. Spam over Internet Telephony, http://net.cs.uni-tuebingen.de/fileadmin/RI/teaching/seminar_mobil/ss07/abgabe/paper\-turino.pdf.

[405] Sun Tzu. *L'Art De La Guerre*. Flammarion, Paris, France, 1972.

[406] S. Ulam. John von Neumann 1903-1957. *Bulletin of the American Mathematical Society*, 64(3):1–49, 1958.

[407] United States Department of Justice. Searching and seizing computers and obtaining electronic evidence in criminal investigations, computer crime and intellectual property section, criminal division, 2002.

[408] J. R. Vacca. *Computer and Information Security Handbook*. Morgan Kaufmann, San Mateo, CA, 2009.

[409] Martin van Creveld. *Command in War*. Harvard University Press, Cambridge, MA, 1985.

[410] Martin van Creveld. *The Transformation of War*. The Free Press, NY, 1991.

[411] Martin van Creveld. *The Changing Face of War*. Ballantine Books, NY, 2006.

[412] Tom Van Vleck. http://www.multicians.org/security.html.

[413] Serge Vaudenay. Security flaws induced by cbc padding - applications to ssl, ipsec, wtls. In *Proceedings of In Advances in Cryptology - EUROCRYPT'02*, pages 534–546. Springer-Verlag, 2002.

[414] Videolan.org. Security advisory 1202, http://www.videolan.org/security/sa1202.html (last visited Jan 2013).

[415] Berthold Voecking. *Algorithmic Game Theory*, chapter 20 - Selfish Load Balancing, pages 517–542. Cambridge University Press, Cambridge, UK, 2007.

[416] Carl von Clausewitz. *Vom Kriege*. Ferd. Dümmler's Verlag, Berlin, 1867.

[417] J. von Neumann. *Theory of Self-Reproducing Automata*. University of Illinois Press, Urbana, IL, 1966.

[418] John von Neumann and Oskar Morgenstern. *Theory of Games and Economic Behavior*. Princeton University Press, Princeton, 1944.

[419] K. W. Dam W. A. Owens and H. S. Lin. *Technology, Policy, Law, and Ethics Regarding U.S. Acquisition and Use of Cyberattack Capabilities.* The National Academies Press, Washington, DC, 2009.

[420] X. Wang, R. Zhang, X. Yang, X. Jiang, and D. Wijesekera. Voice pharming attack and the trust of voip. In *SecureComm 2008*, 2008.

[421] Xin Wang, Guillermo Lao, Thomas DeMartini, Hari Reddy, Mai Nguyen, and Edgar Valenzuela. Xrml – extensible rights markup language. In *Proceedings of the 2002 ACM workshop on XML security*, XMLSEC '02, pages 71–79, New York, NY, 2002. ACM.

[422] Joel Weinberger, Prateek Saxena, Devdatta Akhawe, Matthew Finifter, Richard Shin, and Dawn Song. An empirical analysis of xss sanitization in web application frameworks. Technical report, Technical report, UC Berkeley, 2011.

[423] Joel Weinberger, Prateek Saxena, Devdatta Akhawe, Matthew Finifter, Richard Shin, and Dawn Song. A systematic analysis of xss sanitization in web application frameworks. *Computer Security–ESORICS 2011*, pages 150–171, 2011.

[424] E.W. Weisstein. *CRC Concise Encyclopedia of Mathematics.* Chapman and Hall, Boca Raton, FL, 1999.

[425] Wikipedia. x86 instruction listings, `http://en.wikipedia.org/wiki/X86_instruction_listings` (last visited Jan 2013).

[426] Eddy Willems. Cyber-terrorism in the process industry. *Computer Fraud & Security*, 2011(3):16 – 19, 2011.

[427] Michael R. Williams. *A History of Computing Technology.* IEEE Computer Society Press, Los Alamitos, CA, 1997.

[428] Wired. "Scary hybrid internet worm loose," Sept. 18, 2001 `http://www.wired.com/news/technology/0,1282,46944,00.html`.

[429] G. L. Wittel and S. F. Wu. On attacking statistical spam filters. In *Proceedings of the First Conference on Email and Anti-Spam (CEAS)*, 2004.

[430] K. Wong. The hackers and computer crime. In *Securicom 1986, Paris, France*, pages 11–26. SEDEP, 1986.

[431] Charles V. Wright, Lucas Ballard, Scott E. Coull, Fabian Monrose, and Gerald M. Masson. Uncovering spoken phrases in encrypted voice over ip conversations. *ACM Trans. Inf. Syst. Secur.*, 13:35:1–35:30, December 2010.

[432] Charles V. Wright, Lucas Ballard, Fabian Monrose, and Gerald M. Masson. Language identification of encrypted VOIP traffic: Alejandra y Roberto or Alice and Bob. In *Proceedings of the 16th USENIX Security Symposium*, pages 1–12, 2007.

[433] Tim Wu. *The Master Switch: The Rise and Fall of Information Empires.* Vintage Books, 2011.

[434] Bin Xiao, Bo Yu, and Chuanshan Gao. Detection and localization of Sybil nodes in VANETs. In *Proceedings of the 2006 Workshop on Dependability Issues in Wireless Ad Hoc Networks and Sensor Networks*, DIWANS '06, pages 1–8, New York, NY, 2006. ACM.

[435] Gongjun Yan, Stephan Olariu, and Michele C. Weigle. Providing VANET security through active position detection. *Computer Communications*, 31(12):2883 – 2897, 2008. Mobility Protocols for ITS/VANET.

[436] Wei Yan, Zheng Zhang, and Nirwan Ansari. Revealing packed malware. *Security & Privacy, IEEE*, 6(5):65–69, 2008.

[437] Andrew Chi-Chih Yao. How to generate and exchange secrets. In *Foundations of Computer Science, 1986, 27th Annual Symposium on*, pages 162 –167, Oct. 1986.

[438] Wu Ye, Narayanan Vijaykrishnan, M. Kandemir, and Mary Jane Irwin. The design and use of simplepower: A cycle-accurate energy estimation tool. In *Proceedings of the 37th Annual Design Automation Conference*, pages 340–345. ACM, 2000.

[439] A. L. Young and M. Yung. *Malicious Cryptography Exposing Crytpovirology.* Wiley, Indianapolis, 2004.

[440] S. Young and D. Aitel. *The Hacker's Handbook.* Auerbach, Boca Raton, FL, 2004.

[441] Yevgeny Zamyatin. We. *Mirra Ginsburg, Viking, New York, 1972*, 1972.

[442] K. Zetter. Top Federal Lab Hacked in Spear-Phishing Attack, Wired Magazine, April 20, 2011, `http://www.wired.com/threatlevel/2011/04/oak\-ridge\-lab\-hack/`.

[443] Yue Zhang, Serge Egelman, Lorrie Cranor, and Jason Hong. Phinding phish: Evaluating anti-phishing tools. In *Proceedings of the 14th Annual Network and Distributed System Security Symposium (NDSS 2007)*, 2007.

[444] Michelle Zhou, Prithvi Bisht, and V Venkatakrishnan. Strengthening xsrf defenses for legacy web applications using whitebox analysis and transformation. *Information Systems Security*, pages 96–110, 2011.

[445] Ye Zhu, Xinwen Fu, R. Bettati, and Wei Zhao. Anonymity analysis of mix networks against flow-correlation attacks. In *Global Telecommunications Conference, 2005. GLOBECOM '05. IEEE*, volume 3, page 5 pp., Nov. – Dec. 2005.

[446] Ye Zhu, Xinwen Fu, Bryan Gramham, Riccardo Bettati, and Wei Zhao. Correlation-based traffic analysis attacks on anonymity networks. *IEEE Transactions on Parallel and Distributed Systems*, 21:954–967, 2010.

[447] H. S. Zim. *Codes and Secret Writing*. William Morrow, NY, 1948.

[448] E. Zimmerli and K. Liebl. *Computermissbrauch Computersicherheit: Fälle – Abwehr – Aufdeckung*. Peter Hohl Verlag, Ingelheim, Germany, 1984.

[449] C.C. Zou, W. Gong, and D. Towsley. Code red worm propagation modeling and analysis. In *Proceedings of the 9th ACM Conference on Computer and Communications Security*, pages 138–147. ACM, 2002.

Index